PLACE IN RETURN BOX to remove this checkout from your record.
TO AVOID FINES return on or before date due.

DATE DUE	DATE DUE	DATE DUE
_____	_____	_____
		_____

Close Ties: Railways, Government, and the Board of Railway Commissioners, 1851–1933

Close Ties is the story of how Canadian communities sought to assert some public control over some of the first large private corporations. Ken Cruikshank shows how the close ties between governments and railways generated a number of freight rate controversies and shaped a variety of regulatory responses to those controversies. In an attempt to resolve freight rate disputes governments attempted to stimulate competition in the railway industry, entered into contracts such as the Crow's Nest Pass agreement, fixed tariffs in statutes such as the Maritime Freight Rate Act, and created an independent regulatory agency, the Board of Railway Commissioners. Cruikshank demonstrates that new initiatives did not necessarily displace older ones, but instead created a pluralistic world of regulatory instruments which has governed the Canadian freight rate structure through much of the twentieth century.

The Board of Railway Commissioners, the forerunner of the National Transportation Agency and the centrepiece of the dominion government's regulatory strategy from 1904 onwards, is one of the most important institutional innovations in the emergence of the modern state. *Close Ties* focuses on this commission, describing its origins and examining its efforts to resolve complete freight disputes.

Cruikshank challenges a number of previous interpretations of government regulation, concluding that the history of railway regulation in Canada is neither the story of how powerful business corporations used governments to subvert the people's interests, nor a tale of the righteous people overcoming robber barons. Instead, *Close Ties* presents the more complex and interesting story of how governments tried to accommodate the equally selfish demands of divergent and conflicting interests in a competitive economy.

Close Ties offers important new insights into the development of Canada's railway system, the history of regulation, and the nature of business-government relations in Canada.

KEN CRUIKSHANK is an assistant professor in the Department of History, Trent University.

Close Ties

Railways, Government, and the Board of Railway Commissioners, 1851–1933

KEN CRUIKSHANK

McGill-Queen's University Press
Montreal & Kingston • London • Buffalo

© McGill-Queen's University Press 1991
ISBN 0-7735-0854-6
Legal deposit fourth quarter 1991
Bibliothèque nationale du Québec

Printed in Canada on acid-free paper

This book has been published with the help of a
grant from the Social Science Federation of Canada,
using funds provided by the Social Sciences and
Humanities Research Council of Canada.

Canadian Cataloguing in Publication Data

Cruikshank, Ken, 1957–
    Close ties: railways, government and the Board of
    Railway Commissioners, 1851–1933

    Includes bibliographical references and index.
    ISBN 0-7735-0854-6
    1. Railroads and state – Canada – History. 2. Rail-
    roads – Canada – Rates – History. 3. Board of Rail-
    way Commissioners for Canada – History. I. Title.

HE2807.C79 1991   385'.0971   C91-090323-9

This book was typeset by Typo Litho composition inc.
in 10/12 Baskerville.

To Peggy

Contents

Figures and Maps

FIGURES

MAPS

Tables

Acknowledgments

After so many months spent alone staring at a personal computer screen, it is a pleasure to remember and thank the real people and institutions who contributed to the creation of the book. I am grateful to the Social Sciences and Humanities Research Council of Canada and to the Graduate Program in History at York University for their generous financial assistance, without which I might never have completed the dissertation which forms the basis of this book. The staff at the National Archives of Canada ensured that my research time was effective and productive.

I thoroughly enjoyed my studies at York, and am indebted to all of my fellow students who made that cold and daunting institution a comfortable and stimulating place to work. Greg Johnson always kept me thinking about the practical challenges of historical research and writing. Mark Cox shared his enthusiastic and iconoclastic interest in the subject of regulation with me. He always had an opinion, and always managed to get one out of me.

I wish to thank Christopher Armstrong, Robert Cuff, Tom Traves, Peter George, and Ed Dosman, whose comments during the preparation of my dissertation and at my defence helped shape this book. Duncan McDowall generously took the time to read my dissertation, and his advice greatly improved the quality of this book. I would also like to express my appreciation to the anonymous readers of this manuscript who pointed out some significant factual errors and offered some other important observations. Peter Blaney, Victoria Grant, and Joan McGilvray of McGill-Queen's University Press have provided able editorial assistance, and their enthusiasm for this project has been greatly appreciated by someone new to publishing. I was very lucky that Paul Craven took an interest in this project. I greatly benefitted from his interest in the state, his encyclopædic knowledge of railways, and from his annoying habit of asking all the right questions. I only wish I had answered more of them.

I reserve a special place in this acknowledgment for Viv Nelles. His enthusiastic teaching awoke my dormant interest in the role of the state, and his commitment to his own work has been a constant source of inspiration. He proved to be an ideal thesis supervisor. He left me alone until I needed his advice, and gently prodded me into thinking about the larger issues when there was a danger I would become entangled in the intricate details of my research.

Peggy Sample tried to help translate my turgid writing into prose, tolerated the absent-mindedness and other peculiar habits I develop when working on large projects, and kept me in touch with the present. During the course of the research and writing of this book, she and I learned a great deal – to our great sorrow and joy – about the need for, and value of pluralism in the health care system. For all of these reasons and thousands more, this book is dedicated to my wife, Peggy.

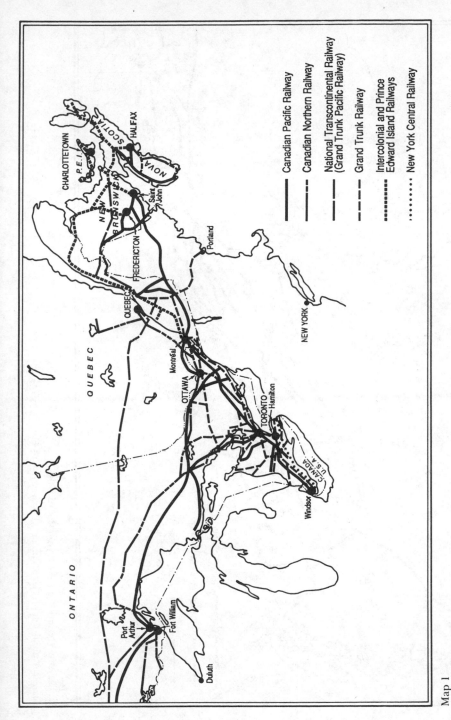

Map 1
Railways in Eastern Canada, 1916 (Main Lines)
Source: Annual Report, Department of Railways and Canals, 1915–16

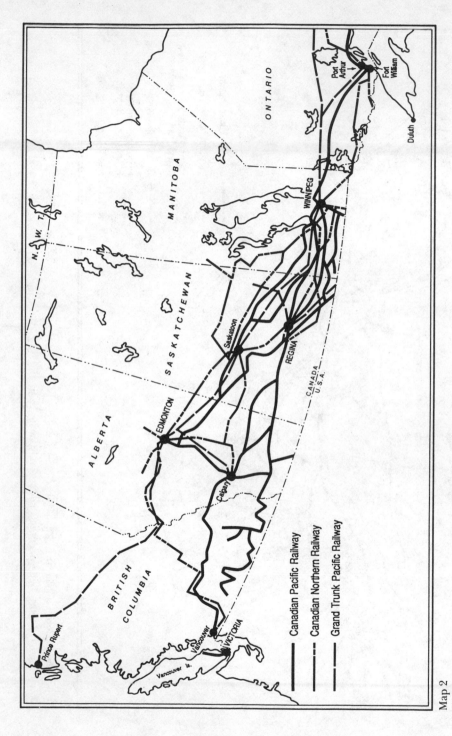

Map 2
Railways in Western Canada, 1916 (Main Lines)
Source: Annual Report, Department of Railways and Canals, 1915–16

Close Ties

CHAPTER ONE

Introduction

The moon was shining brightly on the tin roofs of Montreal's many churches when a crowded train arrived from Toronto late one November evening in 1856. The passengers looked forward to some respite from the exuberant crowds who had mobbed the train throughout the day at each station and village along the route. The travellers had come to join the citizens of Montreal and thousands of other visitors from Ontario and New England in a grand two-day celebration honouring the opening of the Grand Trunk Railway. The festivities began the following morning with an impressive three-mile-long procession, featuring the Knights of St Crispin working at their new sewing machines, local soap and oil merchants exhibiting their wares, the labourers and managers of the Canada Sugar Refinery marching behind a miniature of their works, and hundreds of other representatives of Montreal's industrial and mercantile community. Later that day, 4,000 guests gathered in one of the Grand Trunk's workshops, transformed for the occasion into an enormous banquet hall. Following the dinner, the governor general, the bishop of Montreal, the mayors of Montreal, Toronto and London, and other prominent citizens toasted a new era of prosperity and unity in the Canadas.[1]

Thirty years later, one of the Grand Trunk's original promoters, Sir Alexander Tilloch Galt, presided over a different and less boisterous event. No parades or grand banquets marked the opening of the hearings of the Royal Commission on Railways in October 1886. Appointed by the government of John A. Macdonald "to consider the advisability of creating a Commission with power to ... regulate the system of railway management in its relations to the commerce of the country,"[2] Galt and his fellow commissioners heard the business leaders of Toronto, Hamilton, Montreal, Halifax and other major Canadian cities express their dissatisfaction with the service provided by the railways. The enthusiasm of mid-century was gone; the romance of steam had given way to the reality of freight rate quarrels.

The very excitement generated by the arrival of the steam locomotive bred these later discontents. "Railroad iron is a magician's rod, in its power to evoke the sleeping energies of land and water," wrote Ralph Waldo Emerson, accurately reflecting the almost desperate hope of citizens across the North American continent that the railway could transform their sleepy, backwoods communities into thriving centres of civilization.[3] Merchants, manufacturers, and farmers looked to the railway as a source of power, prosperity, and prestige. Such expectations were easily shattered; such ambitions were easily thwarted.

From the 1850s well into the twentieth century, business and political leaders sought to harness the energies of the "magician's rod." Most Canadian communities initially delegated control over the construction and management of the railways they anxiously sought to private entrepreneurs. Through their governments, they granted private business leaders special authority to expropriate land and to adopt an organizational form capable of undertaking such a large scale enterprise. Through their governments, they also provided railway corporations with an equally critical resource – money. In mid-nineteenth-century Canada, governments were in the best position to attract and secure the substantial amounts of foreign investment required to finance railway ventures. Thereafter, some form of state assistance continued to be critical to the marketing of many railway securities.[4] Railway corporations, dependent on the state for legal and financial resources, were never entirely private ventures. The close ties between governments and the railway industry meant that railways were considered public projects: extensions of local, provincial, and even national ambitions.

Private railway managers, however, did not necessarily respond to the ambitions of those communities that had supported their projects. Instead, they reacted in the best way they knew how to the dictates of the market: they sought to maximize earnings by maximizing traffic. The conflict between the expectations and ambitions of the shipping community and railway corporate policies lay at the core of the dissatisfaction that followed the initial enthusiasm for the steam locomotive in most communities. Railways were "public" projects in private hands.[5]

In order to control the "magician's rod," then, many community leaders concluded that they had to reassert some of the control over railway management that they had delegated to private entrepreneurs. Between 1850 and 1930, a number of business communities turned to governments in an effort to reconcile the freight rate policies of railway corporations with their own economic ambitions. This book recounts the story of those efforts.

The railway companies were among the first business enterprises to be subjected to extensive control by the modern state. The struggle to expand, or perhaps more correctly, to reassert public authority over private corporations which is described here was repeated in other economic fields throughout the twentieth century, in Canada, the United States, and other capitalist societies. While specific outcomes varied, the general consequence was a transformation of governing authority and institutions – the creation of the modern administrative state.

Freight rate controversies resulted in a significant and lasting innovation in the way Canadians were and are governed – regulation by an administrative tribunal. From 1904 onward, the Board of Railway Commissioners, Canada's first national independent regulatory agency, provided the central forum for hearing and resolving freight rate disputes. The board, the direct ancestor of both the National Transportation Agency and the Canadian Radio and Telecommunications Commission, served as the institutional model for many subsequent regulatory initiatives. Considerable attention is therefore given in the pages that follow to the economic, institutional, and ideological origins of the railway commission, and to the subsequent efforts of its members to establish their agency as an effective and acceptable governing institution.

Administrative regulation, however, did not represent the first or only means adopted to control freight rates. Before the establishment of the board, business and political leaders could ask the courts or a special cabinet committee to respond to their freight rate grievances. At the same time, they convinced their political leaders to sponsor the construction of competitive lines and to exchange public financial assistance for rate concessions. The railway commission did not supersede these earlier measures entirely, nor did it prevent shippers and railway officials from asking the dominion government to find other ways of resolving their disputes. The government eventually participated in approving rate advances, began directing the railway commission towards certain objectives, and even fixed some freight tariffs by statute. Business and political leaders did not select one governing instrument but instead relied on a number of different measures to shape railway rate policies. In addition to tracing the origins and early operation of the railway commission, then, this study also outlines the development of "regulatory pluralism." The regulatory pluralism that emerged by 1930 continued as a fact, if not a guiding principle, of Canadian public administration for much of this century.

The study of regulation in Canada, as in other countries, has largely been the preserve of administrative lawyers, political scientists, and economists, rather than historians. Although the earliest work done by scholars in each of these disciplines tended to be highly descriptive, more recent work is highly prescriptive. Scholars offer suggested reforms based on their analysis of regulatory "failure." Lawyers accuse regulators of adopting procedures that fail to protect the rights of their clients, either because those procedures are too cumbersome or, more frequently, because they are too arbitrary. Political scientists observe that because of their relative insulation from the political process, independent administrative agencies gradually acquire the outlook of the industry they are supposed to be controlling. Economists criticize regulatory agencies for being too insensitive to the wider impact of their decisions and seek to demonstrate that regulations distort the healthy operation of the market economy. Lawyers propose either to enhance or weaken judicial review of the administrative process, political scientists call for firmer legislative oversight and guidance, or join the economists in proposing to dismantle the regulatory state entirely.[6]

This historical study does not adopt the mode of analysis of any of these disciplines, although it has been informed and guided by some of the important questions raised in this burgeoning literature. Like other recent histories of regulation, it is an attempt to understand the social and intellectual forces that shaped and sustained those regulatory initiatives and institutions which scholars in other disciplines are so eager to reform or eliminate. It is hoped that it will provide a historical dimension that is often lacking in current regulatory debates. If nothing else, it is also hoped that this study may counter the over-simplified view of regulatory history, and thus of regulation, promulgated by the followers of such disparate critics as New Left historian Gabriel Kolko, consumer advocate Ralph Nader, and the Chicago School economist George Stigler.[7] The history of railway rate regulation in Canada does not reflect their accounts of business corporations using governments to subvert the "people's" interests, any more than it appears as the tale of the righteous people overcoming the robber barons. Instead, it is the rather more complex story of how governments responded to the equally selfish demands of various participants in a competitive economy and tried to promote and accommodate those divergent and conflicting interests.

Chapter 1 introduces the story by analyzing the politics of private rate-making, a politics that generated grievances and demands for greater public control over freight rates. Those who sought this control did not readily abandon the market, and chapter 2 follows a number of efforts to have governments capture the benefits of railway competition, efforts that produced two regulatory landmarks – the 1897 Crow's Nest Pass agreement and the 1901 Manitoba agreement. The following two chapters recount the search for a governing form capable of resolving freight rate disputes, a search that culminated in 1904 with the creation of the Board of Railway Commissioners.

The interaction of the railway commission with its clients, shippers, and railway officials, and with its political masters, cabinet and Parliament, provides the main focus of the remainder of the study. Chapters 5 and 6 describe the regulatory strategy adopted by the commissioners in their efforts to create a viable forum for resolving disputes. The second of these chapters concentrates on the board's initial response to the rate grievances of the prairie west and British Columbia. The action taken by both the government and the railway commission to deal with the extraordinary regulatory demands generated by World War I forms the subject of chapter 7. The final two chapters pick up the story of regional rate controversies in the 1920s, describing the efforts of both governments and the commission to accommodate those protests. Those regional controversies produced two important additions to the Canadian regulatory system – statutory grain rate legislation and the Maritime Freight Rates Act. Throughout the 1920s, the railway commission came under attack from all sides – from those who thought it had developed close ties with the railways and those who thought it had developed close ties with the politicians. The study concludes on the eve of the Depression, with the railway commissioners divided over their regulatory role, and with politicians increasingly involved in resolving rate grievances.

The orientation of the study is decidedly national. The dominion government's jurisdiction included control over Canada's major railway corporations. Quite a few provincial lines were also brought within the jurisdiction of the central government through the use of the declaratory power. As a result, I have not examined the regulatory response of provincial governments to the railways they did control. Provincial governments are not absent from my story, however, for they played an important role in organizing and directing regional rate protests. More than any other rate grievances, those regional protests tested and demonstrated the limits of regulation.

CHAPTER TWO

The Politics of Freight Rates

In the second half of the nineteenth century, Canadians experienced a transportation revolution. Before the Grand Trunk opened its line between Montreal and Toronto in November 1856, fewer than 900 miles of railway were in operation in Canada. By 1905, competition between railway corporations and the communities that frequently supported them produced a network covering over 20,000 miles. Steady advances in railway technology throughout the period transformed the service provided by those corporations. Railway managers acquired the technology to carry more and more freight without corresponding increases in the amount of work performed by their locomotives. As the railway network expanded and technology advanced, shippers were able to send goods by rail for longer distances, more cheaply, with less handling, and with greater attention to the special transportation needs of their product.

For railway companies, the transportation revolution was expensive. Managers adopted the latest technological advances in order to remain competitive or gain a marginal advantage over other railway and transportation companies. At the same time, they continued to lay more rails to reach new areas as well as lucrative markets already served by their competitors. While railway executives lobbied governments and scrambled in securities markets for money to support these developments, their freight officials struggled to attract paying traffic. Because increased traffic did not produce proportionate increases in operating expenses, it represented the key to providing the revenues to cover current and additional financing. For railway managers, freight rate adjustments offered one means of attracting this traffic.

For a number of business owners and local producers, the transportation revolution was disruptive. The railway eliminated the "tariff of bad roads" that had protected and restricted the economic development of hundreds of Canadian communities. Increased competition altered established patterns of economic activity. Better transportation service at lower costs afforded those merchants and manufacturers with sufficient credit and capital new opportunities to trade in or produce goods for enlarged markets. For individual shippers and business communities, freight rate adjustments offered the means of maintaining or advancing their position in the local and national economy.

The expansion of the railway network and continual advances in locomotive technology during the closing decades of the nineteenth century posed different kinds of challenges for shippers and railway freight officers. A growing number of merchants, farmers, and manufacturers in all parts of Canada found that the strategies adopted by railway officers to maximize earnings conflicted with their own business ambitions. As a result, they sought to use public authorities to gain some control over the rate-making process in order to make private railway decision-makers responsive to the shipping communities they served. The transportation revolution gave birth to a struggle over freight rates in nineteenth-century Canada, a struggle that would continue well into the twentieth century. The transportation revolution thus produced and shaped the politics of freight rates.

By the time the colonists in Nova Scotia, New Brunswick, Ontario, and Quebec celebrated, or mourned, the birth of the dominion of Canada in 1867, most major centres in the colonies had been introduced to the new technology of the steam locomotive. Only a few small lines were in operation in the Maritime provinces; one of the terms of the Confederation agreement, however, ensured that a railway "connecting the River St Lawrence with the City of Halifax" would soon be under construction. In 1867, the locomotive played a more immediate role in the newly created provinces of Ontario and Quebec. There were several lines no longer than 100 miles – "portage" railways paralleling sections of water routes, particularly in the Niagara peninsula and Ottawa River regions, "hinterland" lines emanating from various Lake Ontario and St Lawrence River ports a short distance to their immediate inland territory, and Montreal's lines, which linked Canada's industrial and commercial capital to the railway system of New York State.[1] Two major companies, the Great Western and the Grand Trunk, provided some coherence to the patchwork of rails. They carried the bulk of the freight and passengers in Canada. The Great Western provided an international "bridge" across southwestern Ontario, connecting Michigan and New York via London and Hamilton; the Grand Trunk carried freight and passengers from Michigan via Toronto and the north shore of Lake Ontario to Canada's inland port of Montreal, or beyond to the Atlantic seaboard at Portland, Maine. Both companies vied with railways south of the border for a share of the freight traffic between the American Midwest and the Atlantic seaboard.[2]

During the 1870s, the construction of a new railway, the Canada Southern, added to this competition. This railway, which offered a short, efficient connection between Detroit and Niagara Falls, came under the control of the New York Central in the latter part of the decade. In response, officials at the Grand Trunk concentrated their limited resources on improving the interchange of traffic between their line and connecting United States carriers, and on extending their own American lines into Chicago. The Great Western's managers reacted to the new competitor by constructing a better through route parallel to and south of its main line, a strategy that also entailed the acquisition of a number of independents that would connect the old and new lines in the Niagara peninsula. At the same time, the Great Western sought to counter the Grand Trunk's control of traffic northwest of Toronto by acquiring two railways running north from London and Guelph to two Lake Huron ports.[3]

The emergence of the Canadian Pacific as a force in Ontario and Quebec in the early 1880s heightened the territorial competition. During the construction of the transcontinental line from northern Ontario to the Pacific Coast in the early 1880s, the new railway's managers also sought to ensure that their company would have access to the markets of Canada's populous golden triangle in southwestern Ontario and southwestern Quebec. By acquiring a railway under construction between Ottawa and Toronto, and by absorbing a number of independent lines, the Canadian Pacific began to forge a system that would run from southwestern Ontario and from Owen Sound, a Georgian Bay port, to Toronto and then north of Lake Ontario to Ottawa, Montreal, and to points beyond in New England, where various connections could be made to the American seaboard. By 1890, much of that system was complete, and the Canadian Pacific's lines had been extended so as to provide direct access to American traffic at Windsor and to the Atlantic seaboard at Saint John.[4]

In response to the Canadian Pacific's aggression, Grand Trunk officials attempted to consolidate their control over the railway network of central Canada. They managed to negotiate a long-sought amalgamation with the Great Western in 1882 and, in addition, took over some eighteen smaller railways operating in Ontario and southwestern Quebec. By 1890, the railway operated 2,200 more miles of track than it had a decade previously, including two additional routes for through American traffic and numerous lines covering much of Ontario west of Toronto. In spite of the growth of the Canadian Pacific, the Grand Trunk still handled the largest proportion (some 40 per cent) of all rail freight in the country.[5]

In western Canada, the Canadian Pacific responded to intrusions into its territory in much the same way as the Grand Trunk had done in central Canada. During the 1890s, the Canadian Pacific constructed a number of branch lines in British Columbia to counter the attempts of J.J. Hill's Great Northern Railway to tap Canadian freight traffic at the coast and in various interior mining regions. The twentieth century would produce an even more spectacular territorial struggle between the Canadian Pacific, the Canadian Northern and, to a lesser extent, the Grand Trunk. That frenzy of railway construction after 1900 would add a further 23,000 miles to a railway network that had already expanded from some 2,000 to over 17,000 miles between Confederation and the close of the nineteenth century.[6]

However, it took more than the mere extension of track mileage to retain a competitive edge in the railway business. In order to ensure that the quality of their service did not fall behind that of potential rivals, the railways also had to remain abreast of the new technology. In their bid for the traffic of the American Midwest during the 1860s and 1870s, officials at the Grand Trunk and Great Western tried to ease the interchange of freight at the border by investing in ferry services or bridge construction at international gateways, and by changing the gauge of their tracks to meet the emerging North American standard. Faced with the need to offer fast and efficient through service, both railways moved rapidly to replace their iron rails with those made of the more durable steel. After 1880, the Grand Trunk continued to make improvements to its ever-expanding network, including the construction of a tunnel at Sarnia to reduce the travelling time between Chicago and the Canadian border, and the double-tracking of the line between Montreal and Toronto. During the 1880s and 1890s, locomotives were fitted with a third and then a fourth pair of driving wheels, providing them with the power to haul new large freight cars, whose cargo capacity trebled to thirty tons between 1875 and 1905. The use of these larger freight cars and locomotives necessitated further investments in the strengthening of rails, roadbed, and bridges.[7]

The results of these technological changes are reflected in Figure 1. In the 1860s and again in the 1870s, the amount of freight carried on an average Grand Trunk train nearly doubled. With

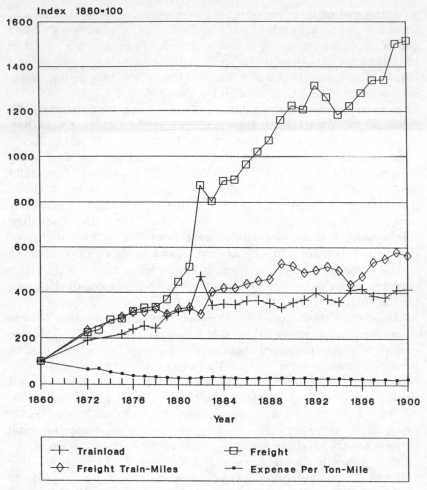

Figure 1
Grand Trunk Railway Freight Operations, 1860–1900
Source: Appendix B, Table B.1.

larger average trainloads, the railway company carried 300 per cent
more freight in 1885 than in 1875, while the total mileage over which
its freight trains hauled traffic advanced by only 33 per cent. Because
railway managers succeeded in keeping the expenses associated with
moving trains relatively constant, traffic volumes increased without
a corresponding advance in the cost of transporting the freight. The
estimated cost of carrying one ton of freight one mile declined significantly in the 1860s and 1870s, stabilized during the next decade,
and declined gradually in the final years of the nineteenth century.

Territorial and technological competition ensured that in each of the final four decades of the nineteenth century, more and more Canadian communities became part of an increasingly efficient transportation system. With each development of the system, shippers were able to send their freight for longer distances more rapidly, with less handling and danger of damage. This revolution in overland transportation created new challenges for railway freight officials, and for the business communities they tried to serve.

Technological improvements and strategic expansion required the investment of considerable sums of money. Railway executives scrambled to raise private capital in American and British financial markets. They frequently relied on bonds or guaranteed securities to entice cautious investors to put money into their projects. The interest on these securities had to be paid regularly and during most years of the nineteenth century absorbed practically all of the net earnings of the Grand Trunk and over half of the Canadian Pacific's net receipts.[8] Railway managers had to meet these fixed financial obligations, regardless of the amount of business they performed.

In addition, managers believed that many operating costs, amounting to as much as two-thirds of total expenditures, did not vary significantly with the amount of traffic carried by the railway. Freight officials, therefore, were encouraged to attract any freight available. To meet both financial and a large proportion of operating costs, it was better to carry some paying traffic than none at all. Efforts to entice shippers away from competing carriers and to encourage the development of new sources of freight could take many forms, but reducing freight rates remained the central strategy.[9]

During the nineteenth century, a number of Canadian and American railways actively competed for enough traffic to remain solvent by slashing their rates. Throughout much of this period, revenues per ton-mile, generally accepted as a rough estimate of the overall rate level, declined faster than the cost of living. As Figure 2 demonstrates, the Grand Trunk received an average of 1.2 cents for carrying a ton of freight one mile in the early 1870s. After 1875, the earnings for the same shipment declined dramatically, averaging 0.72 of a cent during the 1880s and 0.65 of a cent in the final decade of the century. The Canadian Pacific Railway also saw a reduction in its freight revenues from 1.1 cents to 0.75 of a cent per ton-mile between 1886 and the opening years of the twentieth century. The scramble for traffic, then, generally meant that shippers paid less and less to send their goods by rail.

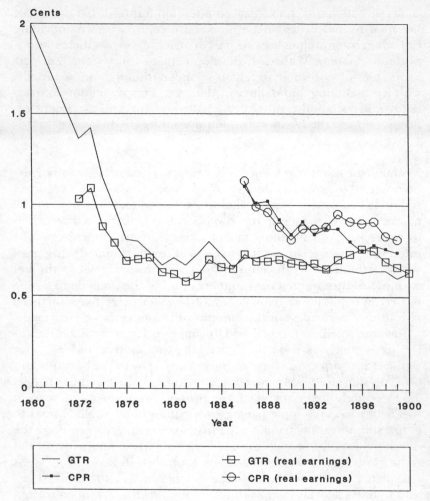

Figure 2
Grand Trunk / Canadian Pacific Freight Earnings per Ton-mile, 1860–1900
Source: Appendix B, Table B.4.

Rate reductions, however, were not evenly distributed among the railways' clients. While the specific rates set out in Tables 1 to 5 confirm the general downward trend, they also reveal considerable variations among both commodities and locations. Between 1860 and 1900, the earnings per ton-mile on the Grand Trunk declined 68 per cent. The charge for carrying building, roofing, and hanging paper between Montreal and Toronto was reduced by more than 50 per cent, while the freight tariff on leather carried from Toronto to Montreal declined only 8 per cent. The cost of shipping sugar

Table 1
Grand Trunk Railway, Examples of Freight Rates, Toronto to Montreal

	Freight Earning per Ton-mile	Grain Spring		Hardware Fall		Paper Fall		PackingHouse Products Fall	
	Index	Dollars	Index	Dollars	Index	Dollars	Index	Dollars	Index
1860	316	0.200	160						
1865	n.a.			0.300	167	0.360	211	0.300	130
1872	216	0.180	144						
1874	183			0.225	125				
1876	129	0.150	120						
1887	112	0.150	120						
1896	100	0.100	80	0.180	100	0.180	105	0.240	104
1900	100	0.125	100	0.180	100	0.170	100	0.230	100

Sources: Tables 1, 2, 4 and 5: Royal Commission Evidence, testimony of John Earls, Montreal, 15 December 1887; CNR, vol. 8546, Grand Trunk Railway, History of Freight Rates in the provinces of Ontario and Quebec, Montreal, 10 January 1912. Table 1: CNR, vol. 2001, 251–61; vol. 10817, minute 389, 13 October 1896. Table 2: CNR, vol. 2001, 132–43. Table 3: CNR, vol. 2001, 300–4; vol. 8146, tariff GS6. Table 4: CNR, vol. 2001, 76–85, 132–43, 351. Table 5: CNR, vol. 2001, 132–43, 388–518.
Note: Dollars per 100 lbs/Index, 1900 = 100

Table 2
Grand Trunk Railway, Examples of Freight Rates, Montreal to Toronto

	Freight Earnings per Ton-mile	Hardware Spring		Paper Fall		Sugar Spring	
	Index	Dollars	Index	Dollars	Index	Dollars	Index
1864	n.a.	0.200	125	0.400	267	0.20	142
1874	183	0.225	141			0.30	200
1887	112	0.120	75			0.10	66
1896	100	0.140	88	0.180	120	0.15	100
1900	100	0.160	100	0.150	100	0.15	100

Source: See Table 1.

and hardware from Montreal to points in Ontario generally declined more sharply for longer distances. But distance did not always account for variations in changes. Oil produced in the Sarnia-Petrolia area was carried by rail to Toronto and Montreal for about 30 per cent less by the end of the century than it had been in the 1860s; the rate to the intermediate point of Kingston showed a sharper reduction of 36 per cent, while the cost for carrying it the furthest, to Quebec City, fell by only 17 per cent.

Table 3
Grand Trunk Railway, Oil Rates from Sarnia / Petrolia

	Freight Earnings per Ton-mile	To Toronto		Kingston		Montreal		Quebec	
	Index	Dollars	Index	Dollars	Index	Dollars	Index	Dollars	Index
1865	n.a.	0.20	143	0.33	157	0.35	140	0.35	120
1891	111	0.12	86	0.22	105	0.21	84		
1898	(100)	0.15	107	0.22	105	0.25	100	0.30	103
1900	100	0.14	100	0.21	100	0.25	100	0.29	100

Table 4
Grand Trunk Railway, Sugar Rates from Montreal (Fall)

	Freight rates per Ton-mile	To London		To Toronto		To Kingston		To Quebec	
	Index	Dollars	Index	Dollars	Index	Dollars	Index	Dollars	Index
1858	(316)	0.50	294	0.30	200	0.20	154		
1864	n.a.	0.25	147	0.25	167	0.24	185		
1874	183	0.40	235	0.30	200	0.23	177	0.25	208
1887	113	0.19	112	0.12	80	0.10	77	0.18	150
1892	103	0.18	106	0.15	100	0.14	108		
1898	(100)	0.16	94	0.13	87	0.13	100		
1900	100	0.17	100	0.15	100	0.13	100	0.12	100

Source: See Table 1.

Table 5
Grand Trunk Railway, Hardware Rates from Montreal (Spring)

	Freight Earnings per Ton-mile	To London		To Stratford		To Toronto		To Kingston	
	Index	Dollars	Index	Dollars	Index	Dollars	Index	Dollars	Index
1865	n.a.	0.25	132	0.31	163	0.20	125	0.16	114
1874	183	0.375	197			0.225	141	0.15	107
1887	113	0.19	100			0.120	75	0.10	71
1893	102	0.18	95	0.21	110	0.14	88	0.12	86
1900	100	0.19	100	0.19	100	0.16	100	0.14	100

Source: See Table 1.

Railway freight agents, then, had to decide where and how much to reduce rates in order to maximize traffic revenues, while keeping costs to a minimum. In making these choices, they gave little thought to the actual cost of transportation, a fact that frustrated those shippers trying to understand the rate structure. Since most trains carried a variety of commodities with different handling requirements, it was practically impossible to establish the precise expense of moving any one commodity on that train. In addition, there were many general operating costs that could only be allotted arbitrarily to specific freight movements. Few Canadian freight officials even tried to estimate freight costs. They made little if any use of the kind of sophisticated cost-accounting system pioneered by the American railroad manager Albert Fink during the 1870s. A veteran freight agent for the Grand Trunk, John Loud, admitted that he never considered general statistics such as the average cost or earning per ton-mile when he fixed rates. George Olds, the Canadian Pacific's freight officer for more than a quarter of a century, explained that it was "troublesome" to calculate the expense of carrying any particular item, and described his own rather crude system of "accounting": "All you know is that at the end of the year you carried so many passengers and have so much money for them, and so many tons of freight over a certain mileage, and you have so much money for them, and you have paid so much interest charges and wages, and what have you left? And that is all you know, and you have not time to consider much else."[10] With one eye on regular year-over-year comparisons of revenues and expenses, freight agents and other traffic officials relied on instinct, precedent, and experience in setting rates, responding as best they could to commercial and competitive pressures.

The pressures facing railway managers reflected their industry's peculiar combination of monopolistic and competitive characteristics. For some communities in the nineteenth century, a single railway company provided the only transportation link to markets and suppliers. Others watched as lines that had once competed amalgamated with each other or entered into various types of co-operative arrangements. Increased self-regulation in the 1880s and the merger of smaller lines into the Grand Trunk and Canadian Pacific systems expanded the opportunities for collusion. Although shippers might experience the railway as a monopoly, many forms of competition nevertheless continued to govern the industry.

Competition between the railways remained strong, particularly for through traffic to the eastern seaboard. During the 1870s and 1880s, the Grand Trunk participated in a series of rate wars that saw through rates on grain and meat plummet. In 1885 the rate on grain from Chicago to New York fell to as low as seven cents per 100 lbs, a figure that included a three-cent terminal charge at New York. The highly competitive rates between Chicago and New York had a wide influence on the Canadian rate structure and provided the basis for most import and export rates on freight carried between Ontario and Montreal, Portland, and other American ports.[11] William Van Horne, president of the Canadian Pacific from 1888– 99, claimed with some pride that rate agreements were better maintained in the territory where his railway and the Grand Trunk competed than anywhere in the United States. By the late 1880s, freight officials from both companies met regularly, and Van Horn threatened his local officials with suspension or dismissal if they varied rates without sufficient evidence of competition or executive approval. Despite this, both railways continued to offer special rates in order to capture the lucrative traffic of major shippers.[12]

The competition of water carriers played an equally significant role in shaping the Canadian rate structure. A complete system of navigation linked Chicago, Duluth, Port Arthur, and numerous other ports on the Great Lakes to Montreal and beyond to the Maritime provinces. For seven or eight months of the year, as one traffic manager lamented, "railways could be dispensed with altogether."[13] As lake and ocean freighters improved their carrying capacity and speed with the introduction of steam and iron, ocean rates both east- and westbound declined dramatically. Although both the Grand Trunk and Canadian Pacific gained some control over the fleets on the Great Lakes and the Atlantic, tramp steamers calling between various ports on the Great Lakes and between Montreal and the Atlantic seaboard maintained competitive conditions.[14] For this reason, many of the largest shippers, such as the milling firm, W.W. Ogilvie Company, admitted that they rarely used the railways when a water carrier was available. Although the railways were able to offer rapid handling of freight, a service of particular interest to smaller shippers, and succeeded in increasing their share of the grain trade to Montreal during the 1880s, they still had to keep their rates close to those offered by the steamers.[15]

Even in the absence of direct rail or water carrier competition, officials sought to ensure the competitiveness of the freight carried by their railway. It was obvious that rates could not be set so high that the goods produced by existing or potential clients were priced out of their final markets, as various shippers successfully argued. Railway agents were particularly anxious to sustain existing sources of traffic. In the 1890s, a number of Ontario millers convinced Grand

Trunk officials that they needed special rebates if they were going to be able to compete with their counterparts in the northwest. Similarly, a leather manufacturer agreed not to move his factory closer to his suppliers and away from the Grand Trunk's line, but only after the railway's managers offered attractive rate concessions.[16]

Railway, water, and market competition did not affect all shippers equally. Although railway managers frequently denied that they offered special rebates to favoured individual manufacturers, the ability of large industries to guarantee large quantities of traffic made such arrangements highly attractive and gave these companies significant bargaining power. The Ogilvie milling firm, Carling Breweries, Massey-Harris, Canadian General Electric, E.B. Eddy, Quaker Oats, Imperial Oil and other large enterprises all enjoyed rate concessions on their business. Special rates were also extended to larger, established merchants who could be relied upon to generate a significant amount of freight traffic and to pay their freight bills regularly and promptly. By the close of the century, for example, most major merchants in Winnipeg paid only a small handling charge to import goods from the east and then reship them to an approved list of prairie shopkeepers at the same freight rate as their eastern Canadian competitors paid on a direct, uninterrupted shipment. Such an arrangement allowed the city's merchants to compete with their eastern counterparts for the trade of the west, and ensured their dominance in their own region. Although railway officials had clearly responded to intense pressure from Winnipeg merchants, they initially saw some advantages in this policy: it provided the Canadian Pacific with a central and convenient distribution centre and, by favouring established merchants, guaranteed some economic stability in the developing and volatile western economy.[17]

The Canadian Pacific's western rate structure provides a unique illustration of the influences that shaped freight rates, since throughout most of the 1880s, the company had a virtual transportation monopoly in the west. Monopoly power never meant, however, that the railway could charge any rates it desired. While seeking to recover some of the company's operating costs, freight officials faced equally important business considerations. In order to create future traffic, to enhance the value of the railway's land holdings, and to ensure that both its land bonds and other securities would attract overseas investors, officials sought to maximize the allure and prosperity of the west, while minimizing complaints and negative reports. They also used their monopoly to attempt western regional development. Coal companies seeking freight rebates had to agree to a maximum selling price for their product in various major communities. The railway offered rate advantages and other assistance to large grain shippers such as the Ogilvie firm in an effort to produce a relatively good and stable price for grain. Ogilvie and other large grain buyers were even monitored by the Canadian Pacific to ensure that they did not abuse the rate advantages they enjoyed by keeping the price paid to the farmer for grain excessively low.[18]

American western freight rates also influenced those adopted in the Canadian Pacific's "monopoly" territory. The rates on livestock bound for the eastern United States were adjusted to meet those of the Northern Pacific Railway to prevent ranchers and other producers from simply driving their cattle to the stations where rates were lowest, regardless of the international border. More significantly, railway officials kept their rates competitive with those south of the border to avoid invidious comparisons. William Van Horne blamed the freight agitations of 1883 and 1884 in Manitoba on the failure of his local freight agent to respond to a reduction in eastbound grain rates on the Northern Pacific. The Canadian Pacific was receiving enough adverse publicity in the English press; its agents were expected to adjust rates so as to avoid provoking rate controversies that might further discourage potential settlers and investors alike.[19]

Railway freight agents, then, had to consider a wide number of factors in making rate decisions. They liked to say that their skill lay not in fixing rates but in understanding how competitive forces set the rates for them. They were probably right in thinking that the ways in which railway, water, and market competition affected the overall rate structure were little understood by shippers, who only saw that some communities, some routes, and some competitors benefited from lower rates. Nevertheless, railway officials enjoyed a considerable margin of discretion in setting rates. Their decisions would be shaped by their views on a number of important and somewhat speculative questions.[20] Was a particular type of freight traffic worth encouraging? Would lower rates make an industry or merchant any more active and thus produce more traffic for the railway? Was the competition from other carriers a real threat in this community or for this product? Would it be better to favour a small number of shippers or business communities or, alternatively to try and equalize conditions among them? Would rate concessions help silence vocal critics of the railway? There were no simple answers.

The railway's clients, of course, were more than willing to try to influence the views of freight agents. Shippers, particularly those offering desirable quantities of freight, used their private bargaining power to negotiate rates. If this approach failed, or if shippers felt they lacked a strong negotiating position, they turned to larger business organizations, to the press, and to politicians in order to bring more pressure to bear. Whatever strategy shippers adopted, rate decisions involved a process of bargaining and compromise. The private negotiation of freight rates involved political controversy and choice; politics always was a part of rate-making.

In a revealing analogy, William Van Horne described the position of railway managers who set rates:

Our problem is very similar to that which a Finance Minister has to solve in providing the necessary revenues to meet the country's expenditures. A railway tariff, like a customs tariff, can never be satisfactory to everybody, however just it may be. Each individual or community looks to the effect upon himself or itself. The farmers in the Northwest think they should have the most favourable consideration. The ranchmen think the development of the cattle interest should be stimulated by very low rates; the lumbermen think the same of their particular industry, and so with the miners and everybody else. The argument is the same in every case. "Give us low rates in order that the business may be developed." But all of our business has to be developed and the Company has to live at the same time.[21]

Van Horne's comparison was apt. When railway freight agents made their choices about the best means of attracting and developing their company's traffic, they reached decisions that had larger consequences for the industrial and mercantile development of the community: such choices were bound to be controversial. Both the government's National Policy customs tariffs and the railways' freight rates could be adjusted to stimulate economic activity. Like the National Policy tariffs, railway rates were the product of a decision-making process that could be criticized for favouring established, influential merchants, manufacturers, sectors, and communities. Unlike the informal and formal bargaining that went into the revision of customs tariffs, however, the final decision about freight rates rested with a private interest, the railway corporation. Shippers who became dissatisfied with rate policies challenged the final authority of railway officials within that process.

During the final decades of the nineteenth century, an increasing number of shippers came to believe that the private system of rate-making placed them at a disadvantage or did not adequately respond to their changing economic situation. In criticizing railway rate policies, business leaders were responding to changes in their broader economic environment: the development of a national economy, the growth of urban centres, and the spread of large-scale industry. The railway locomotive represented one of the most visible symbols of the new economic order; those dissatisfied with the developments of the late nineteenth century readily pointed to adverse rate policies as the source of their misfortunes. The expansion and improvement of the railway system and the general decline in freight rates broke down the trade barriers that poor, costly transportation had created between communities and contributed to the emergence of a more integrated, competitive economy. Companies with sufficient credit and capital had new opportunities to trade in, or produce for, greatly enlarged markets. As the American business historian, Alfred Chandler, demonstrates, modern mass production and distribution depended on the speed, volume, and regularity in the movement of goods that the railway and steamship had made possible. Merchants and manufacturers oriented to local, regional markets faced increased competition from large-scale enterprises, often operating in distant communities.[22]

Partly as a result of the transportation revolution, the fortunes of a number of merchant communities declined in the nineteenth century. In his fine history of the Buchanans' wholesale business in Hamilton, Douglas McCalla demonstrates how the construction of the railway network in western Ontario during the 1860s and 1870s gave their traditional customers improved access to the merchants of Toronto. In 1865, Hamilton merchants such as the Buchanans imported $66 worth of goods for every $100 brought in by their competitors in Toronto. By 1885, and for the remainder of the century, Hamilton distributors handled about $22 in imports for every $100 of freight received at Toronto.[23] In fact, as Figure 3 demonstrates, the merchants of Toronto and Montreal increasingly dominated Canada's import trade, at the expense of most other cities. Halifax, Saint John, Hamilton, Kingston, and Quebec City all experienced a relative decline in their positions as distributing centres. Although changes in the patterns of mercantile trade cannot be attributed solely to the coming of the railway, freight rate policies did contribute to the competitive advantage enjoyed by larger merchant communities. To the extent that the railways needed the considerable traffic volumes supplied by major centres and could more efficiently handle freight loaded at a central point, freight agents became vulnerable to the demands of these communities for rate concessions. Not surprisingly, those merchants who did receive favourable rates accused railway officials of distorting the economy

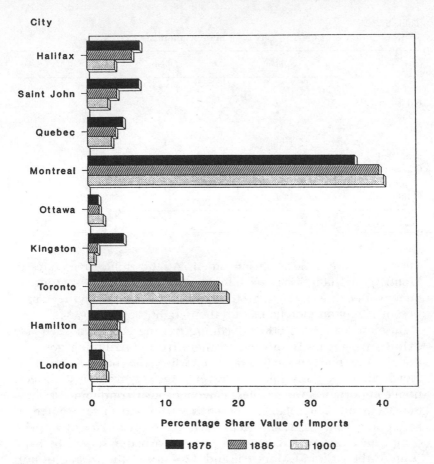

Figure 3
Estimate of Mercantile Activity in Nine Canadian Cities
Source: Canada, *Sessional Papers*, 1876, 1886, 1901, Trade and Navigation Returns.

and depriving them of the trade benefits that should have resulted from their natural geographic location.

The Royal Commission on Railways of 1886 gave shippers an opportunity to criticize railway management publicly. Table 6 shows that business leaders in most declining trading centres were united in their dissatisfaction with the rate structure and called for a railway commission with control over the rate-making process. The complaint of John Tilden, a Hamilton merchant whose firm had been in operation since 1843, was typical. He pointed out that Montreal and Toronto merchants could ship their goods to points nearer Hamilton such as London, Ingersoll, Woodstock, and Windsor for

Table 6
Views of Business Leaders by City on Railway Commission Proposal, 1886

City	Support	Oppose	No Opinion
Hamilton	15	5	2
Kingston	3	11	3
London	3	21	1
Ottawa	11	2	3
Toronto	20	16	6
Montreal	22	33	6
Quebec	14	1	0
St John	10	4	1
Halifax	6	2	2

Source: Royal Commission Evidence.

the same price as local businessmen. At the same time, rates to Montreal and points east were higher than the rates west from the same points, thus protecting Montreal's merchants from the expansion of Hamilton merchants into their trading territory.[24]

Business leaders in other declining trading centres agreed that existing freight tariffs prevented them from distributing goods to their natural markets. In Quebec City, where the construction of the North Shore Railway failed to reverse the city's diminishing economic importance, the business elite vigorously condemned railway management. A number of merchants who had once profited by reshipping iron, sugar, and oil to the north shore of New Brunswick complained that their customers were now better served by Saint John to the east and Montreal and Toronto to the west. Not only was it impossible to reship barrels of oil, one angry Quebec City shipper pointed out, but the through rate from Petrolia was actually lower to the Maritimes than it was to his city. Even in Ottawa and Toronto, two cities which advanced or maintained their position within the distribution network, many business leaders suspected that railway freight officials continued to favour the traditional centre of that network, the city of Montreal. Because of their proximity to this trading giant, Ottawa merchants were particularly disturbed by Montreal's rate advantages. One merchant testified that his Montreal competitors could reship goods from Chicago to Ottawa for less than his own direct cost. Moreover, high local rates out of Ottawa to the smaller communities in the surrounding area gave wholesalers in the nation's capital only a slight margin over their Montreal rivals. In Toronto, a number of small- and medium-sized merchants provided the support for greater government control of freight rates. One merchant, Hugh Blain, complained that on one recorded shipment he had seen, a Montreal competitor enjoyed a six-cent-a-barrel advantage over his Toronto counterpart in shipping twenty-five barrels of sugar to Seaforth, even though the goods were carried 300 miles further.[25]

The belief that railway rate policies deprived certain communities of the competitive advantage that should have resulted from their natural geographic location lay behind many of the rate grievances of the late nineteenth century. Merchants and small manufacturers were motivated to support or reject the existing rate-making process more by the fact of their location than by their specific occupation. An exception was the case of those involved in the traditional flour and grain trade between western Ontario and the Maritimes, where concern stemmed jointly from geographical location and occupation.

Although most shippers in Montreal expressed strong support for railway management in 1886, fourteen of the twenty grain merchants wanted more government control of rates. The publication of low through rates to the Maritimes following the completion of the Intercolonial Railway helped undermine the business of enterprising middlemen in Montreal as well as Quebec City who had been reshipping flour and grain from western Ontario to the Atlantic provinces. As a result, Saint John and Halifax merchants now were in a better position to distribute grain and flour with their own region.[26]

The consequences of these changes for the grain trade of Montreal are clear. Between 1876 and 1886, receipts and shipments of flour remained relatively stable, but the proportion of the commodity being reshipped to the Maritimes declined from 82 per cent to 46 per cent. While Montreal ceased to be a significant entrepot for flour bound for eastern Quebec and the Maritimes, it become an important point of reshipment for grain and flour destined for Europe.[27] Grain merchants operating modest enterprises had difficulty competing for this new export trade. According to one such merchant, Alexander Tough, the maxim that "One man's dollar ought to be as good as another's" did not seem to hold true for the grain trade. Tough and his senior partner testified to the commission that in one instance the railways offered rates three to seven cents below the regular grain tariff to a syndicate of Toronto firms who agreed to fill certain oceanbound vessels. These special rates were made available to other merchants only after the syndicate failed to provide the required quantity of grain. Faced with this situation, small- and medium-sized grain merchants in a number of communities were unable to compete and called for government regulation to counter the growing domination of their trade by large interests.[28]

Many Canadian business leaders also felt that the railways offered disturbing competitive advantages to their American rivals, a number of whom brought their goods into Canada at very low rates. Manufacturers in southwestern Ontario were particularly angry when they found that their competitors just across the river in Detroit shipped goods to Canadian points at lower rates than their own. "In reality," remarked a London hardware merchant, "a part of the subsidies granted to the railways have been given away to the United States distributor to enable people in foreign countries to cut us out." The revitalized Canadian Manufacturers' Association championed the cause of various Ontario manufacturers, arguing that the rate structure was counteracting the benefits of the National Policy tariff.[29]

As in eastern and central Canada, a number of western merchants felt that railway rate policies were depriving them of the competitive advantage they should have enjoyed as a result of their natural geographic location. From the 1890s onward, the merchants of Brandon, Calgary, Regina, Edmonton and other developing western communities all criticized the special freight rates which Winnipeg merchants had negotiated with the Canadian Pacific. They complained that they paid more to reship eastern goods to nearby villages than did their Winnipeg competitors. An agent for McCormick Harvester explained that his company set up an office in Regina to be closer to its market only to find that it was better off distributing its product from Winnipeg. Merchants and manufacturers in Victoria and Vancouver joined in the grievance, arguing that Canadian Pacific officials adopted a rate structure that created clients for Winnipeg and eastern Canada in the British Columbia interior. The rapid development of the west starkly revealed the tendency of rate policies to favour established interests, in this case the Winnipeg business community.[30]

Winnipeg business leaders, who had fought hard for their rate advantages, tried without success to keep the focus of western grievances on other issues. "It would be well to keep in mind that Edmonton was part of the whole country and comparisons should be made with eastern rather than Winnipeg rates," the prominent hardware merchant from Winnipeg, James Ashdown, told his Edmonton business colleagues. Ashdown and his fellow civic leaders sought to rally support for the equalization of the local merchandise freight tariff in the west with the substantially lower tariff used in the east, and for reductions in eastbound grain rates. Both changes would have enhanced the position of Winnipeg's business community, as well as its ability to compete with eastern wholesale houses, without threatening the advantages the city's merchants enjoyed with respect to their other western counterparts. Lower eastbound grain rates would further strengthen grain merchants in Winnipeg, who already had succeeded in making their city a centre for grading and labelling wheat.[31]

Canadian Pacific officials were quick to emphasize the self-interested nature of the "western" rate grievances championed by Winnipeg's merchant community, but were slow to acknowledge the wide appeal of those grievances. Western business leaders and producers were united in their support for Winnipeg's protests. Although merchants in other centres continued to attack Winnipeg's rate advantages, they were willing to call for a general reduction in western tolls as well. For producers, freight rates played a conspicuous role in their livelihood. The price paid to farmers for their grain in most centres was based on the price of grain being paid in England, less insurance, handling, and transportation charges. Farmers looking for a higher price sought to minimize all of these intermediate charges, including freight rates. Winnipeg's "western" grievances attracted support from both farmers and the local business communities hoping to prosper from a healthy wheat economy.[32]

In all parts of Canada, shippers sought freight rate adjustments in a bid to control their increasingly competitive business environment. Some shippers hoped to insulate their business from the new economic order; others felt the rate structure failed to acknowledge changing circumstances and offered too much protection to established interests. Merchants, manufacturers, and farmers attacked the rates enjoyed by their rivals in other communities; they were not concerned about exorbitant rates or excessive railway profits. After all, profits of any kind, let alone excessive profits, were hard to come by for the nineteenth-century railway industry. The expansion of the railway network and the updating of technology burdened railway corporations with substantial fixed capital and operating costs and drove their managers to fight for a share of the limited freight traffic available prior to the turn of the century. Railway freight officials reduced rates in any way that they thought would sustain and attract freight revenues sufficient to cover some of those fixed costs. In responding to a variety of competitive pressures, they constructed a bewildering and byzantine structure of differential tolls, special arrangements, and rebates. The politics of rate-making produced a web of individual bargains and compromises between railway officials and shippers, a rate structure that provoked considerable controversy.

While some shippers continued to rely on private bargaining to acquire favourable rate concessions, during the final decades of the nineteenth century an increasing number of merchants, manufacturers, and farmers turned to their political leaders in an effort to shape rate decisions. They challenged the right of private railway officials to make choices through their rate-making policies about the pattern of economic development. Business leaders and their political representatives searched for a way to use public power to reconcile freight tariff decisions with their own economic ambitions. This politics of freight rates produced a gradual but significant transformation of the state's authority over the economy.

CHAPTER THREE

Public Money,
Private Rights

"The moment one sets foot in the Territories the question of freight rates is raised, and your ears ring with the story until you reach Victoria," wrote the Toronto journalist and intellectual J.S. Willison after returning from a tour of western Canada in 1895. He translated the protests he encountered into a series of articles for the Toronto *Globe* and an 1897 pamphlet entitled *The Railway Question in Canada*. While Willison adopted the western perspective on freight rate grievances, he rejected the west's favoured solution. Canadians, he argued, must turn their minds to "the regulation of rates by statute rather than by the construction of competing roads that will not compete." He maintained that "railway monopoly under efficient regulation," not competition, offered the best means of lowering freight charges.[1]

As Willison observed, freight rate grievances did not necessarily generate demands for regulation by a government agency. Although by the 1890s the concept of a railway commission had been discussed for over a decade, it still met with resistance. Political and business leaders did not readily abandon their faith in the regulatory effectiveness of the market. As the assistant editor of the *Globe* explained to Willison, "It is difficult to get men schooled all their lives in the doctrine of competition to understand that state governed and directed monopoly must be the condition of the future."[2]

Competition, however, was too important a regulatory mechanism to be left to the vagaries of the free market economy. Merchants and manufacturers actively fostered competition by supporting public assistance for the construction of rival lines. Many railway promoters, anxious for and dependent on government largesse, eagerly tapped such pro-competition, anti-monopoly sentiments. Together, ambitious promoters and business communities convinced their political representatives in municipal governments, county councils, provincial legislatures, and the dominion Parliament to fund projects that would not extend rail service to new areas but would offer alternatives to existing lines and, it was hoped, to existing freight rates. This strategy became increasingly sophisticated as business and political leaders learned that new railways did not automatically generate the kind of competition in rates and service they sought. Community leaders used their access to public finance – a resource of critical importance to private railway entrepreneurs – to negotiate regulatory contracts. They required promoters to agree to various conditions, ranging from vague commitments to remain independent, to the adoption of specific rate policies. The benefits of competition were to be enforced by contract.

This regulatory system based on competition and contract evolved during the nineteenth century. It began at the local level, with municipal and county governments attaching rate and service conditions to the subsidies they granted competitive rail lines. These community regulatory initiatives influenced the subsequent approach of the Manitoba and dominion governments to railway requests for public assistance. In subsidizing the Canadian Pacific's construction of the Crow's Nest Pass line in 1897, the dominion government negotiated rate concessions in lieu of creating competition. In 1901, the Manitoba government leased a strategic railway line to the Canadian Northern, a new rival for the Canadian Pacific, but only after the railway's promoters agreed to lower a number of freight rates. While the dominion government chose to impose regulation by contract only, the Manitoba government chose contract as well as competition. Both the Crow's Nest Pass and the Manitoba agreements, landmarks in the history of Canadian freight rates, reflected the dominant regulatory strategy of the nineteenth century, and both agreements demonstrated the limitations of using public money to restrict private rights.

Experience taught that competing roads would not compete, as Willison explained in *The Railway Question in Canada*. The Toronto journalist could have had in mind a number of local controversies surrounding the promotion of independent lines in the 1870s, including both the Hamilton and Northwestern and the Credit Valley Railways. In these and many other cases, community leaders offered generous financial assistance in the hope that alternative railways would resolve their rate grievances, but they soon encountered the determined opposition of the established railway corporations, who sought to restrict competition. They also discovered that even when regulatory contracts were successfully negotiated, they lacked the authority to enforce them.

Perhaps more than any other local railway, the Credit Valley owed its existence to the generous financial support of communities seeking an alternative to the existing rail network. Its chief promoter, George Laidlaw, lived up to his reputation as the "King of the Bonus Hunters." He collected more than $1.6 million from the province of Ontario, eight towns and five counties. The counties of Waterloo and Halton contributed almost $200,000 for a railway that passed within five to ten miles of the Grand Trunk or Great Western routes. The towns of Brampton and Ingersoll parted with a combined total of $30,000 even though both centres were already served by a major railway. The county of Oxford granted a $200,000 bonus, the right of way through Ingersoll and Woodstock, land for stations, and materials for a grain warehouse, all in order to end the Great Western Railway's monopoly of the county's trade. As a condition for most of these bonuses, Laidlaw agreed in writing to make connections with all other existing lines but to maintain the railway's independence. He successfully promoted his railway by promoting the concept of competition.[3]

No other community gave as generously as the city of Toronto, which provided the Credit Valley with two bonuses valued at $100,000 and $250,000. Laidlaw promised the business community of the city that, as well as providing them with half a million new customers, he would "strike a fatal blow" at the rate policies of the Grand Trunk and Great Western Railways. Because the Credit Valley would connect to the Canada Southern, it would offer an alternative route between Toronto and the United States at lower rates than those offered by the established competitors. Laidlaw, aware of complaints that the major railways discriminated in favour of Montreal and other ports, also promised to charge the same low rate per mile on freight shipped for short distances from various points in southwestern Ontario to Toronto as his rivals charged for the longer haul to more distant ports. In a policy designed to appeal to Toronto fuel consumers, Laidlaw guaranteed a permanently fixed and attractively low rate on cordwood, a rate that was subsequently enshrined in the railway's corporate charter.[4]

When he asked to have the charter amended in 1873 so that his company could make agreements with other railways concerning the use of rolling stock, he tried to calm any fears that such agreements might lead to reduced competition. He added a stipulation that the railway not carry foreign through traffic at lower rates than local traffic, thereby responding to a common freight rate grievance.[5]

The first subsidy the Credit Valley received from the city of Toronto in 1872 was given on the condition that the line must reach the city "without using any of the existing lines of railway for that purpose." In 1876, the controversy provoked by a request for a further $250,000 forced the Credit Valley's promoters to offer more specific concessions. Laidlaw sought to make his proposal more attractive to the city council and to the ratepayers who ultimately had to approve the bonus by proposing to bring his railway on an independent line down to the harbourfront, to locate the road's machine shops in the city, and "to carry no Canadian freight at rates which discriminate against the City of Toronto." He eventually succeeded in acquiring the public money his railway required, but only after he had agreed to a number of contractual obligations concerning the organization, construction, and rate-making policies of his railway.[6]

The political and business leaders of Toronto who negotiated the subsidy agreements with the Credit Valley soon learned the fragility of the regulatory regime they had constructed. The managers of the Northern and Grand Trunk Railways weakened their potential rival by denying it independent access to Toronto's waterfront. Both these railways alleged that they owned the once public land over which the Credit Valley was to be constructed, a claim subsequently sustained by the Court of Chancery. The two companies retained the right to keep the Credit Valley terminus two miles away from the commercial centre of the city.[7] A further blow awaited the promoters of the Credit Valley. Although the generous assistance of local governments ensured that the railway was completed in 1881, it was never financially secure. Its route from Toronto to St Thomas via Galt, with a branch from Streetsville to Orangeville, however, made the railway strategically important to the Grand Trunk and the newly chartered Canadian Pacific Railway. In 1883, the Ontario and dominion governments empowered the Credit Valley to amalgamate with the Ontario and Quebec Railway, a line between Toronto and Ottawa controlled by the Canadian Pacific. Higher levels of government ignored protests from the town of Galt, Oxford County, and the city of Toronto and overrode the condition attached to most of the municipal bonuses that the Credit Valley should remain independent and not amalgamate with other lines. Ironically, the dominion government acted in part on the advice of Canadian Pacific officials, who warned that the legislation was "the most effectual means ... of securing a permanent competitive line through [the] older Provinces".[8]

Local community leaders could take little solace from the fact that the new legislation forbad the amalgamation of the Credit Valley and the Grand Trunk. They had generously assisted an independent line in the hope that its alternative rate-making policies would regulate the larger railways. Two of those railways, the Grand Trunk and the Great Western, had already become one. Now they looked on helplessly as their independent line was acquired by the Canadian Pacific, Canada's other major railway corporation. Thus, the fight to establish the Credit Valley as a genuinely independent railway failed. The controversy over the Toronto land demonstrated the determined hostility to further competition of the established railway corporations. In the face of this kind of opposition, business leaders found that it was difficult to muster political support at the provincial and dominion levels for what were primarily local economic ambitions. In fact, the provincial and dominion governments had a greater stake in the overall solvency of the railway industry, and used their authority to override local initiatives, as the ultimate fate of the Credit Valley revealed.

The Hamilton and Northwestern, another independent railway, had a similar history. Hamilton merchants and manufacturers had promoted the line in 1873 to counter the Northern Railway, which Toronto had promoted to capture the trade of the farms and timber operations north of the city to Georgian Bay. Hamilton's business community, anxious to make their city "the Chicago of Canada," convinced their local government to contribute $100,000 and to subscribe for stock of an equal value to finance the Hamilton and Northwestern. At the northern terminus of the proposed route, various communities in the county of Simcoe, most already within reach of the Northern Railway, provided a further $300,000 for the railway. Even though the Northern served both Collingwood and Barrie, local governments there supported the construction of a potential rival to the tune of some $56,000. Local merchants and lumberers looked to the Hamilton and Northwestern to provide competition in rates to Lake Ontario, and to generate competition for their import and export business by giving them access to a second port city, Hamilton.[9]

In exchange for the financial backing, local communities in Simcoe County required that the Hamilton and Northwestern would remain independent of all other lines. An 1878 amendment to the charter of the Hamilton and Northwestern's rival, the Northern Railway, appeared to confirm the policy of competition for Simcoe County.

While Parliament permitted the corporation to make agreements concerning traffic, rolling stock, and other matters with other companies, it stipulated that this latter power "did not extend to the right of making such agreements with respect to any competing lines of railways."[10] Nevertheless, on 23 May 1879, the directors of the Northern and the Hamilton and Northwestern railways ratified an agreement that placed both companies under a joint executive committee. They undertook to share rolling stock, pool their earnings, expenses and debts, and to make rules and regulations governing the working of their traffic. Within a few months, the joint committee increased the freight tariff of the Hamilton and Northwestern road.[11] The railway that was to provide the business communities of Simcoe County with a competitive outlet thus entered into a quasi-partnership with its rival!

One of the directors of the Northern Railway, Charles Campbell, sought an injunction against this agreement. His solicitor, James Maclennan, contended that the arrangement was void because neither railway had been given the power to make such an arrangement in its corporate charter, and because the joint committee resulted in a monopoly. Campbell's motives were less than honourable: he initiated the action in an effort to force the other directors to buy the shares in the Northern Railway that he had acquired at no cost. Nevertheless, the case raised a number of questions of concern to those who had sought to create competition in Simcoe County.[12]

Vice-Chancellor Samuel Hume Blake dismissed the application. He held that a general provision permitting arrangements between railways provided ample power to both companies to enter into such an agreement. As for the 1878 amendment preventing agreements with competing railways, Blake contended that it applied only to a narrow set of inter-railway arrangements. He observed that all legislation designed to restrict railway corporate discretion should be interpreted strictly, allowing "a very considerable latitude as to the mode in which its directors may think best to carry out the purposes of the Acts of Incorporation."[13]

Blake's reasoning regarding the question of monopoly would have dismayed those communities that had offered public money to create competition. Blake offered a lengthy citation from a decision of the Vice-Chancellor's Court of England, *Hare v. London and North Western Railway* that included the following remarks:

I see nothing in the alleged injury to the public arising from the prevention of competition, I find no indication, in the course taken by the Legislature, of an intention to create competition by authorizing various lines ... It is a mistaken notion that the public is benefited by pitting two railway companies against each other till one is ruined, the result being, at last, to raise the fares to the highest possible standard ... I must, therefore, dismiss from consideration the arguments founded on the notion that the companies were under any obligation to carry on their traffic with a view to keep up competition.[14]

Like most judges, the Vice-Chancellor insisted throughout that the court must focus on the relevant legislation and not the broader impact of its decision. His approving citation of *Hare*, however, clearly demonstrated that his statutory interpretation coincided with his own view of the public interest.

Blake's comments suggested that those engaged in the fight for competition could look for little help from the courts. The legal system generally focused on the rights of property and capital. Agreements between municipal governments and railways concerning tangible issues, such as the location of stations, machine shops, or even specific performance requirements were understood and enforced by the courts.[15] Judges found it more difficult to come down on the side of the intangible and entirely local benefits that competition might offer against the will of corporate directors and the interest of investors. They could be expected to favour stipulations with respect to competition only if regulatory contracts contained much stronger language or legislators offered much greater direction.

Although the Simcoe County Council received legal opinions challenging Blake's decision from James Maclennan and the county's solicitor, D'Alton McCarthy, they chose to rely on political lobbying rather than a court challenge.[16] Unfortunately, like the supporters of the Credit Valley project, they found little sympathy for their local ambitions in the national political arena. For the leaders of Simcoe County, the fight for competition ended in failure.

In the view of several observers in southwestern Ontario, the institutions of law through which they had hoped to enforce competition – the courts and the governments – failed at a crucial moment. During the lengthy struggle over the Credit Valley's access to the harbourfront, Toronto City Council, Board of Trade, and Corn Exchange began to agitate for a new forum for the settlement of disputes of the kind in which they had become embroiled. A deputation met with the prime minister and the minister of railways to discuss the creation of a dominion railway commission that would have the power to settle disputes between municipalities and railways, enforce traffic arrangements between railways, and adjust local and through rates. One of the solicitors representing the Credit Valley Railway and the Simcoe County Council was D'Alton Mc-Carthy, who subsequently became the leading parliamentary advocate of a railway commission during the 1880s.[17] In order to regulate the behaviour of private railway corporations, business and political leaders turned from the use of public money to the use of public authority.

Business communities in Ontario were not unique in seeking to generate competition through public assistance. Almost from the moment the Canadian Pacific reached their city, Winnipeg merchants and manufacturers actively sought to create a rival to the all-Canadian transcontinental. Unlike their counterparts in Ontario, however, the Winnipeg business community dominated their province's economy and faced a railway corporation whose monopoly over the region's transportation network was guaranteed by the dominion government. From the outset, therefore, they exercised their considerable influence with the provincial government to promote competition. After a protracted struggle and an initial setback, the Manitoba government learned how to wield public money to limit private rights.

In order to generate any kind of railway competition, Manitoba's leaders had to challenge the Canadian Pacific's monopoly clause. In 1880, Prime Minister John A. Macdonald had been determined to have a transcontinental railway constructed, having witnessed almost a decade of delays and false starts. As a result, he had offered the promoters of the Canadian Pacific a number of generous concessions. Among them was a guarantee that for twenty years no other railway would be constructed within fifteen miles of the border, effectively protecting the new all-Canadian transcontinental from rail competition via an American route. Merchants and farmers in Manitoba, frustrated by the poor harvests and the low commodity prices of the mid- to late 1880s, had a ready political demon in this monopoly clause, which allegedly resulted in exorbitant rates on the Canadian Pacific.

Disgruntled shippers turned to the provincial government to fight the Canadian Pacific. During the early 1880s, the Manitoba legislature issued charters for several railways that were projected to connect with American lines, but in each case, the Macdonald government lived up to its agreement with the Canadian Pacific and used its constitutional authority to veto the provincial legislation. Manitoba's premier, John Norquay, under increasing pressure to take some decisive action, in 1886 challenged the dominion government by issuing a charter for the Red River Valley Railway that would operate between Winnipeg and the boundary with the United States. He threatened to construct the railway as a public work, should Ottawa intervene. An angry George Stephen, president of the Canadian Pacific from 1881–88, warned Prime Minister Macdonald that a delegation from Winnipeg was trying to convince the Northern Pacific to build all or part of the Red River Railway and reroute western traffic south of the Great Lakes. The Macdonald government, deeply committed to the success of an all-Canadian transcontinental route, again used it constitutional authority of disallowance to veto Norquay's legislation and also helped prevent the sale of the provincial bonds needed to support the proposed railway.[18]

Canadian Pacific actions did little to ease tensions. In May 1887, Van Horne, the company's vice-president, ordered his local superintendent to do some "house cleaning at Winnipeg," temporarily reducing the amount of work done in the Winnipeg shops and laying off a substantial portion of the work force, while in the same month, Stephen threatened to remove the workshops from Winnipeg permanently. Moreover, in the face of what they considered to be the uncivil demands of a small group of Winnipeg merchants, railway officials steadfastly refused to make any freight rate concessions. Rate reductions, Stephen told Macdonald, would provide neither an "ounce of prevention" nor a solution to the real problem facing western farmers – low world grain prices. The intransigence of Stephen and Van Horne, one Conservative politician told the prime minister, only contributed to the "fever heat" in Manitoba.[19]

The inability of the Manitoba government to break the deadlock with the Canadian Pacific and the dominion government eventually led to the defeat of first Premier Norquay, and then the Conservative administration in Manitoba. The new Liberal premier, Thomas Greenway, promised to forge ahead with the construction of the railway. As the railway controversy showed every sign of continuing unabated, the value of Canadian Pacific stock declined sharply. Seeking a way out of the impasse, Stephen proposed that his railway would give up its monopoly clause if the Macdonald government would guarantee $15 million in bonds. This would be used to purchase additional rolling stock and finance a number of other improvements, thus ostensibly preparing the Canadian Pacific for the new competitive environment. The government approved the proposal in April 1888.[20] Through the persistent efforts of the provincial government, Manitoba's business community had been successful in exerting enough pressure to have the monopoly clause eliminated from the Canadian Pacific's charter.

The railway controversy in Manitoba had already forced the Canadian Pacific to make some limited rate concessions. Although railway officials denied that there was any connection, in the fall of 1887 the company had reduced its grain rates from western points such as Winnipeg, Brandon, and Regina to Fort William by three to four cents per hundred pounds. By the autumn of 1888, a new tariff was adopted on freight shipped between Manitoba and the Lakehead that decreased rates on grain from one to three cents per hundred-weight and on general merchandise from 10 to 13 per cent. The 1888 changes were a direct response to the rates established by the Northern Pacific Railway, which had agreed to complete the Red River Valley line in exchange for a long-term lease.[21]

Beyond these initial adjustments, the costly fight for competition produced meagre results. Unfortunately for those seeking genuine competition, Northern Pacific officials acquired the Red River Valley line to counter the Canadian Pacific's power over transcontinental rates. Should the Canadian Pacific line cut its rates on the Pacific Coast, the Northern Pacific could now retaliate at Winnipeg. This balance of power did prove effective in stabilizing rates. Ironically, the Manitoba government had leased its line to a railway whose main objective was to prevent, not promote, competition.[22] Although Manitoba battled the dominion government and the Canadian Pacific for the right to competition in their province, and went to the length of actually constructing a portion of the competitive line itself, once built, they did little to ensure that it would provide real competition, or produce the lower rates they sought. Like their counterparts in Ontario, Manitoba business and political leaders discovered that rival railways did not necessarily compete. In future, the Manitoba government would not spend public money without acquiring some control over freight rates.

The next opportunity came in the late 1890s when the Northern Pacific asked the Manitoba government to either assist its proposed extension to Duluth, Minnesota or to permit the company to sell its money-losing lines in the province. Neither the administration of Thomas Greenway nor that of his successor, Conservative Rodmond Roblin, would accept any arrangement that did not include firm guarantees of tariff reductions, which the Northern Pacific refused to negotiate.[23]

By the early months of 1901, officials from two Canadian railway companies were courting the Manitoba government. Each sought a long-term lease of the Northern Pacific lines in Manitoba. Thomas

Shaugnessy, who had succeeded Van Horne as president of the Canadian Pacific in 1899, feared that any new rival might engage in a costly rate war. In exchange for a long-term lease, he proposed to reduce grain rates by four cents per hundredweight over the next five years, as well as to immediately lower salt and coal rates between Manitoba and the Lakehead. Furthermore, Shaugnessy agreed to contribute $5000 annually towards the salary of a government appointed official with the authority to investigate and enforce reasonable freight rates in the province.[24]

The Canadian Pacific faced a rival bidder, the Canadian Northern Railway, which had been organized in 1898 by two ambitious railway contractors, William Mackenzie and Donald Mann. Because the creation rather than the reduction of railway competition remained an important government objective, Mackenzie and Mann possessed a decided advantage in dealing with the Roblin administration. In the contract that they successfully negotiated with the Manitoba government in February 1901, Mackenzie and Mann promised both rate concessions and competition in exchange for a 999-year lease of the Northern Pacific lines, and a provincial bond guarantee to finance the expansion of their fledgling railway. By the terms of this contract, the government of Manitoba could adjust the freight rates charged within the province and between the province and Fort William as it saw fit, on condition that it subsidize any resulting deficiency between revenues and operating and capital costs.[25]

Although the contract was short on specific rate concessions, the Manitoba government and the Canadian Northern negotiated a freight tariff that produced reasonably significant reductions. It was agreed that grain rates would be reduced by two cents per hundredweight in 1902 and again in 1903, thus matching the Canadian Pacific four-cent concession in half the time. The Roblin administration also convinced Canadian Northern officials to reduce the tariff on all other merchandise by a total of 15 per cent: 7.5 per cent in 1901 and a further 7.5 per cent in 1902. To bring its other western rates somewhat into line, the Canadian Northern unilaterally reduced its general merchandise tariff in the Northwest Territories by 7.5 per cent. The Canadian Pacific retaliated by meeting the new rates.[26]

In negotiating this regulatory contract, the Manitoba government did succeed in bringing about a relatively significant reduction in western rates. The government did have the advantage of having rival applicants seeking to outbid one another, one of which was a fledgling railway whose future expansion depended on generous public assistance. Although Mackenzie and Mann were much more interested in their immediate financial needs than in the impact of freight rate reductions on the operating fortunes of their prospective railway, they did drive a shrewd bargain. Not only did they get the assistance they required, but they protected their railway by having the Manitoba government agree to cover any losses of revenue attributable to low freight rates. In that way, the provincial government would be equally committed to a profitable rate structure.

The Manitoba agreement represents one of two significant landmarks in the history of the nineteenth-century approach to regulation. A provincial government appropriated the technique employed by local governments and used public funds to ensure a degree of control over the freight rates of a private railway. This agreement, along with its attached specific rate concessions, had been preceded and partly inspired by another landmark of the strategy of competition and contract – the Crow's Nest Pass agreement, negotiated between the dominion government and the Canadian Pacific in 1897.

The Crow's Nest Pass agreement emerged as a result of the Canadian Pacific's desire to tap the markets and minerals of the booming mining district of southern British Columbia. Shortly after the election of Wilfrid Laurier's Liberal administration in 1896, Canadian Pacific executives approached the new dominion government with a special request for government assistance to build a line through the Crow's Nest Pass to the Kootenays. This request provoked unexpected opposition and a debate over railway competition in Canada. Canadian Pacific officials found that in order to acquire public funds, they would have to agree to the kind of regulatory contract that railway promoters often made with local governments.

By 1890, both the dominion government and Canadian Pacific officials had recognized the potential value of rail access to the mining districts of British Columbia, and the danger of losing that trade to American railways. The disorganization of the Conservative government in Ottawa in the years following the death of Macdonald in 1891 and the commercial depression after 1893 prevented significant public or private investment in a railway into the region. The Canadian Pacific's William Van Horne and Thomas Shaugnessy took the first opportunity following the election of Wilfrid Laurier in 1896 to press ahead with their project. They asked the new government for a subsidy of $5,000 per mile and a loan of $20,000 per mile to help construct a proposed 327-mile line through the Crow's Nest Pass to the East Kootenay district.[27]

Although Canadian Pacific officials actively encouraged boards of trade throughout Canada to support the project and courted influential Liberals, their campaign met with resistance. Business and political organizations in many parts of British Columbia, the prairie west and Ontario demanded that either the government or a different private company construct and operate the new line. They contended that any private railway should have its rates controlled by the government, and should guarantee "the perpetual maintenance of unrestricted competition."[28]

While only a few members of the government, most notably the new minister of railways and canals, Andrew George Blair, appear to have supported public construction, other Liberal members of Parliament opposed the Canadian Pacific's proposal. A.T. Wood, a Hamilton MP and hardware merchant with agents in Winnipeg and British Columbia, explained to Laurier that he and other traders did not want the railway to have exclusive control of the growing trade with the mining districts of the Kootenays. "I know that when you are aware of the feeling of the country," Wood wrote, "you will be the last man to surrender to the leader of the great monopoly, which like a great octopus is squeezing the very heart out of the business in the Northwest and British Columbia." Laurier assured Wood and other correspondents that the government would not make a deal that would increase the Canadian Pacific's monopoly power.[29]

The anti-Canadian Pacific, anti-monopoly sentiments expressed by Wood and others shifted the focus of negotiations over the Crow's Nest Pass subsidy to the question of competition and freight rates. Providing genuine rate competition in the area would be difficult. As Canadian Pacific officials willingly pointed out, any independent line still needed to make arrangements with either the Canadian or an American transcontinental railway for through traffic. The influential Liberal journalist J.S. Willison, sceptical of the effectiveness of railway competition anyway, suggested an alternative approach. He recommended that Parliament help the Canadian Pacific construct the line, but only on the condition that the company reduce its charges for hauling grain and other western products, accept permanent government supervision of its through and local rates, and abandon the section of its charter that prevented public control of rates unless profits exceeded 10 per cent of capital. By mid-March of 1897, Willison estimated that newspaper editorials throughout Canada favoured such a proposal by a ratio of twenty to one.[30]

Although Canadian Pacific president William Van Horne initially balked at negotiating rate reductions, he was anxious to make a deal.

Failure to reach an agreement would have reinforced the impression abroad among investors that the new dominion government was hostile to the company. Moreover, as Van Horne told one Canadian Pacific director, Donald Smith, "control of the traffic of Southern British Columbia is of too great importance to us to justify any risk whatever of losing it." The Kootenay district, a source of fuel for the railway, the site of potentially valuable mining properties, and the centre of a lucrative traffic in ores and merchandise, was simply too valuable a territory to lose to any competitor.[31]

Laurier entrusted his minister of the interior, Clifford Sifton, to negotiate with Canadian Pacific executives. In the final agreement, Sifton and Van Horne tried to appease various regional interests without seriously undermining the financial condition of the Canadian Pacific. In exchange for a subsidy of $11,000 per mile, the Canadian Pacific agreed to reduce its rates on eastbound western grain by three to fourteen cents per hundredweight, and to lower its westbound tariff from the Lakehead and eastern Canada on green and fresh fruits by one-third, on coal oil by one-fifth, and on agricultural implements, cordage and binder twine, wire, window glass, hardware, building and roofing paper, paints, livestock, woodenware, and household furniture by one-tenth. These reductions were intended to appeal to farmers and other consumers in the west, as well as to merchants and manufacturers in eastern Canada who hoped to profit from expanded trade with the Canadian west. Winnipeg merchants, whose trading interests were neglected in these adjustments, had to settle for informal guarantees that the railway would continue to protect their central position in the distribution of westbound goods.[32]

At the conclusion of the negotiations, Van Horne reported to Donald Smith that "All of us here feel well satisfied with the bargain." Though all the while Van Horne warned Sifton of the disastrous financial consequences of lower grain rates, he informed Smith that the reduction would have been forced upon the railway by other causes. He regarded the adjustments in the railway's other commodity rates as nominal, adopted in response not to the negotiations for the Crow subsidy, but to the government's alterations of Canada's trade tariff.[33]

Furthermore, Van Horne succeeded in limiting the government's future control over the railway's freight tariff. Only the maximum local and through tolls charged on the Crow's Nest Pass line were to be regulated by the government. The exemption from regulation on the rest of the railway contained in section 20 of the company's corporate charter remained intact. As to guaranteeing other railways access to the Crow line, the agreement largely confirmed those rights already guaranteed in the general railway law of Canada.[34] Clearly, Canadian Pacific executives believed they had given up very little in exchange for a substantial subsidy arrangement.

The limited contractual obligations negotiated in the Crow's Nest Pass agreement demonstrated that railway promoters still had a fairly strong bargaining position in negotiations with governments. While the newly elected Laurier government was anxious to appear as a defender of the people against the previous Conservative government's pet railway, it also hoped to gain the politically invaluable support of the Canadian Pacific. The Canadian Pacific never really faced a serious rival in negotiating the construction of the Crow's Nest Pass. Moreover, the project was seen to be of considerable importance to the overall health of an economy just emerging from a commercial depression. In a memo to the prime minister, Sifton underlined the "tremendous" effect the large monthly expenditures for the construction of the new line would have on the trade of Canada, "in its present condition."[35]

In spite of its limits, the Crow's Nest Pass agreement represented a significant development in the nineteenth-century regulatory system. For the first time, the national government adopted the local government strategy of attaching rate-regulatory conditions to a financial subsidy. If it had the political will, the federal government was in a better position to enforce its contract because the railway company could not escape its obligations through an appeal to a higher governing authority. Although those who supported competition in the Crow's Nest Pass failed to achieve their objective, the controversy that they generated resulted in the government asserting some measure of control over freight rates on one of Canada's major railways. Furthermore, what Van Horne regarded as relatively harmless maximum rates would acquire an unexpected significance after World War I.

While it could hardly be called laissez-faire, Canadian business and political leaders adopted a market-oriented approach to the regulation of railway freight rates in the late nineteenth century. They did not readily abandon the market system in favour of government intervention but rather looked to familiar business mechanisms – competition and contracts – to resolve their freight grievances. The dependence of many of Canada's railways on public assistance provided the means of introducing some controls on private behaviour. Nevertheless, railway executives continued to enjoy considerable influence and bargaining leverage when it came to dealing with governments. However much railway promoters might need public money, the governments with whom they negotiated frequently needed the railways just as badly. Local, provincial, and national politicians depended on the successful construction of the new lines to fulfill election pledges and to promote the overall development of the economy; they also sought to maintain friendly relations with politically influential railway corporations. They could not let the negotiation of regulatory concessions interfere with these other objectives.

Well into the twentieth century, business and political leaders continued to try to shape railway corporate behaviour by creating competition. "Will any man tell me that the towns of Oshawa, Bowmanville, Port Hope, Cobourg, Belleville, and lively Kingston need another railway to move their traffic?" one prairie lawyer asked as the Canadian Northern successfully whipped up local support and acquired public funding for the construction of a third railway line along the north shore of Lake Ontario. The same question could have been asked as the same railway received generous government support to construct branch lines into areas already served by the rival Canadian Pacific in the prairie west. In British Columbia, Canadian Northern promoters were generously assisted by the provincial government to construct a line from Vancouver to the prairie west, in order to provide competition for the Canadian Pacific. Although the dominion government did require the Grand Trunk to build its transcontinental through new areas, many parts of the line were located within twenty miles of, and parallel to either of its rivals. The government even rerouted part of the line to provide a rival for the Canadian Pacific between Winnipeg and Portage La Prairie.[36] As J.S. Willison had been told, it was difficult for men schooled in the doctrine of competition to fully abandon the principle.

Business and political leaders continued to use public money to acquire regulatory concessions. In exchange for a substantial bond guarantee, the British Columbia government asserted exclusive control over the rates to be charged on the Canadian Northern's line in the province. Before the dominion government began financing the Grand Trunk Pacific project in 1903, its promoters had to agree that the new line offer freight rates and facilities to promote the routing of traffic through Canadian ports. In the same year, the Laurier administration stipulated that its financial assistance to the Canadian Northern was conditional on the railway charging rates no higher that "the rates or tolls which may be fixed in the contract to be made ... under this Act," although no such agreements ever were negotiated.[37]

Faith in competition and contract continued into the twentieth century, and complicated the task of those who sought to regulate the railways. The belief that competition would regulate railway behaviour helped produce an extraordinary amount of duplication within the Canadian railway network in the years preceding World War I, eventually creating enormous problems for public policy-makers. At the same time, public regulators grappled with a rate structure that was shaped by a network of contractually governed agreements, most notably the Manitoba and Crow's Nest Pass agreements.

CHAPTER FOUR

Public Authority, Private Rights

The creation of competition and the enforcement of its benefits through contract did not challenge the private rate-making prerogative of railway companies. Indeed, governments implicitly recognized corporate powers by "purchasing" a limited measure of public control through formal contracts. Nevertheless, it remained possible for the Canadian legal authority David Mills to argue that "the State" stood in a different relation to railways than "to other species of private property." Writing in 1872, Mills contended that railway corporations received generous government assistance and the sovereign power to expropriate property "upon grounds, not of private necessity, but of public utility." The private power of railways had always been derived from, and circumscribed by, public authorities. At a minimum, the railway industry possessed certain definite public responsibilities, grounded in English common and statutory law. Mills interpreted the state's proper role more broadly. "One of the most important duties now devolving upon Parliament," he concluded, "is to determine within what range railway corporations shall be confined."[1]

While the creation of competition and contractual obligations remained a dominant strategy of regulation throughout the nineteenth century, the concept of the railway as a public utility provided the basis for a quite different form of public control. As dissatisfaction grew with the emerging rate structure and the effectiveness of competition as a regulatory mechanism, business and political leaders sought a clearer definition of, and a more efficient means of enforcing the traditional legal obligations of railway corporations. For their part, railway officials resisted any serious effort to restrict their existing private power. The result was that although Parliament clarified the legal obligations of railways and experimented with a new institutional means of responding to rate complaints, the railways continued to accept only a narrow definition of their legal responsibilities. By the end of the nineteenth century, the response of the government and the railway industry to the freight rate controversy demonstrated the extent of private power and the limits of public authority.

Canadian legislators, like their counterparts in Great Britain and the United States, granted extraordinary discretion to private organizations to finance, construct, and operate railways. Vigilant British administrators encouraged and pressured Canadian legislators to ensure that the ultimate supremacy of the state, implicit in the act of granting charters, was made explicit. In response, colonial legislators included provisions in many early railway charters, including that of the Grand Trunk, that reserved the right of the government to assume ownership and control of the company in the future.

Until World War I, however, governments did not exercise their right to take direct control of private railways. Public ownership remained an exception, resorted to only when a private entrepreneur could not be interested in a particular project. In order to fulfill a promise embodied in the British North America Act, for example, the dominion government constructed and then operated the Intercolonial Railway, which provided an all-Canadian rail link between the Maritimes and central Canada. At the turn of the century, the dominion government also built the National Transcontinental Railway across the northern regions of Ontario and Quebec, but only on the understanding that upon its completion, it would be operated by the Grand Trunk.

Because governments engaged in the railway business reluctantly, they did not look upon public ownership as a means of regulation. A number of different governments rebuffed attempts to have the Intercolonial Railway adopt a fixed mileage tariff, equalize long- and short-haul rates, or even refrain from offering preferential tariffs. The railway's public managers did not envisage any special developmental objective in setting rates. Like their private counterparts, they were anxious to encourage traffic if it promised to generate greater revenue for the railway. The railway's general manager summarized his approach to rate-making: "The Intercolonial is looking after its own interests and has no desire to work against or for any particular place, but merely to take care of itself to the best advantage."[2] Similarly, when the Borden administration assumed the task of operating the National Transcontinental in 1915, it refused to have the railway play a developmental, regulative role. Although a number of interests pressured the government to use the railway to help reduce the cost of transporting grain through Canadian ports, the National Transcontinental did not set a competitive pace by introducing low developmental rates on western grain between Lake Superior and Quebec City.[3]

Whatever rhetoric they might use, then, most governments regarded public ownership as a necessary evil and not as a positive assertion of state sovereignty. In fact, the few examples of government operation that did exist became symbols of the inherent evils of the whole principle of public ownership. Critics of government railways were variously motivated by an interested or principled opposition to the extension of public control, a concern over increasing public expenditures on government railways, a partisan desire to highlight a governments's incompetence, or a sense that their particular region or community failed to benefit from existing policies. Armed with far more information than they might ever have about a private railway company, these critics created an image of government railways as patronage-ridden, inefficient enterprises. Even many of those who favoured public ownership advocated a more "businesslike," independent approach to government railway operations. Public railways were to behave as if they were private ones; market competition rather than government intervention would regulate their operating and rate-making decisions.[4]

Direct public acquisition of railways remained an anomaly, and peripheral to the debate over rate regulation throughout the nineteenth and early twentieth centuries. From the onset of railway construction in Canada, legislators included in railway charters other means of asserting public control over private companies. The province of Canada's 1851 Railway Clauses Consolidation Act, which provided the basis for the dominion of Canada's railway act, outlined three specific provisions with respect to rates that were to be incorporated into every subsequent railway charter. These measures, imported from British statutes, represent the basic foundation of the nineteenth-century regulatory system.

The first of these empowered Parliament to intervene and reduce the tolls charged by any railway whose net income from all sources exceeded 15 per cent of the capital actually expended in its construction. When the Canadian Pacific Railway received its charter, this provision was made more restrictive by adopting the British standard of a net income of only 10 per cent. Given the poor financial returns on all Canadian railways throughout the nineteenth century, Parliament never had an opportunity to use this power. Railway officials went so far as to argue that Parliament could not interfere in any way with their rate-making powers until their profits exceeded the allowable limit. This legal interpretation, most frequently pressed by the Canadian Pacific Railway, was never tested in the courts, but it remained a potent argument.[5] What was intended as a restraint on private power became a potential restriction on public authority.

A second measure granted the executive of the government extensive authority over railway rates by providing that freight tariffs had to be approved by cabinet and were subject to its revision. Although potentially important, this form of control remained a passive and feeble restriction on railway operations throughout the nineteenth century, largely because governments made little effort to enforce the provision. As a result, many railway companies operated under tariffs that had never been sanctioned. For example, although in 1888 the government discovered that the only Canadian Pacific western tariff it had ever approved had expired four years previously, by 1894 neither the government nor the railway company had bothered to correct the situation. It made little difference anyway, since in practice, governments only approved the maximum tariff. High maximum levels and generally falling rates ensured that railway officials retained a good deal of flexibility in adjusting tolls. At the turn of the century, Grand Trunk and Canadian Pacific officials had little difficulty charging rates in Ontario and Quebec well within the general tariff approved for use in 1884.[6]

The executive and legislative regulatory measures concentrated on the absolute level and overall profitability of the rate structure. The relative level of rates offered to different shippers and communities, however, lay at the core of rate grievances. Individual shippers were expected to resolve these complaints by taking legal action in the courts, relying on the third specific provision required in railway charters, which stipulated that the rates charged be "payable at the same time and under the same circumstances upon all goods and persons, so that no undue advantage, privilege or monopoly may be afforded to any person or class of persons."[7]

Yet, although government investigations uncovered numerous rate complaints in Canada's industrial and mercantile heartland in southwestern Ontario, shippers rarely used the courts to resolve rate disputes. Of 266 suits brought against railway companies in the courts serving Toronto, Hamilton, and London between the 1850s and 1900, only two involved the question of rates. Nineteenth-century Canadian legal commentators relied on English precedents to interpret rate law, since so few reported Canadian cases existed.[8] In the single most important Canadian rate case, the interpretation offered and English authorities followed help explain the reluctance of shippers to resort to the courts.

In its 1873 ruling in *Scott v. Midland Railway*, the Ontario Court of Queen's Bench responded to an attempt to enforce two of the public obligations of railways: the requirement that tariffs have government approval and that shippers receive equal treatment. The executors of a Lindsay businessman sought to recover the amount of freight costs he had paid to the Midland Railway. They based their suit on two arguments. First, they alleged that prior to 1867, the railway had no right to collect any tolls, as the government had never approved the rates on the Midland Railway. Second, they contended that after 1867, two different railway rate policies constituted undue discrimination under the law. For several years Midland officials had charged less to carry lumber to Lake Ontario from Port Perry than from Lindsay, even though the haul from Port Perry was thirty miles longer. As well, because the Lindsay lumber merchant had refused to sign a four-, five-, or ten-year agreement to ship his freight exclusively by rail, he had paid thirty cents more per hundredweight than those dealers who did. The Lindsay merchant, it was contended, had been the victim of discrimination that was both personal and based on his geographic location.[9]

The judicial interpretation of the railway's legal obligations strictly limited the effectiveness of public control. The court ruled that in the absence of a government-sanctioned by-law, railway companies were, as common carriers, still entitled to receive a fair and reasonable compensation for any services they performed. This fine distinction between statutory tolls and common law compensation for services ensured that railway officials could collect money for carrying freight without having their tariff approved. In failing to fulfill their public responsibility, they simply forfeited some powers and procedures established under statute in the case of nonpayment of tolls. The railway companies did not have to reimburse charges paid in the absence of a formally approved freight tariff, unless the aggrieved shipper could prove those charges were unreasonable.[10]

In considering the provisions of the Railway Act that dealt with equality and non-discrimination, the Ontario Court of Queen's Bench followed the strict and limited interpretations offered by the English courts. Mr Justice Morrison concluded that the provisions only required that the railway charge an equal amount to all persons for carrying similar freight between precisely the same points. Such a narrow definition defeated the first allegation of discrimination based on location. Morrison then cited with approval English judicial statements that even between the same points, a railway corporation might vary the rates it charged in relation to the quantity of freight shipped, or as part of the kind of exclusive carrying contracts the Midland Railway signed with various lumber merchants.

Furthermore, in order to maintain a charge of discrimination, the court ruled that any aggrieved shipper had to provide concrete evidence of the transactions involving differential rates, prove that all other circumstances were identical, and clearly show that the lower rates gave an "undue advantage" to those shippers enjoying them.[11] Considering the potential difficulties in meeting even the first criterion – establishing what freight rates competitors actually paid – the judgment imposed a heavy burden of proof on plaintiffs, while affording railway companies a number of possible defences against such complaints. Such rigid and strict criteria required to establish a case of discrimination both discouraged shippers from using the court system, and reinforced the traditional suspicion of many business leaders that the courts represented an ineffective forum for resolving their rate disputes.[12]

Judicial enforcement of the equality clause, cabinet approval of freight tariffs, or parliamentary initiative in the event of excessive profits did not seriously restrict the private rate-making prerogative of railway corporations. The formal regulatory system established at the outset of Canada's railway age did not offer the kind of public control favoured by a growing number of shippers and their political representatives by the 1870s and 1880s. As the fight for competition also appeared to have revealed, neither governments nor the courts seemed willing or able to restrain private power in the public interest. By the closing decades of the nineteenth century, the transportation revolution and rate-making process generated grievances against the kind of power that railway corporations exercised in Canadian society. That dissatisfaction merged with a concern that existing public institutions were failing to restrain that power.

The ensuing debate concentrated largely on the creation of a body that would be capable of enforcing the state's existing legal authority. The Conservative member of Parliament D'Alton McCarthy contended that railway companies were becoming "practically beyond all law by reason of the want of a proper tribunal to carry it out." He saw the need for a forum "more readily accessible, more expeditious and less expensive than any now existing for the settlement of disputes between the public and the railway companies." Throughout the 1880s, McCarthy championed his alternative – a "Court of Railway Commissioners" – and stimulated a serious debate over the regulation of railways.[13]

D'Alton McCarthy's immediate interest in the railway commission proposal emerged from his involvement in the fight for competition. He was a prominent lawyer who practised both in Barrie and Toronto, and provided legal advice to the Simcoe County Council when it sought to prevent the amalgamation of the Northern and Hamilton and Northwestern lines, and to the Credit Valley Railway in its bid to acquire access to Toronto's harbourfront. Frustrated by the response of the courts in both these cases, he became determined to create a more practical forum for handling public disputes with railways.

McCarthy called for the creation of a special "Court of Railway Commissioners," with jurisdiction over freight and passenger rates, railway amalgamations, and a number of other matters that were a frequent source of disputes, such as the location of railway crossings. The new tribunal would resemble a court of law in its powers and procedures, and the three commissioners would enjoy the political independence of judges. Only one commissioner would be an experienced lawyer, however; the other two, a railway official and a man of "common sense," would bring a practical approach to disputes. McCarthy also hoped to make his new institution more accessible than an ordinary court through another innovation: any municipal government, agricultural association, board of trade, or other business organization would be permitted to present the complaints of their members.[14]

The proposal for a court of railway commissioners resembled others being considered in Canada, many of which were inspired by the creation in 1873 of the English Railways and Canals Commission.[15] McCarthy provided the supporters of such an alternative with an influential, if somewhat enigmatic, champion. Throughout the 1880s, the relatively young politician was a power in the ruling Conservative party: he was selected to represent the government in a number of important legal controversies with the Ontario government, helped found the pro-Conservative Toronto *Empire* when the Toronto *Mail* broke with the party, was offered but refused a cabinet appointment, and was sometimes touted as a successor to the aging prime minister. McCarthy had an independent streak that always kept him from the centre of power and later led to his alienation from the party when he engaged in his well-known crusade against the extension of French language and education rights.[16]

It was this relative political independence that allowed McCarthy to become the champion of the railway commission proposal. He introduced a private member's bill on the Court of Railway Commissioners in each session of Parliament between 1880 and 1886, in spite of the opposition of Charles Tupper, the minister of railways, and other key members of the Conservative government. McCarthy received the support of over a dozen Conservative and Reform members of Parliament, the boards of trade of Toronto and Ottawa, as well as numerous municipal and county councils.[17] In 1883, the Grand Trunk's general manager, Joseph Hickson, who like most other Canadian railway executives strongly opposed the measure, warned the prime minister not to underestimate McCarthy's influence. He thought it would be dangerous to dismiss the proposal out of hand, but instead urged that it be referred to the powerful House of Commons Standing Committee on Railways, "where it may stay for a while." There, Hickson promised the railway companies would "leave no stone unturned and use all the influence they can on the Members of Parliament."[18]

Prime Minister Macdonald, nicknamed 'Old Tomorrow' for his willingness to avoid controversy by procrastinating, readily followed Hickson's advice and convinced a reluctant but still loyal McCarthy to allow the Railway Committee to study his bill. Railway officials then arranged for what one reporter called "the largest aggregate of deputations ever assembled in Ottawa" to oppose McCarthy's proposal. The presence of 150 railway officials and shippers, combined with the attendance of nearly 100 members of Parliament, forced the committee to move from the large Railway Committee Room to the Chamber of the House of Commons.[19]

Officials from the Grand Trunk and Northern railways warned the assembled politicians against importing a regulatory system that had been designed for England's "fully developed trade and its enormous and profitable railway system." The current laws and court system did respond to aggrieved shippers, they argued, and McCarthy's proposals would simply inhibit the profitable American through traffic and frighten away the investment capital desperately required to develop the Canadian railway network. A group representing well over 100 shippers from all parts of Ontario and Quebec then told the committee that "the cure it [the bill] proposes would be far worse than the disease." These business leaders feared the proposed commission would outlaw the special rates railways fixed in response to shipping and market conditions. Larger shippers, grain merchants, and lumber dealers did not want to lose the benefits such flexibility in rate making offered.[20]

Sustained railway opposition and serious divisions among shippers guaranteed the failure of McCarthy's proposal. On 3 April 1883, seventy-six parliamentarians, including the prime minister, the minister of railways, two other members of cabinet, and a former Reform Party leader and prime minister, rejected the bill. Only a small group of six Conservatives, five Reformers and one Independent, all but one of them representing Ontario constituencies, voted in support of the bill.[21] McCarthy could take some comfort when the government amended the Railway Act during the same session of Parliament to include a revised equality clause he had proposed in his bill.[22]

McCarthy continued to champion the railway commission proposal in spite of the adverse vote. Three years later "Old Tomorrow" Macdonald adopted a second delaying tactic. In 1886, he appointed the aging but still enterprising railway promoter and loyal Conservative, Alexander Galt, to head up a royal commission to study the matter. This was one of two major royal commissions appointed in 1886; the other was asked to investigate the "Relations of Labour and Capital." On the eve of an election, Prime Minister Macdonald sought to appease disgruntled Conservatives as well as important segments of the electorate, and to defuse potentially explosive controversies over the economic transformation of Canada.[23]

Only days after the Royal Commission on Railways commenced its hearings, Galt complained that they were "very long and troublesome," and confessed to his wife that if he could devise an excuse, he would resign. Instead, he simply did not attend most of the hearings and left Egerton R. Burpee (of the prominent Saint John business family) to chair the meetings. Assisting Burpee in hearing witnesses were George Moberly, a Collingwood lawyer with extensive business and transportation interests, and Collingwood Schreiber, a trusted career civil servant. Schreiber, responsible for the operation of the government's own railway system, sympathized with private railway officials and understood the kinds of controversy rate-making practices generated.[24]

No clear consensus emerged from the testimony heard in Toronto, Montreal, Halifax, Saint John, Quebec, Hamilton, and London. Of the 277 merchants, manufacturers, farmers, and community leaders who appeared, 131 supported and 112 opposed the proposal to create a railway commission. Moreover, as one reporter noted, the testimony was frequently vague, puzzling, and contradictory. In Halifax and Saint John, for example, a number of witnesses understandably interpreted the creation of a railway commission as involving a reform in the management structure of the government-operated Intercolonial Railway. Elsewhere, shippers presented their own particular rate grievances; few showed signs of having given any consideration to the proposal for a railway tribunal. When pressed by the commissioners, advocates of the railway commission spoke generally of the need for an institution that was "come-at-able," an accessible, expeditious, and inexpensive forum of "common sense."[25]

As in 1883, the proposal for a railway commission divided shippers. Opponents preferred to leave rate making to the good sense of railway managers, rather than create "a circumlocution office for business which we might have to transact with the railway companies." Many shippers, particularly grain and lumber merchants, continued to fear that a railway commission would interfere with the special rates upon which their business depended. Railway officials played on these fears and took some part in orchestrating the appearance of witnesses whose testimony, in the words of Canadian Pacific Assistant General Manager Thomas Shaugnessy, "will be reasonable and just to the companies, and will tend to show how ridiculous is a large amount of the evidence given by interested and incompetent people."[26] In this way, they continued to resist any expansion of public control over their rates. The adoption of the Interstate Commerce Act in 1887 in the United States only increased their opposition to any changes in Canadian law. Because American railways were now subject to a law forbidding the charging of higher rates for the shorter than for the longer haul, the Canadian Pacific and Grand Trunk hoped to offer lower through rates and capture a share of American oceanbound traffic.[27] Testifying before the royal commission inquiry, both Canadian Pacific Vice-President William Van Horne and Grand Trunk General Manager Joseph Hickson argued vehemently that Canadian legislators should not adopt a similar long- and short-haul clause.

Nor did the railway managers believe any increased government regulation was necessary. The current system of laws, they argued, provided ample protection to those few shippers who genuinely encountered discrimination. Further government interference would simply fail. Van Horne noted that wherever local legislatures and railway commissions in the United States had attempted to fix "hard and fast rules" with respect to rates, "they have been obliged to squint at deliberate violations of their enactments or rules." Hickson concluded that any central authority like the newly created Interstate Commerce Commission "would find itself overwhelmed with work and with complaints with which it would be wholly unable to deal."[28]

In the face of vague testimony, conflicting opinions within the shipping community, and the determined opposition of the railway industry, the members of the royal commission produced a cautious report. After favourably comparing the construction costs and low freight tariffs on Canadian railways, the report suggested a few amendments to clarify the law with respect to rates and offered a compromise on the major question of a regulatory commission. Instead of creating a special independent agency, the report recommended that new authority be given to an old institution – the Railway Committee of the Privy Council. This special cabinet committee already formally certified the safety of all new rail lines, ensured the proper construction and maintenance of public crossings, and required railway companies to submit returns of accidents. The Royal Commission recommended that the committee also be authorized to resolve disputes between railway companies and between shippers and railway companies over freight tariffs and classification.

Galt and his colleagues admitted that the Railway Committee was not a perfect institution. Its members were cabinet ministers with other responsibilities who had to remain in Ottawa, might be expected to be somewhat partisan, and could not concentrate exclusively on railway matters. To overcome the first of these problems, it was suggested that the Railway Committee be authorized to appoint officers in each province to hear and determine local complaints. The other limitations, the commissioners concluded, were outweighed by two general advantages. First, widening the authority of the Railway Committee would involve "the least possible disturbance to existing methods." Second, members of the committee were directly accountable to Parliament, preserving a fundamental principle of responsible government. Since a railway tribunal was experimental, the royal commissioners concluded, it seemed "undesirable to remove its operation, in its inception, beyond the direct criticism and control of Parliament." Under their proposal, Canada would "avoid the hasty creation" of a new system of railway regulation.[29]

Perhaps because the Report of the Royal Commission on Railways was so moderate, most of its recommendations were embodied in the revised dominion Railway Act of 1888. The sections of the law with respect to rates were amended to establish more clearly what constituted discrimination. The act provided more specific measures to prevent the practices that were most offensive, both to shippers and to railway officials – the granting of secret rates, rebates, and individual privileges. In contrast to the 1887 American railway act, Canada's new legislation explicitly authorized the offering of proportionately lower tolls for longer hauls and for larger quantities of freight. Differential rates between localities "which, by reason of competition by water or railway, it is necessary to make to secure traffic" were also not to be considered discriminatory. For the most part, then, the revised Railway Act simply translated the narrow definition of discrimination accepted in the English and Canadian courts into statutory language.[30]

The new legislation authorized the Railway Committee of the Privy Council to enforce the law. The committee, to be composed of the minister of railways and canals, the minister of justice, and two other members of cabinet, was to deal with matters as diverse as crossings, fencing, rates of speed through municipalities, as well as the adjustment of tolls, and unjust discrimination. Little was done to make the Railway Committee more accessible to the public. The legislation did not include a provision such as McCarthy had proposed permitting associations and organizations to appear on behalf of their members. Nor did it incorporate the royal commission's recommendation concerning the appointment of regional officers to hear and determine local complaints.[31]

With the 1888 Railway Act, Canada took a timid first step towards expanding the regulatory authority of the state. Although Hickson of the Grand Trunk pressed the government to postpone its initiative, the new legislation did not seriously interfere in the private sphere of railway operations.[32] The Railway Act formally sanctioned a number of private rate-making practices, and the enforcement of all of its new rate provisions rested with the cabinet, hitherto sympathetic to railway company concerns. In the regulatory debate of the 1880s, private rights were maintained against public authority.

The government's cautious experiment with the Railway Committee of the Privy Council proved to be important, for it set the stage for the final debate over the the creation of a railway commission. During the 1890s, the Railway Committee amply demonstrated that its limitations as a regulatory body outweighed its advantages. Of equal importance, the government's experience revealed flaws in the overall extent of public control which had been established in the nineteenth century.

During the entire fifteen years that the Railway Committee's jurisdiction included rate matters, it received fewer than twenty complaints concerning passenger or freight tolls. Only half of the complaints were set down for a hearing, and four of these were dismissed when the complainant failed to appear.[33] Shippers, large numbers of whom willingly voiced their complaints to the Royal Commission on Railways in 1886 and 1887, shunned the Railway Committee, just as they had the courts.

The treatment of the rate complaints from two western farm organizations provides important insights into the operations of the Railway Committee. In June of 1893, the Manitoba Farmers' Central Institute asked the government to end the discriminatory practices of the Canadian Pacific against a number of communities on its western line. The government instead referred the matter to the Railway Committee, which asked the organization to formulate and prove a specific case. Although providing a few more details, the Institute's secretary insisted "It lies with the Government as the Guardian of the people's interests to make the enquiry." Although the committee did have the power to institute inquiries, it did not take up the challenge. Instead, when no one appeared for the Farmers' Institute at three scheduled hearings, the case simply was dismissed.[34]

Unlike the Farmers' Institute, the members of the Regina County Association of the Patrons of Industry formulated their grievances into a detailed brief and arranged for two western Conservative politicians, Senator Charles A. Boulton and Nicholas F. Davin, to represent them. The Conservative government responded more quickly to pressure from their own colleagues and from a farm organization with growing influence in the west. The Railway Committee heard the complaint just over a month after receiving it. In presenting their case, Boulton and Davin rested the Patrons' allegation of discrimination on a series of rate comparisons which allegedly demonstrated that freight charges were higher in western Canada than in either eastern Canada or the western United States. These comparisons raised some emotional and complex questions about the overall equity of the Canadian freight rate structure. Similar arguments would haunt Canadian regulators and politicians for years to come.[35]

Any substantive questions, however, were lost in a sea of procedural and jurisdictional questions raised by the Canadian Pacific Railway's chief solicitor, the Honourable Mr Justice George M. Clark. Clark emphasized that the cabinet Railway Committee was not sitting to hear and settle political questions; as a judicial body, it must follow legally accepted standards. The Patrons, he noted, had no more right to present their complaints to the committee than to a court of law because they lacked a direct and material interest in the question. Furthermore, the complaints were based only on a comparison of published freight tariffs, whereas a court required evidence that a specific transaction or set of transactions had actually occurred under the cited freight tariffs. Finally, Clark argued that as a Canadian court, the committee must follow English authorities, which had already ruled that rate comparisons between different regions did not constitute a charge of unjust discrimination.

When Boulton protested that the presentation of the complaints of the people should not be "bound down by the technicalities of the representatives of the Canadian Pacific Railway," the chairman of the Railway Committee, Railways Minister John Haggart, reminded him that as a legal tribunal the Railway Committee was bound by those technicalities. He adjourned the case until such time as the Patrons could provide evidence of specific transactions and could show that the rates were discriminatory in ways other than by mere comparison with different regions. The editor of one Patron newspaper, the *Canada Farmers Sun*, expressed outrage at Haggart's "unceremonious treatment" of the facts.[36]

As politicians, the members of the Railway Committee adopted a somewhat less harsh response to the Patron's complaints. Prior to the formal Railway Committee hearing, the deputy minister of railways, Collingwood Schreiber, broached the idea of a government inquiry with Canadian Pacific officials. While both Vice-President Shaugnessy and President Van Horne objected to the appointment of a royal commission, they agreed to go along with a "factual" investigation by officers of the Department of Railways or the Railway Committee.[37] On 15 November 1894 the Conservative government authorized a committee of three civil servants, all from the Department of the Interior, to hold public hearings in the west and undertake an investigation of western rates. Through the winter of 1894–95 the three men, P.S. Archibald, William Pearce, and W.H. Allison, listened to allegations of high and discriminatory rates at over twenty prairie communities from Winnipeg, Regina, Calgary, and Edmonton to Morden, Wawanesa, and Moosomin. The three commissioners were obviously unimpressed by what they heard, for in their final report of May 1895, they completely vindicated the rate policies of the Canadian Pacific. Their report included only those favourable comparisons of the freight tariffs in the western United States and Canada presented by railway officials, although the conflicting evidence they heard suggested that comparisons between carefully selected points could produce just about any result. To make matters worse, the government did not append the complete proceedings of the inquiry to the report, only the testimony of Canadian Pacific Vice-President Thomas Shaugnessy. Although the commission undoubtedly received some flawed evidence and spurious complaints from western shippers, the Toronto journalist J.S. Willison offered a fair verdict in concluding that "the report is a railway rather than a public document, and does not show any exhaustive consideration of the questions at issue."[38]

Although the complaints of western farm organizations prompted this minor if rather ineffective inquiry, they also revealed the degree to which the Railway Committee intended to emulate fully judicial procedures. While the committee's approach might have worked well in settling crossing, traffic, and other property questions between railway companies or between railways and municipal governments, it hindered the effective resolution of rate complaints from private shippers. The onus to provide evidence of actual business transactions and to demonstrate clearly how they contravened the law frustrated progress on most complaints sent to the Railway Committee.[39] "In regulating rates, in preventing discrimination, in protecting the individual shipper or the individual community against the calculated injustice or the insidious aggression of railway managers", J.S. Willison concluded in 1897, the Railway Committee of the Privy Council "is inert and impotent, a farce and a failure."[40]

One final, spectacular rate controversy revealed the weakness of the Railway Committee and the entire system of public control that had been patched together in the nineteenth century. The controversy arose from a secret agreement senior officials of the Grand Trunk and Canadian Pacific forged with representatives of the Standard Oil Company at Montreal's Windsor Hotel during September of 1898. Standard officials threatened to ship their company's oil exclusively by tankers to key markets such as Montreal, unless the railways agreed to cut by one-third freight rates from Standard's newly acquired refining facilities at Petrolia and Sarnia. While rejecting this proposition, railway officials anxiously sought to retain the lucrative traffic offered by a company that dominated the American oil industry and was in the process of acquiring a monopoly of Canadian petroleum refining operations. Following extensive negotiations, Standard Oil and railway officials reached a secret agreement.[41]

In October 1898, the railway companies introduced a new freight tariff that appeared to increase all oil rates. Rates from Petrolia and Sarnia, where Standard Oil had acquired refineries, only increased by one-fifth, however, whereas the Canadian portion of the rate on oil shipped from independent operators in Pennsylvania advanced by between one-third and one-half. Furthermore, railway officials also privately reduced by one-sixth the new rates from Standard's Canadian refineries to all centres where water competition was effective, including the lucrative markets of Toronto and Montreal. If anyone doubted the intent of the rates introduced in October of 1898, in January 1899 railway officials completed their bargain by slapping a higher rate on "American oil" than on "Canadian oil" shipped within Ontario and Quebec.[42]

Standard Oil, therefore acquired a significant competitive advantage for shipping oil from its new Canadian facilities over imports from independent operators. A Montreal merchant estimated that the net result of the agreement amounted to an additional customs duty of 1.125 cents per gallon on the oil that he imported from independent refiners in Pennsylvania and Ohio. An American refiner summed up the impact of the agreement succinctly: "I cannot sell oil in Montreal under these conditions." The situation outraged not only Standard's competitors but manufacturers such as Massey-Harris who consumed considerable amounts of fuel oil.[43]

The adverse impact of the deal on independent refiners and on manufacturers, the secretive nature of the agreement, and the spectre of the Standard Oil Trust arriving in Canada, ensured that the government would be expected to act. Clifford Sifton, a moderate member of Prime Minister Wilfrid Laurier's cabinet with respect to railway matters, urged J.S. Willison to fight the Standard Oil controversy to the finish in the editorial pages of the *Globe*. Railways Minister A.G. Blair actively encouraged a Hamilton distributor of American oil, the Sun Oil Refining Company, to formulate a case for presentation to the Railway Committee.[44]

Within three weeks of the Sun Oil Company's making a formal complaint, Blair convened a hearing of the Railway Committee. From the outset, the Canadian Pacific's Judge Clark and the Grand Trunk solicitor B.B. Osler stonewalled, using procedural and jurisdictional arguments. Counsel for Sun Oil, they argued, failed to present evidence of a specific transaction involving the allegedly discriminatory rates. Furthermore, the railway counsel pointed out that the Railway Committee lacked jurisdiction over rates from points in the United States such as those contained in the October tariff. Blair pressed the lawyers to admit that the advances prevented American oil from competing with Standard's Canadian oil. The effect of the rates was of no concern to the Railway Committee, responded Osler, because it had no legal right to regulate them. The hearing adjourned after one day, with the Railway Committee reserving judgment on the crucial question of its jurisdiction.[45]

In April, the Railway Committee opened the door to a further hearing by ruling that the Canadian portion of through rates from American points were subject to the provisions of the Dominion Railway Act and therefore, were within its jurisdiction. In spite of warnings from Canadian Pacific President Thomas Shaughnessy that any interference with the rate agreement might "close up every oil well in Canada," the government pressed ahead. The Laurier administration provided technical and financial assistance to both Sun Oil and a second importer, Gall-Schneider of Montreal, so that they could present their case to the Railway Committee. When the hearing, held on 30 January 1900, became entangled in procedural wrangles, Blair adjourned the case to allow counsel for Sun Oil, H.L. Staunton, and Gall-Schneider's lawyer, Liberal politician L.-P. Brodeur, to amend and better prepare their case.[46]

Finally, for three days beginning on 20 March 1900, the Railway Committee of the Privy Council listened to the substance of the allegations against the Grand Trunk and Canadian Pacific Railways. Lawyers for Sun Oil and Gall-Schneider maintained that the railway corporations had ignored their legal obligations in three ways: by unjustly discriminating between localities in their October 1898 tariff, by failing to get cabinet approval for that tariff, and by granting Standard Oil a secret rebate. During the course of testimony, Staunton and Brodeur succeeded in establishing the details of the agreement reached between railway and Standard Oil officials at the Windsor Hotel. The Railway Committee, the lawyers contended, must strike down a rate agreement that discriminated against oil importers such as their clients, and that, by limiting competition and threatening to increase oil prices, was contrary to the broader public interest.[47]

Railway counsel contended that the question before the Railway Committee was "not what the public are interested in, but what are the powers of the railway company and whether they are going beyond their powers under the railway act."[48] They noted that the lower rates from Petrolia and Sarnia had been granted to meet water competition, and thus constituted a type of discrimination clearly sanctioned by the Railway Act. Furthermore, they contended that the courts in England had ruled that railway companies were entitled to look after their own interests, as long as they did not intend to give a particular person or locality an advantage. Railway officials had not conspired to benefit the Standard Oil Company or injure importers of American oil, but had merely increased some rates in order to compensate for the lower rates forced upon them by competition from water carriers. The increased American rates, they pointed out, had applied to Standard's substantial imports as well as to others. Under the law, then, it was the intent and not the effect of the agreement that the Railway Committee must consider.

Committee Chairman Blair frequently intervened during the proceedings, challenging the railway's arguments and expressing his own views. The railways minister expressed obvious dismay at the way in which railway counsel ignored the broad impact of the agreement with Standard Oil and relied upon legal precedents to justify their actions. Yet it became equally clear that he too doubted whether the Railway Committee, in its capacity as a judicial body, could resolve the dispute satisfactorily. Blair, however, insisted that "there must be a power somewhere to redress a wrong if the wrong is shown to exist."[49] If under the law the Railway Committee could not resolve the problem on legal grounds, he indicated that the cabinet committee might ask the full cabinet to use its political authority to revise the rates.

Judge Clark was understandably irritated by such a suggestion. Throughout the hearing, Clark complained, it had become apparent that "we are not here to try the question whether we have already done something contrary to the law as it stands but whether we did not do something which would induce some one to have the law altered or to have our rights limited." "You need hardly put it that way," Blair responded sharply, "Your rights are just as they may be determined by the proper constituted authority, and what you call your rights can vary from time to time ... The rights of railway companies are not to be paramount over every institution."[50]

The exchange reflected the more fundamental conflict that provided the subtext for the proceedings. Beyond their objections to the appropriate jurisdiction of the Railway Committee, Clark and Osler rejected any government interference with the rate-making prerogative of the railways, unless there were a clear violation of the Railway Act. On the other hand, while Blair accepted that the Standard Oil agreement might be legally defensible, he regarded the case as a test of the government's right to restrict private power in the public interest. In the end, Blair and his four colleagues on the Railway Committee did resort to the cabinet's wider authority. On 1 May 1900, the Laurier government approved and imposed the oil rates to be charged by the Canadian Pacific and Grand Trunk Railways. The new tariff, which had been recommended to cabinet by the Railway Committee, required Standard Oil to pay the published tariff rates of October 1898, while restoring the rates from American points prior to that date.[51]

Nevertheless, the resolution of the Standard Oil case revealed serious weaknesses in the Railway Committee as a regulatory forum. The complainants in this case had a substantial stake in the outcome and could afford legal counsel. Even so, they had difficulty formulating a case that met the judicial standards followed by the committee. Even after three sets of hearings, it was not clear that the complainants succeeded in proving that the offensive agreement between the Standard Oil Company and the railways violated any laws. Blair and his colleagues resorted to the ultimate authority of cabinet rather than confronting the legal issues. If anything, the remedy they adopted implied that the specific statutory restrictions did not outlaw the kind of agreement reached between the Standard Oil Company and the railways.

The Standard Oil agreement demonstrated the narrow view the railway companies might be expected to adopt of their public responsibilities when those responsibilities conflicted with their need to maintain the lucrative traffic of a powerful shipper. The agreement underlined the degree to which the private interest of the railways need not produce rates that were beneficial to the wider community. Supporters of a railway commission pointed to the Standard Oil agreement as further evidence of the need for an institution capable of enforcing the public's interest in private railway operations.[52]

The government's response to the Standard Oil agreement discredited the existing means of enforcing the public responsibilities of railways. The proceedings taken against the railway companies confirmed that the Railway Committee could be as unresponsive and cumbersome as the courts. Just as important, the hearings revealed a substantial tension between the technical requirements of the law and what both the complainants and members of the government regarded as a just resolution of the question. Laurier's enigmatic and volatile railways minister, A.G. Blair, who was now determined to create an independent regulatory commission, would remember this experience well. To effectively enforce the public responsibilities of railway corporations, Parliament would have to do more than create a new "come-at-able" tribunal of "common sense." For regulation to be effective, Parliament would have to redefine the nineteenth-century boundaries of public authority and private rights.

CHAPTER FIVE

Railways, Politics, and Administration

Late in 1901, Simon James McLean, professor of sociology and political economy at the University of Arkansas, turned down a job opportunity in his home town of Ottawa. A fellow student and acquaintance from the Universities of Toronto and Chicago, William Lyon Mackenzie King, was looking for a successor to Albert Harper, his second-in-command in the Department of Labour. The ambitious McLean frankly explained to King that he was reluctant to abandon his own area of expertise, railway policy, for "one in which your hand has shown its cunning."[1] At that date, the bright railway economist saw better prospects in the Canadian public service than playing second fiddle to the fledgling deputy minister of labour.

The year 1901 had been a promising one for McLean, who since 1898 had been angling for a position as a member of, or secretary to, a proposed Canadian railway commission. In January, Railways Minister A.G. Blair had indicated in an interview that the recently re-elected Laurier government intended pressing ahead with a long-promised policy – the establishment of a railway tribunal. Almost simultaneously, a leading Liberal newspaper, the Toronto *Globe*, ran a series of editorials and articles on excessive and discriminatory freight rates, most of which concluded with a call for an independent regulatory agency. In March, the House of Commons had unanimously supported a resolution calling for the creation of a Board of Railway Commissioners. In the summer, the government had appointed McLean, who already had prepared a study on railway commissions for Blair's Department of Railways, to investigate freight rate grievances in Canada.[2]

When McLean turned down King's offer in late December, he knew that early in the new year, the railways minister intended to make public both his studies on railway commissions and rate grievances. He also understood that shortly thereafter, the Laurier government planned to introduce legislation establishing a Board of Railway Commissioners, legislation that McLean was then helping to draft. Although the thirty-year-old political economist accepted an appointment at Stanford University early in 1902, he clearly hoped his future lay with the new government agency he had promoted assiduously.[3]

Like many intellectuals who achieve a measure of influence with governments, Simon McLean was in the right place at the right time. By the turn of the century, a growing coalition of shippers looked to the creation of a railway commission as an alternative to the existing regulatory system. Neither the courts nor the Railway Committee of the Privy Council had proved able to resolve rate disputes effectively. Although the Crow's Nest Pass and Manitoba agreements had breathed new life into the traditional system of competition and contract, many business and political leaders disliked using public finances to purchase rate concessions. The general demand for a regulatory agency was frequently short on specifics, and it was McLean's task to translate this demand into a specific set of proposals. He brought to the design of the new government agency an understanding of the regulatory experience in other countries and ideas concerning the reform of public administration. It remained for the government, in particular the railways minister to guide the proposals through a political system that was sensitive to pressure from powerful and organized interests such as the railway industry. The final form, mandate, and powers of Canada's first regulatory commission were a product of the interplay between McLean's Progressive ideas, economic interests, and Canadian politics.

Simon McLean belonged to a generation of Canadian intellectuals who emerged from the University of Toronto's Department of Political Economy during the 1890s, a group that included urban reformer Samuel Morley Wickett and labour reformer William Lyon Mackenzie King. Born in 1871, McLean was raised and educated in the Ottawa area. In 1890, he enrolled in the recently created Honours course in History and Political Science at the University of Toronto, which provided the first four years of a five-year law program. McLean's fourth-year paper on "The Tariff History of Canada" won the Bankers' Scholarship in 1894 and was published in the Toronto University Studies in Political Science series the following year. With the assistance of a Mackenzie Fellowship, he completed his degree in 1895, and like Wickett and King, continued his education outside of Canada. In 1896 he received his Masters degree in Political Science at Columbia University, and in the following year he majored in economics at the University of Chicago, completing his doctoral thesis on the "Railway Policy of Canada" in June of 1897. In the fall of that year, McLean received a posting as a professor of political economy and sociology at the University of Arkansas.[4]

McLean was an academic who, he admitted, "was more and more attracted by problems of practical interest," and was intent on establishing his expertise in the field of government railway policy. While he was teaching at the University of Arkansas, he published a number of articles, some of them drawn from his doctoral thesis, which provided historical and non-evaluative descriptions of railway policy in Canada and the United States. The enterprising academic saw an opportunity to further his career by assisting the Canadian government in creating a railway commission. As the son-in-law of the auditor general, he had some connections in Ottawa but in fact his introduction to key members of the Laurier government came from none other than J.S. Willison, the influential Liberal journalist well known for his advocacy of a railway commission.[5] Prime Minister Laurier responded coolly to Willison's suggestion that he make use of McLean, arguing that government action with respect to a railway commission was "premature." Railways Minister Blair appeared more anxious than the prime minister to press ahead with the initiative. He agreed that McLean should undertake a preliminary study on the organization and operation of regulatory tribunals in the United States.[6]

Completed within a few months, McLean's report described and assessed the regulatory experience in the United States as well as Great Britain, and Canada. He concluded that all of these countries had resorted to some form of regulation because neither the competitive principles nor the economic self-interest of railway corporations had adequately safeguarded the public interest. The result was that unrestricted competition eventually led to extremely limited competition as railway companies made both formal and informal traffic agreements. Competition created other injustices by requiring railways to charge high local rates to compensate for drastically reduced revenues on through rates. In Canada, where railway companies could reduce expenses and enhance net profits by favouring large industries and urban centres, their rates contributed to the declining population of wealth-creating, agricultural communities. "What the railway wants is the greatest profit," McLean concluded, "What the country wants is the greatest good for the country and the most uniform development of its resources."[7]

In McLean's view, the greatest good for the country in transportation policy could only be accomplished in one of two ways – "State ownership or Commission regulation." It is unlikely that he ever seriously considered the former method: he had studied under economist J.L. Laughlin at the University of Chicago whose students were strongly discouraged from entertaining such notions. In his report, McLean avoided discussing the question of public enterprise by concluding that the large amount of private investment in the Canadian railway industry simply made state ownership an impractical alternative. Therefore, the only real option was a properly organized railway commission. The compromise adopted by Canada in 1888 of delegating regulatory control to a cabinet committee was doomed to failure, McLean observed, because "regulation is essentially an administrative function; an intermingling of this with political duties leads to lack of harmony and efficiency."[8]

McLean's emphasis on harmony and efficiency, on the separation of administration from politics, revealed the Progressive assumptions upon which his study rested. His graduate education at American universities had brought him into close contact with this current of ideas; at Columbia University McLean may even have studied under a leading Progressive intellectual, Frank Goodnow. Goodnow and other members of an emerging community of academic social scientists in the United States questioned the ability of governments to respond to the problems of the increasingly interdependent, urban and industrial society. They contended that governments needed to provide constant supervision over a number of economic activities, a supervision which neither legislators nor the judiciary were equipped to provide. While the administrative functions of governments must be enlarged, this was impossible so long as partisan politics was allowed to interfere with the bureaucracy. Patronage did not simply undermine the morality of the nation, as an older generation of reformers had argued. It undermined the capacity of governments to provide efficient public service to an industrializing nation. Progressives advocated civil service reform and called for the creation of new governing institutions that would be insulated from partisan, patronage politics, would offer continuing supervision of economic problems, and would be composed of, or rely on, experts. By arguing that administration was different from politics, Progressive intellectuals attempted to reconcile their proposals for new institutions that would be unaccountable to the electorate with traditional democratic values.[9]

Canada was not immune from these intellectual currents. "As the scope of legislation grows more perplexing every year," one Canadian intellectual wrote, "the scope of law-making widens, the complexity of each subject increases with the growing complexity of the industrial community, the need of expert guidance through the maze of statutes becomes cumulatively greater." The emphasis on the importance of expert investigation and administration was reflected in calls for the creation of a special tariff board, for civil service reform, for public operation or regulation of major utilities through independent commissions, and for the appointment of special expert agencies to investigate industrial combines, labour disputes, and the depletion of Canada's natural resources.[10]

McLean's report on railway commissions also reflected the Progressive attitude towards expert investigation and public administration. The creation of a fair and reasonable rate structure, he concluded, could not be left to legislators. The complexity of rate-making had defied efforts in other countries to fix tariffs by statute or according to cost of service principles. Rate-making involved compromise and a balancing of interests, and therefore required constant supervision. The best legislators could do would be to establish broad policy outlines and leave their specific application to a permanent agency.

In McLean's view, the members of such an agency must be both independent and possess considerable technical expertise. Even technically qualified members would require time to obtain the practical experience necessary to supervise railway rate policies. In contrast to many American state governments which had failed to provide adequate tenure to those who had been appointed or worse still elected to their railway commissions, the three commissioners who would sit on Canada's railway agency should be as secure from political interference as the judiciary, and should be granted lengthy, preferably life, tenure. They would exercise all of the powers of the Railway Committee of the Privy Council, and be given further control over all aspects of the railway industry, from stock and bond issues to labour disputes. While the agency would receive rather than solicit submissions from aggrieved parties, it could choose to try to settle disputes informally, or initiate its own investigations in response to general complaints about rates or service. Furthermore, McLean argued that the burden of proof should be shifted away from shippers to the railway companies, who should now be required to prove to the commission that disputed rates were reasonable or non-discriminatory.[11]

As a result of his examination of the regulatory experience of other countries, McLean also felt that the new commission would require protection from judicial interference. While the courts had obstructed the work of the Railways and Canal Commission in England, Canadian observers such as McLean were more concerned over a repetition of the American railway commission's experience. The United States Supreme Court had defeated the purpose of administrative regulation by treating the Interstate Commerce Commission's proceedings as "meaningless preliminaries" when it heard appeals. The court required the parties to present their cases all over again, admitted new evidence, and willingly set aside any of the commission's findings. When the railway commission found existing rates to be unjust or discriminatory, the court ruled that new rates could not be prescribed to resolve the problem. Shippers faced the prospect of repeated appearances before the commission and the court if the railway did not voluntarily correct the problem to their satisfaction. By the turn of the century the United States Supreme Court had reduced the Interstate Commerce Commission to "a mere statistical-gathering agency."[12] To avoid the development of a similar situation with a Canadian railway commission, McLean advised that the enacting legislation clearly declare that the agency's decisions on questions of facts should be final. Although appeals on matters of law should be allowed, he insisted that the regulatory agency itself be the sole authority in determining what constituted a matter of fact or law. Since McLean regarded the regulation of rate-making and other related industry activities as a matter of administration, he proposed the creation of an independent and expert authority that would be free from the unwarranted interference of both the legislative and judicial branches of the government.[13]

In February 1899, Railways Minister Blair received McLean's report outlining a proposed Canadian railway commission. At this time, however, Blair was not in a position to proceed any further. He was preoccupied with the extension of the government-owned Intercolonial Railway to Montreal, a highly controversial proposal that he had championed in spite of opposition from within the cabinet and the Conservative-dominated Senate. Blair feared that McLean's scheme would face the same kind of opposition as had the Intercolonial proposal. Although Prime Minister Laurier denied rumours that the cabinet was divided over the measure, it seems likely that the concept of expanded government regulation met with opposition from such traditional liberals as Finance Minister Fielding, Trade and Commerce Minister Richard Cartwright, and the prime minister himself. Therefore, in spite of growing public support for the railway commission proposal in the late nineteenth century, McLean's report received no official response, nor was it subsequently even published.[14]

McLean's fortunes brightened following the re-election of the Laurier government in 1900. Blair, still railways minister, announced that the government would press ahead with the commission proposal, and the House of Commons subsequently gave its unanimous support to the principle of a railway commission. McLean convinced the government to appoint him to undertake a second study, this one related to rate grievances in Canada. Although Laurier privately disapproved of the idea of a railway commission, he could not ignore the enthusiasm for the proposal in both Ontario and the west, two areas of the country upon which the Liberal party relied for electoral support, and in which there had been some slippage in the 1900 election. He agreed to a minor, departmental investigation as a means of postponing further action while demonstrating the government's continuing concern.[15]

During the summer months of 1901, merchants, manufacturers, and farmers in southwestern Ontario and western Canada voiced their grievances to the government's special commissioner. The inquiry lacked the status and prestige associated with a royal commission, and many business communities were unable to prepare formal briefs on the short notice they received. McLean remained undaunted by these limitations. Unlike one Canadian Pacific official who sardonically observed that "The general drift of the complaints is they want lower rates – like Oliver Twist, they want something more," McLean took the rate grievances very seriously. Within a few months after the hearings, he produced a report that classified and summarized the shippers' complaints.[16]

Not surprisingly, McLean used this second report to reiterate many of his earlier statements. Throughout his description of the problems associated with rebates, freight classification, proportionately higher rates on short hauls and small quantities, and the low transcontinental rate structure, McLean continually emphasized that the "untrammeled and arbitrary discretion" of the railways led to abuses. He noted that the railways justified a considerable seasonal disparity in their freight tariffs because of competing water carriers in the summer and the increased cost of movement in the winter. Both of these reasons involved questions of fact, McLean argued, facts that an independent regulatory agency would be able to investigate, or at least require the railways to prove. He treated the various rate grievances largely as technical questions, which did not involve fundamental policy issues; in his view, such problems could be resolved most effectively by an expert commission. He also placed greater emphasis on the specific regulatory powers the railway commission should be granted with respect to rates. The existing provision of the Railway Act governing approval of maximum tariff schedules did not provide an effective basis for regulation. Under the new system, advance approval would be required for all rates, except those special rates on freight such as grain and lumber that had to be changed rapidly in response to market conditions. All rates, including the special competitive ones, could be reviewed, altered, and amended by the railway commission as it saw fit.[17]

It is probable that the greater emphasis on rate powers that McLean was proposing simply reflected the fact that he was then in the process of drafting the actual railway commission legislation. The new importance he assigned to broad regulatory discretion, however, suggests the impact of the intervening Standard Oil controversy on McLean's employer, Railways Minister Blair. Following that hearing before the Railway Committee of Privy Council. Blair was concerned that any future regulatory agency have the legal means to resolve any rate grievance that it determined was legitimate. Blair's influence and a greater sensitivity to political considerations also appear to have modified McLean's view on one other important issue – the right of appeal. The Railway Act already provided an appeal to cabinet from the decisions of the Railway Committee. McLean now argued that subject to such an appeal, all decisions of the new regulatory agency should be final. By allowing the cabinet to review the decisions of the commission on appeal or on its own initiative, independent regulatory control would be reconciled with the Canadian tradition of ministerial responsibility. As well, the cabinet would be more readily accessible to aggrieved shippers than the Supreme Court, and would be in a position to consider any broader questions of transportation policy that might be implicit in the decision being appealed.[18] In light of the fact that McLean had not given any consideration to this type of appeal in his 1899 report, it seems clear that these arguments were largely rationalizations. An appeal to cabinet simply made use of a traditional practice in an attempt to satisfy many supporters of the commission who were hostile to judicial review, while at the same time assuring the railway companies of some recourse from the commission's decisions.

In March 1902, the minister of railways tabled both of McLean's reports. The following month, he introduced, for discussion purposes only, new legislation creating a Board of Railway Commissioners, which largely followed McLean's recommendations. The bill stipulated that three commissioners enjoying the independence of judges would be appointed for a ten-year term and given the powers of a court to enforce Canada's railway laws. The agency would have the authority to review and amend all railway rates, and appeals could be directed only to the cabinet. The proposed new law would create a new regulatory agency, and give that agency real control over railway rates.[19]

The draft legislation reflected the views of two government actors, McLean and Blair, on the subject of regulation. Progressive assumptions about public administration, an understanding of the American regulatory experience, and the lessons derived from the Railway Committee of the Privy Council's previous efforts to control freight rates all shaped the institutional form and authority of the proposed railway commission. For the first time since the 1880s, the railway commission proposal had been given a precise form. The new agency would not be just the specialized court D'Alton McCarthy had conceived in the 1880s; it would be granted a very wide authority with respect to rates, broad discretion in responding to complaints, and would be carefully protected from judicial interference. The railway companies now faced the spectre of a more effective method of public authority over their private rate-making prerogative.

Railway officials viewed the release of McLean's reports and the government's draft legislation with considerable hostility. Grand Trunk officials had already refused to co-operate with McLean's rate inquiry, not wanting to encourage "agitators to go through the country soliciting grievances, when the public are only too prone as a rule to fly to the Press to air their grievances." Following the tabling of the reports, General Manager Charles M. Hays expressed his continued confidence in the Railway Committee of the Privy Council as a regulatory agency and warned that a commission would only create more government positions and increase taxes.[20]

Canadian Pacific officials adopted a different strategy. As early as 1901, President Thomas Shaugnessy had welcomed the "appointment of a non-partisan railway commission" that would remove popular misconceptions concerning rate matters and defend the railways from unwarranted criticism, but it became clear that what the Canadian Pacific's president really wanted was only an outward appearance of regulation. Western Canadian communities were demanding government support for competitive rail lines, and American railway competitors were seeking legislation that would limit the Canadian Pacific's ability to do business in their country. Shaugnessy hoped that the existence of regulation would weaken the case for their proposals. However, he argued that the requirement that the railway commission sanction all tolls would be unworkable. Instead, he suggested that while all tariffs should be filed with the regulatory authority, it should only be granted the power to approve and disapprove maximum rates. He also insisted on a right of appeal to the Supreme Court, as otherwise the new railway commission "would be clothed with power of a most extraordinary and dangerous character."[21] Thus, although Shaugnessy decided not to oppose openly a proposal that had acquired wide popular appeal, he sought to limit the real power the commission would wield.

By the turn of the century, railway officials had every reason to resist a significant expansion of public authority over their operations. Having survived the uncertain economic growth of the 1880s and the depression of the 1890s, the industry was now sharing in the general economic prosperity of the country. Freight traffic growth was advancing well, and railway officials were managing to keep the relationship between operating expenses and revenues relatively stable. The results were encouraging: beginning in 1899, in each year the net revenues of the Grand Trunk topped $2 million for the first time since 1883, while the Canadian Pacific netted earnings of over $12 million, nearly doubling the annual profits it had recorded during the first five sluggish years of the 1890s. The prospects for future growth and financial stability looked extremely promising for 1903 and beyond.[22]

In a highly influential study, historian Gabriel Kolko contends that in the United States many railway companies supported regulation to resolve the internal problems of their industry, and particularly to prevent destructive rate competition. In Canada, the industry engaged in its own private quest for rate stability. Although a brief rate war between the Grand Trunk and Canadian Pacific Railway erupted in the late 1890s, throughout the late nineteenth century the railway corporations modified and formalized their own regulatory mechanisms. The Association of General Freight Agents, originally formed in the early 1880s to develop a uniform freight classification and act as a railway clearing-house, was reorganized into the Canadian Freight Association in 1898. Retiring Grand Trunk freight officer J.M. Earls became the association's first permanent chairman, and minutes of the meetings began to be published. The association provided for greater co-operation within the industry, improved co-ordination of traffic between railways, and permitted shippers to present their grievances and rate requests to joint committees of freight traffic officials. By the turn of the century, the association's freight committee had succeeded in bringing some order out of the chaos of special rates on particular types of freight traffic in Ontario and Quebec, and in the process managed to effect some rate increases. Through such measures of self-regulation, the railway companies limited "ruthless competition" within their industry, and in the process believed they were also accommodating the grievances of shippers. Government intervention, therefore, appeared to be unnecessary.[23]

The overall corporate strategies of Canada's major railways, however, limited the degree to which they could resist the government's regulatory proposals. The Canadian Pacific, the Canadian Northern, and the Grand Trunk railways all had reason to maintain friendly relations with the Laurier administration. During 1901 and 1902, the Canadian Pacific required government approval for a proposed substantial increase in its capital stock, while the two other railway systems had even greater plans. Both the Canadian Northern and Grand Trunk sought to capture a share of the greatly increased traffic between western and eastern Canada by transforming their regionally based lines into transcontinentals that would rival the Canadian Pacific. Neither railway could afford this kind of expansion without substantial public assistance. Officials from both companies were negotiating large and controversial financial-aid packages with the Laurier administration at the same time as the government was pressing ahead with its railway commission proposals. It is interesting to note that, although historians frequently emphasize the dependence of governments on railways for support, in this case, the relationship cut two ways. Each of Canada's three major railways was aware that its rivals were also currying government support, and none was anxious to alienate the Laurier government in a heated battle over the commission proposal: they did not want to put their more fundamental corporate plans at risk.[24]

Despite this, there were attempts to weaken the legislation. Officials from the major railways agreed to a common front on the commission proposal, and adopted Shaugnessy's strategy. A legal committee formed by the railways contended that "The agitation which has arisen of late years for amendments of the laws respecting railways has been substantially confined to the creation of some tribunal such as that of the new Board." and therefore the government should "confine the Bill to the constitution and jurisdiction of the Board of Railway Commissioners, leaving for future consideration any substantial changes in the other parts of the present law."[25] While accepting the inevitability of a railway commission, they sought ways to limit its real authority.

The minister of railways introduced a revised version of the railway commission legislation on 20 March 1903, and despite the criticism that railway officials had expressed, the legislation, as amended, remained largely unaltered. The new Act made two modifications to the appeal process, granting the proposed commission the discretion to refer disputed questions of law to the Supreme Court, and allowing those appearing before the commission to request the Supreme Court to review for jurisdictional errors. The major appeal route on questions of law and fact, however, continued to be through the cabinet rather than the courts, and the expanded authority granted to the commission to regulate freight rates also remained intact.[26]

Representatives of the Farmers' Association, United Fruit Growers' Association, Ontario Fruit Growers' Association, Dairymen's Association, Dominion Livestock Association, Toronto Board of Trade, and Canadian Manufacturers' Association all strongly supported the Laurier government's initiative. The Toronto Board of Trade and a number of wholesale shippers appointed lawyer J.L. Staunton to represent their interests, primarily to protect the bill against major changes in Ottawa.[27] What opposition Blair did face in the House of Commons reflected the general popularity of the measure: the minister of railways publicly defended his bill against proposals to give even more power to the new regulatory authority.[28]

At the same time, Blair privately defended his bill against railway proposals that would have restricted the commission's powers. For one and one-half months while the railways minister guided the legislation through the House of Commons, he and the minister of justice, Charles Fitzpatrick, negotiated with the joint committee organized by Canada's railway companies. Railway officials were not entirely comfortable with this arrangement; they urged the government to refer the legislation to a special committee of the House of Commons. Blair anticipated the outcome of such a strategy, and refused to become a party to "any procedure which is either designed or would have the effect of delaying the legislation and putting it over."[29]

Having failed to prolong and possibly stall legislative progress on the bill, railway officials zeroed in on two contentious issues: the broad-rate regulatory authority that would be granted to the commission and the right of appeal to the Supreme Court. They contended that the new railway commission's powers should not exceed the government's traditional statutory authority: it should approve just and reasonable maximum tariffs and prevent discrimination by enforcing the existing provisions of the Railway Act. Railway lawyer F.H. Chrysler told Blair that it would be an unnecessary and dangerous mistake to substitute the judgment of a board of railway commissioners for the practical knowledge of railway traffic officials.

When Blair countered that railway officials determined policy solely from their own private point of view, Chrysler retorted: "Why shouldn't they, Sir?" "Because," the railways minister replied, "they are enjoying privileges, exercising franchises practically compelling the user of these franchises in the ordinary business of the country, and it is right that they should recognize some general supervision and control over their actions. It is in accordance with the fitness of things."[30] Blair recognized that the railways had still not accepted the principle of genuine public control. In defence of the authority being given the railway commission, he noted that such powers were not, in fact, new. Whatever practice might have developed in the past, the government had always reserved the right to alter any and all of the railway's tariffs. In Blair's view, the unrestricted authority assigned to the new commission would be a powerful weapon with which to prevent discrimination and other unjust practices. Bearing in mind the Railway Committee's difficulties in the Standard Oil case, he frankly explained to the railway lawyers that "the ingenuity of you fellows is so inexhaustible and limitless that we must make the words general."[31]

In the face of Blair's determined views, railway officials suggested an alternative proposal. They recommended that the commission be permitted to disallow their general tariffs and prescribe alternative rates as it saw fit, but should only interfere with the lower rates offered on many commodities if there was proof that the rates were unreasonable or contrary to the discrimination clauses of the Railway Act. The commission would have no authority to alter the special rates offered to shippers of products such as grain and lumber in response to changing market conditions, although the railways would be required to file notice of these rates. Blair was wary of these suggestions. Much of the proposed language was derived from the American Interstate Commerce Act, and he feared the Canadian Supreme Court would be able to substitute its own definitions of unreasonable and discriminatory rates for the standards established by the commission just as the American court had done.[32] While he considered making some amendments to the government's legislation, he also insisted that the commission must be able to alter any railway tariff, and be free of judicial interference.

Although Blair did agree to make some modifications to the bill, he preserved the commission's authority in the final wording of the statute. Standard tariffs required the prior approval of the Board of Railway Commissioners, whereas commodity tariffs would go into effect automatically unless they had been disallowed. Blair chose to let the railway commission prescribe its own procedures governing special rates set to meet competitive markets, since he and the rail-

ways could not agree on a proposal. However, he left no doubt as
to the ultimate power of the regulatory tribunal. The Board of Railway Commissioners acquired the authority to disallow any railway
tariff, be it standard, special, or competitive "which it considers to
be unjust or unreasonable, or contrary to the provisions of this
Act."[33] This carefully selected language made it clear that the Board
would be the sole judge of what amounted to unjust rates or what
rates contravened some other part of the act.

The new legislation included other measures to ensure that the
"very large discretion" invested in the board would be exercised
without judicial interference. The new railway commission enjoyed
the exclusive authority to determine, "as questions of fact," what
constituted "unjust discrimination, or undue or unreasonable preference or advantage, or prejudice or disadvantage, within the meaning of this Act." Furthermore, the commission alone could decide
under what competitive conditions lower rates might be charged for
the long haul than for the short haul, or when other forms of discrimination might be condoned "for the purposes of securing, in the
interests of the public, the traffic."[34] In spite of serious opposition
from Canada's railway industry, Railways Minister Blair had significantly expanded the regulatory power of the state, and sought to
insulate this new authority from legal challenges.

It was not surprising then, that the second point of controversy
between the government, shippers, and the railway companies involved the question of appeals. Railway officials demanded the right
of appeal to the courts except with respect to a limited number of
safety-related, engineering matters such as crossings, fencing, and
construction plans. At a minimum, they sought the right to appeal
on questions of law with the leave of the commission or of the
Supreme Court. It was very unusual, F.H. Chrysler noted, to create
a court, place millions of dollars of property in its hands, and then
deny the right of appeal. The railways minister refused to move on
the issue. Any change in the procedure, he told railway officials
frankly, was politically impossible. Moreover, he repeated that every
effort had been made in the new Railway Act "to avoid affording
facilities for hanging up proceedings and practically paralyzing the
arm of the Commission by promising and providing for appeals on
all sorts of questions." The railway commission would be reasonable
and would agree to refer any serious questions of law to the courts.
If it did not, the railway companies could always appeal to the cabinet. Blair insisted on protecting the new regulatory tribunal from
excessive judicial interference.[35]

Railway officials took their battle over the question of appeals
directly to Parliament. They appealed to both the entrepreneurial

and constitutional sensibilities of the business leaders and lawyers in the Conservative-dominated Senate. In October, the Senate adopted a railway-inspired amendment that would allow parties appearing before the railway commission to appeal questions of law, provided either the commission or two judges of the Supreme Court approved the appeal. The Laurier government, pressured by railway officials to prevent the commission from acquiring "autocratic power without precedent" and by shipping organizations not to allow any change, chose to side with the shippers. Members of the House of Commons and Senate held three conferences to resolve this and other differences between their respective versions of the Railway Act, with the result that the Senate finally abandoned its amendment with respect to appeals. Subject to three exceptions, then, the decisions of the Board of Railway Commissioners would be final: its decisions could be appealed to the cabinet, challenges to its jurisdiction could be taken directly to the Supreme Court, and the board could initiate legal references to the Supreme Court. To further underline the authority of the board, the Railway Act required that in considering questions of law and jurisdiction, the Supreme Court "may draw all inferences as are not inconsistent with the facts expressly found by the Board."[36]

The railway companies made two united and sustained attempts to limit the regulatory authority of the new railway commission. In spite of preferred access to the legislative process, and their considerable economic influence, they failed. In Canada, the regulated industry neither sought the regulation nor subverted the final regulatory legislation.

In part, the limited effectiveness of railway industry lobbying demonstrated that their influence within the state was now balanced by other powerful business interests.[37] The freight rate controversy of the late nineteenth century in Canada produced a politically influential coalition of merchants, manufacturers, and farmers who relied upon the transportation services which the railways provided. Their support for a railway commission gave the government a strong bargaining position, a position Railways Minister Blair exploited with considerable skill and determination. He ably defended the legislation, and thus retained the form and authority that he and his expert assistant, Simon McLean, envisioned for the new regulatory tribunal. The Board of Railway Commissioners acquired substantive, and not just nominal, regulatory power.

The creation of the Board of Railway Commissioners did not end the regulatory struggle. Instead, it shifted the struggle to a new institutional forum. The procedures adopted by the regulatory agency, and the meaning that it would give to general phrases such as "unreasonable rates" and "unjust discrimination" now became critically important to Canadian shippers and the railway companies.

A.G. Blair, the political champion of the railway commission, had an opportunity to influence the direction the commission would take on such critical questions. A public feud with Laurier over the government's decision to support the Grand Trunk Railway's transcontinental ambitions led to his resignation from the railways portfolio in July 1903. In spite of their disagreement, or perhaps to limit the political damage resulting from it, Laurier appointed Blair as the first chief commissioner of the new agency. The appointment was a popular one: shippers admired Blair's history of standing up to the major railway corporations while railway officials appreciated the moderate interpretations he had suggested should be given to much of the new Railway Act.[38]

Simon McLean, the intellectual champion of the railway commission, was forgotten in the initial appointments to the commission and its staff. He ended up taking the academic position at Stanford he had been offered in 1902, and four years later returned to Canada to assist his mentor, James Mavor, in the Department of Political Economy at the University of Toronto. He never lost his enthusiasm for "practical matters": he worked on railway valuations for the United States government, and in Canada served as chairman of one of his friend King's labour conciliation boards. In 1908, the Laurier government expanded the membership of the Board of Railway Commissioners and sought to respond to demands from the chief commissioner and from railway officials for someone with some expertise in railway rate-making. McLean became that expert commissioner. Having finally reached the position that he had wanted for so long, McLean never looked back. He was to become the only commissioner to be reappointed for a second ten-year term. During his second, and then third term, McLean served as assistant chief commissioner. He had to retire in 1936, although he continued to serve as an honorary consultant to the commission until his death in 1946.[39] From 1908 onwards, Simon McLean contributed the technical and practical expertise he had argued was essential to the success of the Board of Railway Commissioners – Canada's first national regulatory agency.

CHAPTER SIX

"A Board of Arbitrators"

We, who have cast upon us the grave responsibility of interpreting and executing the law, cannot enter upon experiments without the utmost caution, lest what we may do should prejudicially affect either general business or the proper railway interests of the country. In our judgment, these interests rightly understood and properly regulated, are not hostile or adverse, but in the largest sense complementary to one another, helpful and concurrent. Insofar as we are endowed with capacity for the purpose, it shall be our endeavour in this sense so to administer the law.[1]

With these opening remarks, Chief Commissioner A.G. Blair convened the first public session of the Board of Railway Commissioners on 9 February 1904. In subsequent regulatory proceedings, Blair and the other judges, lawyers, academics, and retired politicians who served on the Board of Railway Commissioners soon learned that in a competitive economy, restoring harmony among contending interests could prove to be a herculean task. Shippers in various communities and regions challenged the freight rates enjoyed by their competitors as discriminatory, and sought the marginal, but potentially significant, competitive advantage rate adjustments could provide. Railway officials defended much of their traditional managerial discretion and many existing tariffs, although they willingly joined in, or sponsored attacks on, those rate arrangements that they regarded as money-losing propositions. The railway commission provided a new and alternative site for the political controversy that had always surrounded freight rate decisions.

The claims and counterclaims of competing economic interests set the regulatory agenda. It remained for the railway commissioners to formulate the specific regulatory responses. Their task was not an easy one, for they were expected to resolve a bewildering array of disputes over matters as broad as the general tariffs used in central and western Canada, or as specific as the proper price to be paid for the transportation of gramophones, automobiles, and peanut butter. The Railway Act left procedural matters almost entirely to the discretion of the board, provided only a few clues concerning the standards it should use to define rates as "discriminatory" or "unreasonable," and offered various remedies once the commission made such a determination. Furthermore, as Chief Commissioner Blair noted early in the board's history, because the commission's counterparts in England and the United States enjoyed quite different and generally more restricted powers, there was "practically no experience ... upon many important questions from which we can profit and to which we may look for guidance."[2]

In attempting to resolve freight rate disputes, the commissioners sought to define a legitimate regulatory sphere that was both separate from, yet central to, the policy-making sphere of governments and the rate-making sphere of the railways. In an age of democracy and science, elections offered some legitimacy to government decisions, and the influence of apparently impartial market forces offered some legitimacy to railway corporate policies. The Board of Railway Commissioners tried to find an acceptable niche in Canadian society for an institution whose members were unelected and who had been given wide authority to overrule the market.

Like the Railway Committee of the Privy Council which it replaced, the Board of Railway Commissioners supervised and controlled a wide range of railway activities, including the location and protection of level crossings, the installation of safety devices, the establishment of rules and regulations for employees, the inspection of new lines, and the investigation of accidents. Special divisions of the agency – the Engineering Department, the Accident Branch, the Railway Equipment and Safety Appliance Department, the Law Department – were established to handle these myriad responsibilities. The jurisdiction and workload of these divisions expanded in the years prior to World War I. In 1904–05, its first year of operation, the commission received 1,009 applications and made 405 orders; in 1913–14, its tenth year, it handled over 5,500 applications, and generated some 2,800 orders. The commissioners and their Ottawa-based staff quickly outgrew their temporary offices in the West Block of the Parliament Buildings, but it was not until the fall of 1911 that the board finally abandonned its cramped and ill-lit quarters and moved to more spacious offices in the upper floors of the Grand Trunk's new Union Station that included an official "courtroom."[3]

Table 7
Board of Railway Commissioners, Rate Cases 1904–1909, Nature of Grievance

Year	1904	1905	1906	1907	1908	1909	All
Geographic Discrimination	1	4	3	2	5	15	30
Reasonableness	3	1	2	1	3	20	30
Special Rate	4	7	2	2	5	3	23
Classification	0	1	4	3	6	6	20
Personal Discrimination	1	1	0	1	0	0	3
Procedure/Appeal	0	0	1	0	1	3	5
Other	1	3	2	2	1	10	19
Total	10	17	14	11	21	57	130

Source: Calculated from Canadian Freight Association, *Decisions of the Board of Railway Commissioners*, vols. 1 to 3.

The work of the Traffic Department, established in 1904 to handle freight and passenger tariff and service matters, reflected the general growth of the railway commission. By World War I, officials in the department no longer dealt only with railway companies, but also handled applications and complaints with respect to the service provided by companies engaged in the express, telephone, telegraph, and hydroelectric business. To cope with these new duties, a total of nine new clerks was added to the original three members of the staff. Much of their work was fairly routine. Several clerks must have been kept busy simply keeping track of the 395,000 schedules of charges that were filed with the commission between 1904 and 1914,[4] which included 285,000 railway freight tariffs.

Freight rate regulation, then, remained only one part of the railway commission's mandate. No more than 1 or 2 per cent of the applications processed in any given year by the board involved this subject. Nevertheless, in contrast to the courts or the Railway Committee of the Privy Council, shippers did use the railway commission as a forum for their rate grievances. Freight tariff cases became, as Chief Commissioner Blair predicted in 1904, the "most publicly visible element" of the commission's work,[5] and the commission's ability to handle complex rate disputes became an important measure of its success as a regulatory agency.

Although Table 7 underestimates the work of the board by including only those complaints that resulted in a formal order, it does give some indication of the variety of rate disputes handled by the commissioners. Three different types of cases dominated the regulatory agenda: cases where shippers alleged that the rate structure resulted in unfair or unequal treatment between those businesses operating in different locations; cases where railway officials sought to have the commission sanction either the introduction or cancellation of the various special rates negotiated with individual shippers; and cases where both shippers and railway officials applied for changes in the Canadian Freight Classification, which, by the turn of the century, listed the class rate and other special conditions of carriage to be applied to some 2,000 commodities, from "Absorbent Cotton" to "Zinc Ashes." In the course of considering these three types of cases, another major issue frequently emerged as the real point of contention – the reasonableness of the disputed toll.

The approach the board adopted to these disputes was shaped by the commissioners, their staff, and their clients. Within this regulatory community, lawyers and freight traffic officers played an important role, each offering a somewhat different perspective on the nature of the board's work. The Grand Trunk's M.K. Cowan, the Canadian Northern's F.H. Phippen, the Canadian Pacific's A.G. Blair (who resigned as chairman of the railway commission after only one year), and F.H. Chrysler (retained by a number of railways for regulatory cases), all became familiar figures at board hearings.[6] Because these men were generally expected to preserve the existing rate structure and rate-making prerogative of the railways against critics, they had an interest in seeing the board adopt court-like standards and procedures. They tried to have cases postponed or dismissed if they had not been adequately notified or informed about the complaint. They asked the commission to impose high burdens of proof on those with grievances, and insisted on the binding nature of any favourable rulings on procedural and substantive matters. Because they felt comfortable in a courtroom atmosphere, they frequently had a strong interest in having the board emulate the judiciary.

They might have expected a sympathetic response to their demands from certain key members of the commission, since the two chief commissioners who served on the board between Blair's resignation in 1904 and 1912 were both experienced judges. During his tenure between 1904 and 1908, Albert Clements Killam, the noted Manitoba jurist and former Supreme Court justice, dominated the three-member commission in much the same way as Blair had done. Following Killam's death in 1908, James Pitt Mabee of the Ontario High Court of Justice assumed control of the board. Although the expansion of the board from three to six members in the same year diminished some of Mabee's authority, the legal perspective remained well represented. The Railway Act required that whoever was appointed to be the new assistant chief commissioner should also have at least ten years' standing at the bar. The Laurier government appointed D'Arcy Scott, the solicitor at Ottawa for the Canadian Pacific and New York Central Railways and, not coincidentally, the son of the retiring secretary of state, Sir Richard Scott, to fill the position.[7] The courts provided the most obvious institutional model for these judges and lawyers to follow. Trial-type hearings offered a familiar guarantee of procedural fairness, as well as a structured means of allowing the disputants to state their views, to present the kind of information they considered relevant, to challenge the explanation of each situation that was offered. The adversarial process was also a useful mechanism for isolating general and potentially explosive issues into single cases; the number of participants to a dispute, could be restricted and attention focused on a limited set of questions. Similarly, the commission could hope to make its decisions appear more authoritative by resorting to written judgments, replete with interpretations of the statute and references to any available precedents. By establishing some firm precedents, the commission had an opportunity to eliminate altogether certain types of recurrent questions from the administrative arena, thereby ensuring a more manageable caseload.

However, the legal perspective, was not the only one available to the commission. The regulatory community also was composed of career railway officials, who offered a quite different approach to regulation. The Grand Trunk's John Loud, the Canadian Pacific's G.M. Bosworth, W.R. MacInnes, and Frank W. Peters, and the Canadian Northern's George H. Shaw, all with years of experience working in railway traffic offices, became just as familiar to the commissioners as their legal colleagues.[8] These men proved invaluable to the board, for having been frequently involved in the setting of many of the disputed tariffs, they were often in a position to untangle their complicated history, or provide the corporate rationale for the rates. Moreover, it was they and their colleagues in the Canadian Freight Association who would subsequently have to translate the commission orders into practical rate changes. Shippers across the country also relied on the railway freight officers to help them formulate their individual grievances before the commission. For example, the Toronto Board of Trade hired a former railway official with some forty years' experience in the Grand Trunk's Toronto freight office to help prepare some of its first presentations to the commission. The Canadian Manufacturers' Association, and the Winnipeg and Vancouver Boards of Trade went even further and retained permanent transportation "experts," also drawn from railway company freight offices, to present complaints to the board and to monitor other regulatory proceedings on behalf of its members.

Such men were preferred to lawyers because they had an intimate understanding of the operations of railway freight offices.[9]

The railway commission had its own rate expert on staff. James Hardwell, generally referred to as the board's chief traffic officer, played a critical role in supporting the members of the commission, few of whom had any practical rate-making or even railway experience. It was he who undertook special investigations into the freight rate cases handled by the board, preparing the reports and recommendations upon which the commissioners often depended. Hardwell's own career had paralleled that of the freight officials who assisted both the railways and various shippers. From 1874 until 1897, he had worked as a clerk or chief clerk in local and regional freight offices on both the Grand Trunk and the Canadian Pacific railways. Between 1898 and the time of his appointment to the board in 1904, he was first a divisional freight official and then the assistant general freight agent on the dominion government's Intercolonial Railway. Although his four years with the public railway gave Hardwell a somewhat independent perspective, he could still be expected to share the outlook of other career railway officials, such as the Grand Trunk's John Loud, or, for that matter, the Canadian Manufacturers' Association's John Marlow.[10]

The perspective of those trained in railway freight offices differed from that of the lawyers. Whereas lawyers by nature paid considerable attention to the *means* of, or the procedures for resolving disputes, freight officials were essentially concerned with the *ends*. These officers became the buffer between shippers and other railway managers, and sought any solution that would satisfy the demands of shippers while protecting railway revenues. Since they were not accustomed to arguing the merits of their rate decisions in a public courtroom, they were more anxious than were lawyers to settle disputes through private bargaining. While legal counsel might hope to use particular disputes to establish favourable general principles, railway officials studiously avoided general policies and preferred to silence aggrieved shippers by making isolated rate concessions. They had been trained to find workable compromises through negotiation. The railway commissioners could see some value in the approach to problems adopted by railway freight officers. They knew that many supporters of the railway commission sought an institution that would avoid the kinds of judicial proceedings that entangled the parties in costly, time-consuming, and ultimately pointless debates over technical rules. Moreover, the commissioners were in much the same position as freight officers, anxious to satisfy aggrieved shippers without alienating those railway managers who sought to maintain existing revenues. They also had a stake in encouraging negotiation and in achieving workable compromises.

The lawyers and the railway officials who gradually gathered around the new agency all offered perspectives that could be expected to influence the commission's regulatory strategy. The judicial model offered a means of satisfying the desire of the commission's clients to be treated fairly and predictably, while the freight officer's less formal approach seemed capable of producing the kinds of final results those same clients sought. In seeking to establish an acceptable and effective agency, the members of the railway commission attempted to achieve their own particular blend of the two approaches. The regulatory strategy of the railway commission was formulated in response to the specific demands of railway officials and shippers, and therefore can best be appreciated through an examination of a number of illustrative cases.

Many students of regulation have observed that the regulatory approach adopted by administrative agencies tends to favour certain interests. Prior to the publication in 1965 of Gabriel Kolko's *Railroads and Regulation*, an influential study of the American railway commission, many scholars had concluded that the procedures used and decisions reached by most administrative tribunals gradually began to favour the industry that the agency was supposed to be regulating. The regulated industry thus "captured" the government agency. Kolko, whose work continues to attract an ideologically diverse group of critics of government regulation, eliminated the notion of a gradual alignment of the interests of the regulators and the regulated, arguing that the function of government intervention was always to serve the interests of the industry. Whether the industry in fact supported the regulation all along or, as is the current theory in *Monopoly's Moment*, a recent study of Canadian utilities by H.V. Nelles and Christopher Armstrong, it reluctantly accepted government intervention as inevitable, the argument still seems to be that once in place, regulation proved to be very useful to the regulated. These theories suggest that, in examining the early behaviour of the Board of Railway Commissioners, attention should be paid to the ways in which the board furthered the interests of private railway companies.[11]

There is no doubt that Canadian railway officials tried to turn the new regulatory regime to their own advantage. Prior to 1 February 1904, a Canadian Pacific freight officer told the commissioners, "many things were done which will not be done again, rebates paid and special rates made which should not have been made." Shortly after the enactment of the new Railway Act, a divisional freight agent of the Grand Trunk received instructions to remove "inconsistencies" in the rate structure. These "inconsistencies" included rates that might be considered discriminatory under the law, or rate practices which, if made general, would seriously affect the revenues of the railway companies.[12] Traffic officials hoped to use the new Railway Act to systematize an often chaotic rate structure, a process they had begun on their own in the 1890s through the Canadian Freight Association.

Many of the commission's cases involving questions of special freight tariffs or reasonableness were a result of the attempts of railway officials to eliminate rates which they believed had outlived their usefulness. Because many of these private rate arrangements were contrary to the anti-discrimination clauses of the Railway Act, the board generally sanctioned their cancellation. In doing so, however, the commission reserved the right to review the "reasonableness" of the resulting readjustments and did not automatically allow railway officials to "line up the rates" as they desired. In early judgments, the board adopted the position that shippers could point to the longevity of a particular rate arrangement as evidence that it was reasonable and profitable. This placed the onus on those seeking to change the existing tariff structure: railway officials would be expected to show that the rate they sought to cancel was both discriminatory and unreasonable. Otherwise, they could be challenged for not eliminating the discrimination by leaving the lower toll in place and realigning the rates for all other shippers downward.[13]

A case involving the William Davies Company illustrates the process by which the commission reviewed rate adjustments. Shortly after the new Railway Act came into force in 1903, officials from the Grand Trunk and Canadian Pacific Railways cancelled a special rate enjoyed by the Toronto packer on its products shipped to Montreal for export on the grounds that the rate was discriminatory, since a similar reduction had never been granted to other Ontario packers. The company appealed to the railway commission to reinstate the rate. Two transportation experts, one hired by the Davies Company and the other by the Canadian Manufacturers' Association, presented the packer's case at a three-day oral hearing that was convened in April and then reconvened in May 1906. They argued that the railways had to show that the old rate was unreasonable. Through the testimony of the assistant general manager of the company, they established that the rate had been introduced in the early 1890s and that the circumstances surrounding the transportation of the product had not changed. Moreover, they pointed out that the old rate still produced a significantly higher earning per mile for the railway than similar goods shipped from Chicago. The Davies Company had sought these rate advantages to assist it in competing against American and European packers for a share of the lucrative English market. The company was not concerned about Canadian competition in the export trade, so was quite willing to insist that the railways should correct the discrimination by lowering the tariff available to the other Ontario packers.

After lawyers for the Canadian Pacific and Grand Trunk failed to have the charge quashed on the basis of insufficient evidence, they proceeded to examine a number of their companies' freight officials. Not surprisingly, these "expert" witnesses contended that the new rate was reasonable, since the relatively lower rates enjoyed by Chicago packers were made possible by stiff competition from water transport at the American port and did not reflect the higher costs of operation in Canada. Representatives of the Davies Company then concentrated on demonstrating that the views of the railway officers could not be substantiated with concrete evidence. Under questioning, the freight agents admitted that no packer ever used a water carrier and that they could not prove that operating costs were higher in Canada. John Loud, a freight officer for over twenty-five years, admitted that he had no idea what the average costs and earnings on his railway were. When asked on what basis he and his officials arrived at a reasonable rate, he vaguely responded that he took all "things" into consideration and made a personal judgment. "What is the reason assigned for believing a rate is fair?," the Davies Company's representative asked the railway commissioners, "It is a reason that would not satisfy a kindergarten scholar." Lawyers for the railways tried to make a virtue of their difficulties. In cases such as this one, they argued that precisely because there was no "scientifical, methodical, mathematical mode" of establishing rates, the railway commission should intervene only when it had been furnished with conclusive evidence that rates were excessive or discriminatory. The rate structure was depicted as a complex product, the result of hundreds of business compromises, and a structure that should not be disturbed except under exceptional circumstances.[14]

Very early in the proceedings, Chief Commissioner Killam suggested that the whole question be turned over to the board's own traffic expert for investigation. Railway counsel, however, regarded the dispute as an important test case because of the attempt to use American rates as a standard of reasonableness. They successfully pressed the board to hold a trial-type hearing, complete with the examination and cross-examination of witnesses, and the presentation of formal concluding statements. Although several commissioners openly complained about the length of time devoted to this case, they did not deny the railways the right to proceed as they wished. The quasi-judicial approach did not prevent the traffic managers representing the Davies Company from participating fully in the hearings, even though they did not have any legal training.[15]

In the end, the board avoided altogether the issue of the use of American rate comparisons that had concerned railway officials. Instead, without any formal justification, the commission ordered the railways to grant the William Davies Company a rate somewhat higher than the packer had previously enjoyed but lower than the new rate the railway companies had introduced. The export rate paid by other Ontario packers was accordingly adjusted slightly downward. Rather than establishing some "scientifical" solution to the dispute, or taking the opportunity to comment on standards of reasonableness, the board simply devised its own compromise, and sanctioned that compromise as reasonable.[16]

In this and other cases, the commission concluded that it would not "determine the reasonableness of a rate aside from the concrete conditions it is concerned with."[17] Such a principle maintained a wide sphere for regulation, and ensured that the commission could consider the specific circumstances surrounding each case. How the board would learn of the particular conditions, and what factors would be considered as important to a particular case, was left open, although the commissioners did indicate a clear preference for investigation rather than formal hearings. In placing the onus on those seeking change, the board made it more difficult for railway officials to use legislation outlawing preferential rates and rebates to eliminate unremunerative tolls. In fact, railway officers risked having to reduce some of their other, non-disputed rates in raising an issue at all. The railway commission did not prove to be a co-operative client of the railway industry.

The effort to eliminate special rate arrangements represented one of the few ways in which railway officers sought to turn the new regulatory regime to their advantage prior to World War I. In fact, in many of the disputes handled by the commission, particularly those raising the question of discrimination based on geographic location, it was the shippers who sought to use regulation for their own private ends. They laid charges of "discrimination" in an attempt to gain a freight rate advantage over competing businesses. Under these circumstances, the railway commissioners found themselves embroiled in trade disputes between shippers. Railway officials also had a stake in such cases, of course; they sought to ensure that any proposed readjustment did not significantly diminish their companies' freight earnings.

In responding to the various demands of shippers for rate adjustments, the railway commission established and tried to follow a number of broad regulatory principles, while leaving a considerable degree of managerial discretion with railway freight officers. Regulators, the commissioners asserted, should only supervise rates, not initiate them. The board, therefore, generally denied attempts by shippers to have the commission compel railway officials to grant them special favours, or to introduce lower rates that might help develop an individual business. The commission also rejected the contention of a number of shippers that the railways should be required to fix lower rates in communities where they competed with water carriers or American railways.

Finally, the board repeatedly stated that it would not fix tolls so as to compensate some shippers for geographic or other disadvantages in their costs of operation. In each case, the railway commission contended that while it would not adjust rates based on any of these considerations, railway officials remained free to do so.[18] In principle, the commissioners would only interfere with a railway decision to offer special favours, or to meet water, American rail, or market competition if and when such decisions gave some specific shippers an unfair rate advantage, or if it could be established that the rates complained of were unreasonable. In trying to leave decision-making with railway officers, the commission sought to define a regulatory, as opposed to a rate-making, sphere, although it still retained a considerable discretion over freight rates. In practice, these clearly enunciated regulatory principles proved to be more ambiguous, and far less protective of railway company interests, than would first appear. Two cases involving applications for rate adjustments from British American Oil and Dominion Sugar help to illustrate the challenges facing the commissioners in resolving freight rate disputes, and the resulting strategy they adopted.

In 1908, the British American Oil Company expanded its Toronto operations from the simple marketing of American products to the refining of American crude oil. Although at this time Standard Oil dominated the Canadian oil industry through Imperial Oil, the increasing consumption of oil in Canada during the early twentieth century provided an opportunity for smaller companies such as British American to carve out a share of the market.[19] As part of its corporate strategy, British American asked railway officials to give its Toronto operation the same kind of preferential rates that were enjoyed by refiners in Petrolia and Sarnia. Railway officers offered to put all the refineries on an "equal" footing by cancelling all of the commodity tariffs on oil and simply charging regular fifth-class rates. This proposal would have produced an absolute rate advance of five cents per hundred pounds for oil products shipped from Petrolia and Sarnia to key markets such as Ottawa and Montreal and, more significantly, would have increased the difference between the rates from Petrolia and Toronto from two to seven cents. British American, which stood to gain from the change, and Imperial Oil, whose Sarnia operation did not rely on rail transportation, accepted, but objections were raised by Canadian Oil Companies, a struggling Petrolia refiner reorganized in 1908 by the National Oil Refining Company of Cleveland. Canadian Oil asked railway officials to continue granting special commodity rates to its firm while charging its Toronto competitor the relatively higher fifth-class rates, in order to equalize the competitive position of each of the refiners in their largest markets.[20]

When negotiations reached an impasse, officials from British American turned to the railway commission for assistance.[21] In a brief oral presentation, the company alleged that existing rates discriminated against their Toronto refinery. Before proceeding any further with the case, the railway commission attempted to "pour water on troubled oil." It sponsored an informal conference to encourage the parties to negotiate a settlement, attended by Commissioner McLean and Chief Traffic Officer Hardwell. Officials from Canadian Oil Companies remained intransigent, and refused to accept a compromise devised by Hardwell or any other plan that would either advance its rates or in any way enhance its Toronto competitor's rate advantages. When this attempt at mediation failed, the railway commission allowed the formal hearing to proceed. A representative of Canadian Oil then tried to delay the proceedings by demanding that British American file a formal petition of complaint. Chief Commissioner Mabee explained that such procedural manœuvres were out of place in commission hearings. "Anything is satisfactory to us as long as we can get rid of the thing," Mabee remarked. "If anyone is taken by surprise when things come up of course we give him a chance to answer."[22]

Proceeding with their presentation, several officials from Canadian Oil noted that British American already enjoyed a rate advantage in most consuming markets. Any adjustment in that company's favour would shut the Petrolia firm out of its former markets and reduce competition, resulting in increased prices for the consuming public and a decline in the value of the refinery's existing capital investment. Canadian Oil officials encouraged the railway commission to adopt the same kind of rate structure as existed in the United States, where similar rates were granted to competing oil refining points. In response to these presentations, officials from British American maintained that the Petrolia and Wallaceburg refineries asked "not for justice but for special treatment.[23]

In Commissioner McLean's final judgment in the case, he affirmed that "As a matter of general policy the Board should not attempt to define the illusory phrase 'benefit of geographical position', or to delimit the distributing area of a particular industry." The railway proposal to apply fifth-class rates everywhere was consistent with that principle. McLean went on to argue, however, that although the existing commodity rates represented "a series of more or less illogical compromises," the board could not ignore that they had existed for years and an established business had developed under them. To resolve the issue a readjustment was ordered along the lines originally proposed by Hardwell. The change minimized the advances facing the Petrolia refinery while granting the Toronto company a slight reduction in some of its current rates.[24] The "justice" meted out by the board did not grant British American the kind of rate advantage it sought, did not equalize conditions in the way Canadian Oil proposed, nor did it allow railway officials to advance or maintain existing tolls. As in the William Davies case, the board resorted to compromise rather than set out clear regulatory standards.

An application to the commission from Dominion Sugar for a rate adjustment combined similar elements from both the Davies and British American cases. Like British American, Dominion Sugar was a relative newcomer to the Canadian industry, having been established in 1901 at Wallaceburg in southwestern Ontario. It sought freight rates that would ensure it a large enough share of the small but expanding Canadian market to keep its capital-intensive refinery solvent. Officials from Dominion Sugar became particularly dissatisfied with the freight tolls paid by Canada Sugar of Montreal on shipments to Ontario's two principal markets, Toronto and Hamilton. Although the Wallaceburg refinery was located over 100 miles closer to both cities than its Montreal rival, it enjoyed a rate advantage of only one cent in Toronto and three cents in Hamilton. In 1909 and 1910, railway officials voluntarily reduced Dominion Sugar's freight tariff when the company threatened to ship its products by water. This special arrangement was subsequently cancelled and Dominion Sugar applied to the railway commission for reinstatement of the preferred rate or for a readjustment of the existing rates so they would more accurately reflect the actual distance the railway carried the freight.

Although officials from Canada Sugar took an interest in the case, they preferred to let railway officials oppose Dominion Sugar's request. Citing the board's ruling that railway agents were free to decide whether or not to meet competition from water carriers, counsel for the railways pointed out that just such a competitive threat led their companies to grant the special rate in the first place. When officials determined that they had little to fear from such competition, they withdrew their rate concession. As for the charge of discrimination in favour of Montreal, the railways' lawyers contended that the existence of more competitive water transport from Montreal than from Wallaceburg fully justified any difference in the rates from those points. Here was a classic example of the type of case that Commissioner McLean, who sat in on the brief April 1913 hearing, had always envisioned for the railway commission. The central point of contention – the existence and extent of water competition – was based on facts that could be investigated and verified. The board's expert, Hardwell, was asked to undertake a thorough inquiry into the actual conditions under which sugar was carried from both Montreal and Wallaceburg. On the basis of this study, Commissioner McLean concluded that the quantity of sugar shipped over water from Wallaceburg to Hamilton and Toronto was declining and had always been much smaller than the amount carried from Montreal. He therefore ruled that the more intense shipping competition from Montreal justified the sugar rates that were proportionately lower from Montreal than from Wallaceburg.[25]

Dominion Sugar contested the "factual" conclusions reached by McLean in his judgment, and won an early rehearing of its case. In October 1913, a refinery official attempted to demonstrate that water competition remained very effective from Wallaceburg. He also stressed the advantages that his Montreal competitor enjoyed in getting lower rates on raw sugar via New York and Halifax and in having a large local market. Chief Commissioner Drayton rejected the use of such arguments, and affirmed that "The Board has not in its past nor should it in the future attempt, by a process of rate-scaling, to overcome natural economic conditions, or to do away with geographical or natural advantages which one location may have over the other." Nor was the chief commissioner impressed by the new evidence concerning water competition, although he did conclude that since the low rates from Montreal were in force throughout the year, they could not be attributed solely to this factor. Insofar as the rates resulted from "an understanding between the Montreal sugar refiners and the railway companies," Drayton ruled they were discriminatory. Dominion Sugar was, therefore, granted a reduction in its rates, not as great as had been requested, but the same percentage of reduction from the class rates as Canada Sugar enjoyed.[26]

The Dominion Sugar case was unusual in that a rehearing was necessary before the commission offered rate concessions. More frequently, the board found a way to order a compromise solution in its initial decision, even if it ruled against the complainants on the main question at issue in the case.[27] As all three cases considered here help illustrate, where possible, the commissioners relied on the methods of mediation, conciliation, and arbitration, rather than adjudication. They frequently encouraged and sponsored informal conferences between railway and shipper representatives in the belief "that compromises which are worked out in round-table discussions are often more satisfactory than the conclusions which are hammered out on the anvil of justice." If that approach failed, the commissioners used their broad discretionary authority over rates to award settlements that offered something to all parties involved in the dispute. The board refused to impose rigid standards and principles on complex situations, or to become a "mere arbiter of logic." Instead, the commissioners and their staff tried to assess existing business conditions and develop their own compromise solutions.[28]

The regulatory strategy adopted by the commission did not necessarily serve the railway industry's interests. Mediation, conciliation, and arbitration prevented railway freight rate regulation from becoming the kind of winner-take-all, zero-sum game that the "capture" thesis often suggests. Before addressing the question of the role and interests of the regulators and the regulated more fully, however, it may be useful to provide a final illustration of the commission's early work. While the cases described above were fairly typical of the kinds of disputes dealt with by the commission in that they involved a very specific industry and a freight tariff limited in its application, the cases that became part of the International Rates order involved a widely held grievance and challenged the entire rate structure that existed in Ontario and Quebec. In contrast to these more individualized disputes, therefore, the stakes were much higher, particularly for the railway industry.

The persistent efforts of the Canadian Manufacturers' Association and the Toronto Board of Trade resulted in the establishment of the International Rates order. These two organizations had been strong supporters of a new railway commission in the first place, and sought to turn the new regulatory regime to their advantage. They challenged the board to resolve a number of long-standing grievances about the freight tariffs used in Ontario and Quebec, and in the process seriously tested the effectiveness of regulation by the administrative commission.

When the railway commission travelled to Toronto for the first time in 1904, the city's board of trade presented a lengthy petition, complaining of such matters as the generally higher freight tariff charged in Ontario compared to Michigan, the rates charged on general merchandise to and from Toronto, and the existence of American rates to Canadian points that were lower than the tariff from Canadian points.[29] The commissioners, not knowing how or whether to address such broad questions, gave the railway companies time to respond to these complaints but took no further action once they had received their responses. In November 1905, the board of trade again approached the commission, this time with a more specific complaint: the rates on freight shipped by merchants from Toronto were unreasonable because they had not been reduced since 1884; and they were discriminatory because their Montreal rivals enjoyed a lower tariff. Once again, the railway companies were given an opportunity to respond to the complaints, and when it again appeared that no further action was contemplated, the board of trade demanded that the railway commission use its powers to investigate and resolve the matter. Instead, the board chose only to convene an oral hearing of the parties in May 1906, a procedure that also resulted in little significant progress.[30]

The board of trade took the opportunity provided by the hearing to criticize the railway commission's handling of their case. While Chief Commissioner Killam did not attempt to defend the delays, he did try to outline the regulatory agency's general approach to disputes. He pointed out that the commission generally heard complaints in oral or written representations, and then carried out its own investigations. While railway officials frequently accepted the responsibility for justifying the rates complained of, regardless of the legal onus of proof, Killam noted that they sometimes insisted that shippers provide formal evidence in support of their complaint. The board had "investigated one or two complaints in that way," Killam remarked, "and the result to my mind has been unsatisfactory." He rejected the attempt by the railway companies to have all complaints treated "as a trial of case at law, and dismissed on grounds of insufficiency of evidence"; the commission's only policy was to carry out inquiries in a way that was both just to all parties and ensured that complaints of a public nature received a full investigation. He did authorize Hardwell to study the matter and the chief traffic officer quickly concluded that the true solution to the problem was "to be found in a general rearrangement of all the class rates between all points, not merely as they affect Toronto, or Toronto, Hamilton and London."[31] A second rate dispute, initiated in the same month as the final hearing of the Toronto Board of Trade case, provided the commission with an opportunity to effect such a sweeping alteration of Ontario's freight tariff structure.

In May 1906, the transportation expert of the Canadian Manufacturers' Association, John R. Marlow, arranged to have the owners of a group of companies from Windsor, Walkerville, and Chatham describe how they paid higher tolls than their American competitors in shipping goods to the same Canadian destinations.[32] Marlow hoped that these specific illustrations would lead the commission to consider and readjust the general tariff applied on freight from the United States and in Ontario.

Railway officials feared the results of such an adjustment. If they were required to lower the rates between Windsor and Montreal to equal the current rates from Detroit, the tariffs between all intermediate points would have to be reduced; otherwise, the railway companies would be violating the section of the Railway Act that required that tolls set for the shorter haul must not be higher than those for the longer haul. The elimination of the apparent discrimination against some particular Canadian shippers, therefore, would threaten to "destroy the entire fabric of rates at present existing in Eastern Canada."[33] Counsel for the Grand Trunk challenged the board's right to consider the case. F.H. Chrysler contended that because the commission had no jurisdiction over international rates, it could not rule that the lower rates from Detroit and the American Midwest violated the long- and short-haul clause of the Railway Act. The board, he concluded, could act only if it found that the Canadian portion of the rates were unreasonable, and since the existing freight tariffs barely permitted the Grand Trunk to pay any return on its investment, they could hardly be considered to be unreasonable. Given its financial position, Chrysler emphasized, the Grand Trunk could not afford the kind of drastic alteration being proposed.[34]

Chief Commissioner Killam remained unmoved by such pleas. At the conclusion of the case, he noted that while the commission would consider the jurisdictional arguments, the contested rates did seem to violate both the long- and short-haul clause and "natural justice." Railway officials, he strongly intimated, should try to remove the alleged discrimination themselves, without waiting for the board to suggest a course. The railway companies agreed to co-operate with the commission. Corporate counsel may have concluded that it would be difficult and, given the board's wide discretion to determine what constituted unreasonable or discriminatory rates or to alter any freight tariffs, futile to press the jurisdictional question. Co-operation would ensure some control over the final adjustment, so that railway officials could minimize the disruption and impact on their revenues. For its part, the commission agreed not to consider the case further for three months, giving Canadian railway officials an opportunity to develop their own solution to the problem and to negotiate any necessary changes with their American counterparts.[35] This strategy permitted the board and the railways to avoid a direct confrontation over the commission's authority.

Because Canadian and American railways used very different systems for establishing their basic freight rates, the task of equalizing rates from Detroit and Windsor was complicated.[36] After several months of negotiations with their American counterparts, railway officials developed the broad outlines of a solution to the problem. In general, their proposal would reduce rates from most communities in Ontario to Montreal and points further east, but would at the same time increase rates from those same communities to Toronto. The freight tariff between most other towns in southwestern Ontario would also be increased.[37] Not surprisingly, railway officials sought a solution that would protect their overall freight revenues.

The railway commission avoided both a direct confrontation with the railways and a considerable degree of work by allowing representatives of the Canadian Freight Association to develop a solution to the problem of international rates. In seeking a compromise, however, the commissioners did not abandon their responsibilities. They refused to accept the first proposal offered by the railways and insisted that certain minimal conditions be met. After a brief hearing in November they facilitated conferences between railway officials, the traffic expert of the Canadian Manufacturers' Association, and the commission's own expert. While Marlow and Hardwell accepted the basic outline of the proposal, they wanted still lower class rates to Montreal and no advance in the rates from Toronto. At this stage, Hardwell also sought revisions that would address the various complaints that had been raised in the earlier hearing by the Toronto Board of Trade. After considering all these suggestions, railway officials concluded that "The results would be so disastrous ... [that] neither the officers of the Grand Trunk or Canadian Pacific Railways feel that they can assume the responsibility for the loss of such a large amount of net revenue ... At the same time they fully recognize the authority of the Board's orders, but in that case the Board, of course, assumes the responsibility of the results."[38]

At this critical stage in the negotiations, Hardwell adopted a more active role. In March, he told the transportation committees of the Toronto Board of Trade and the Canadian Manufacturers' Association that they had two options: they could challenge the railway companies' estimates of the impact of the new rates, engaging themselves and the railway commission in months of expert investigation, or they could authorize the railway commission to negotiate a more acceptable solution. Both organizations agreed to the latter course. Hardwell then helped develop a plan that would group the rates from points west of Toronto, thus avoiding the kinds of increases that the railway companies had originally proposed, while limiting the extent of the reductions that the adoption of a straight mileage basis would produce. At an informal meeting of the Board of Railway Commissioners in July 1907, Hardwell and railway officials announced that they had agreed on a new scale of rates to be adopted in Ontario and Quebec.[39]

Table 8 illustrates some of the results of the negotiations between the board's chief traffic officer and railway officials. The final settlement produced a reduction in freight rates between most Canadian points. The differential rates between Windsor and Detroit were eliminated, although not in the manner that the railways had first proposed. In responding to the complaints of the Toronto Board of Trade, the adjustment did not eliminate some of the advantages enjoyed by Montreal merchants, as the board continued to sanction lower westbound than eastbound rates. Nevertheless, as the rates to Brantford and Collingwood help illustrate, some other complaints of the Toronto Board of Trade were dealt with with respect to its relative position in the Ontario trading network. Through a judicious use of its powers, the regulatory tribunal encouraged the development of a compromise that, for the most part, proved acceptable to both the shipping community and the railways.

In the International Rates order, two organizations that actively supported the creation of a railway commission, the Canadian Manufacturers' Association and the Toronto Board of Trade, demonstrated the utility of the new regulatory regime. With the active support of a public agency, these organizations acquired a bargaining power that they hitherto lacked and were able to get railway officials to undertake the arduous task of restructuring their tariffs in Ontario and Quebec to eliminate a number of longstanding grievances.

In other commission cases, the railway companies had also been required to become more responsive to the demands of various

Table 8
International Rates Adjustments
Cents per 100 Lbs, Fifth-Class Freight

	Original	Railway Proposal	Final
To Toronto from			
Detroit	13	21	18
Windsor	20	21	18
To Montreal from			
Detroit	23.5	29	29
Windsor			
Winter	35	29	29
Summer	30	29	29
Toronto			
Winter	25	–	22
Summer	20	–	20
London			
Winter	33	–	27
Summer	28	–	27
To Brantford from			
Toronto	14	–	11
Hamilton	08	–	08
London	13	–	11
Windsor	18	–	17
To Collingwood from			
Toronto	16	–	14
Hamilton	16	–	15
London	19	–	17
Windsor	25	–	21

Source: NA, Records of the Canadian Transport Commission, RG 46, Board of Railway Commissioners, Central Registry Files, vol. 1542, file 710, Report of Chief Traffic Officer re International and Toronto Board of Trade Rate Cases, 27 June 1907.

organizations, such as those representing the producers of grain, fruit, and livestock. Rather than serving the interests of the railway industry, then, regulation actually provided a measure of what American historian Ellis Hawley has termed "counterorganization," since the creation of the commission helped foster a greater balance of power between a number of smaller shippers and the railway industry.[40]

The commission did not ignore the interests of the railway companies. Although railway officials grumbled about the final settlement in the International Rate order, their co-operation and participation in the process nevertheless ensured that onerous terms were not imposed on the industry.[41] Similarly, even in cases where negotiations failed and the commission did have to order rate adjustments, it remained sensitive to the revenue needs of the railways and rarely accepted the complete remedies demanded by shippers. The resort to conciliation and compromise, which the International Rates order exemplified, allowed the commission to respond to the grievances of shippers, without completely alienating the railway industry.

"This court is not constituted as a common court," Deputy Commissioner M.E. Bernier explained in 1904, but "is rather a tribunal of conciliation." Seven years later, Chief Commissioner Mabee echoed Bernier's view, remarking "It is more in the nature of a Board of Arbitrators that we sit here."[42] This common perception corresponded to the regulatory role that the board adopted throughout its first decade of operation. Although the commissioners enunciated a number of standards and seriously considered their own precedents, they frequently sought to find a way to accommodate competing demands. They preferred to act as mediators and conciliators in the first instance, and willingly took an active role in facilitating negotiated settlements. As a last resort, they served as arbitrators, imposing their own solution on the disputants.

The regulatory strategy adopted by the commission can best be understood in terms of the interests it served, but not in the simple way the theory of regulatory "capture" suggests. Political scientist Roger Noll has suggested that rather than being a universal phenomenon, "capture" actually requires a very particular, and, one could argue, extremely rare situation in which "only one interest group has sufficient per capita interest in the issue to be effectively represented" and in which "only interest-group pressure ... can activate politicians, other bureaus or the courts to affect agency decisions."[43] It is clear that freight rate regulation did not meet even the first of these conditions. Shippers had a strong interest in the outcome of the cases; they sought the potentially important competitive advantage that rate adjustments could provide. In the regulatory arena, the railway industry was not always the main focus of the contest: the commission had to resolve disputes between contending shippers. Furthermore, because the commission travelled around the country to hear cases and adopted relatively flexible procedures in handling complaints, it was not that difficult for shippers of varying sizes to be effectively represented. While some large businesses such as the William Davies Company employed a traffic official to deal with the transportation companies or to present the company's case to the commission, smaller shipping interests could also present their grievances, either on their own or with the assistance of officials appointed by the business organizations to which they belonged.

The board required the continued co-operation and support of all of its clients – both railway officials and shippers – if it hoped to survive as an effective and politically acceptable governing institution. Mediation, conciliation, and arbitration provided convenient strategies of regulation for a new tribunal whose authority remained untested and which sought to balance the competing interests it served. The commissioners preferred bargaining to litigation in order to avoid creating clear losers who might refuse to comply with its orders or challenge its decisions, either in the courts or in Parliament. The board placed the onus on those seeking to disrupt the existing rate structure, and offered compromise solutions so as to protect the capital investment of all of its clients – merchants, manufacturers, and railways alike. In seeking the middle ground, the board aimed to offer some satisfaction to each of the parties engaged in freight rate disputes.

Throughout the nineteenth century, the politics of freight rates had been contained largely in the private sphere, except on occasion when disputes spilled over into the legislative arena. The creation of the railway commission provided a new, permanent, and public forum for the political controversy and choice surrounding freight rate decisions. In making its decisions, the commissioners adopted an approach to the freight rate issue as flexible and malleable as that of railway officials, and found themselves facing many of the same dilemmas. The regulatory process emulated the rate-making process it governed, and, in doing so, involved as much politics as administration.

The legitimacy of the commission's decisions, therefore, did not rest on any special technical skills but rather on the board's ability to serve as an effective conciliator betwen competing shippers, and between shippers and railway officials. It remained to be seen whether, and to what extent, such a regulatory strategy could contain the often bitter controversies surrounding freight rates, and prevent them from spilling over from the administrative into the legislative arena. In the years prior to World War I, a series of disputes in western Canada most seriously tested the separation of politics and administration.

CHAPTER SEVEN

"A Question of Figures"

During the Board of Railway Commissioners' first decade of operation, no other freight rate controversies matched the intensity and complexity of those of western Canada. The phenomenal economic and demographic growth of the prairie west and the continued expansion of the British Columbia interior between the turn of the century and World War I shaped the grievances. Merchants and manufacturers on the British Columbia coast, in Winnipeg, and in eastern Canada all competed for rate advantages that would guarantee them a substantial share of these attractive and land-locked consumer markets. At the same time, ambitious entrepreneurs in smaller prairie towns promoted the construction of railways and then sought rate policies that would transform their communities into major distribution and service centres. Intense interregional and inter-city competition generated sharp and passionate freight rate disputes.

Western rate grievances engaged the attention of the railway commission from its first tour of the region in 1904. For the next decade, the commissioners sought to resolve bitter disputes between merchants and manufacturers in Portage La Prairie, Regina, Edmonton, and Vancouver, and their competitors in Winnipeg. These conflicts involving allegations of geographic discrimination were similar to others dealt with by the board, which, however, soon became entangled with a quite different and controversial question – the tariffs applied to traffic in British Columbia and the prairie west that were higher than the tariffs applied to freight carried in central Canada. Throughout western Canada, local governments and business organizations demanded that their tariffs be reduced to equal those in Ontario and Quebec, except for the portion of the rates that could legitimately be attributed to higher costs of operation in the west.

In January 1912, the Board of Railway Commissioners responded to these demands by initiating a general inquiry into western rates. The dominion government, which had been asked to legislate rate equality, instead assisted in the investigation by hiring special public counsel and an independent freight traffic expert.

The assumption underlying the western rates investigation was that any impartial inquiry into the earnings and expenditures of the Canadian Pacific Railway would "verify" that its operating costs did not justify the higher freight rates in the region.[1] More than any previous case, this investigation raised questions about the relation between freight rates, railway revenues, and the overall cost of transportation. "It must come to a question of figures in the end," explained one dominion government lawyer, "and evidence will not be of great use if we can produce the figures and work them out so that the Commission will have the figures all before them reduced to a point."[2] During the course of the investigation, the dominion government's traffic expert challenged the railway commissioners to abandon their mediatorial approach to regulation and to fix rates on the basis of actual costs. Faced with months of testimony and reams of statistics, the Board of Railway Commissioners tried to determine whether rate regulation really could be just a "question of figures."

Western grievances were complicated by the rapid growth of the region in the two decades following 1900.[3] During this period, the balance of the prairie western population shifted with the large influx of immigrants; the fortunes of a number of towns and businesses rose and fell; and much of the railway network remained under construction. Railways and their freight rate policies were viewed as one means to boost a particular community's economy. In a booming and unsettled business environment, the railway officers who made rate decisions had to deal with a considerable degree of uncertainty.

During the years 1900–10, almost one million settlers migrated to the prairie west, tripling the population. Hundreds of new villages appeared and a number of existing towns grew at spectacular rates. In 1901, Winnipeg–St. Boniface, with nearly 45,000 inhabitants, was the only city that had a population in excess of 6,000 persons. Within just five years, the population of another five centres exceeded that figure: Brandon nearly doubled and Edmonton more than doubled in size, Calgary and Regina tripled their population, and Moose Jaw grew five-fold.

Throughout this period, Winnipeg retained its position as the mercantile and manufacturing centre of the prairie west. The largest western merchants and the agents of many eastern-based towns channelled much of the trade between western Canada and eastern North America through the city. By 1911, Winnipeg was Canada's third most populous city, the third largest importer of goods, and the fourth largest manufacturing centre. The Winnipeg business community worked hard to maintain this dominant position in the face of new rivals. Regina and Edmonton, one-twentieth and one-tenth the size of the Manitoba capital in 1901, both boasted a population only one-fifth as large by 1911. By that date also, Calgary had emerged as Winnipeg's largest rival on the prairies, with one-third the population, and about one-quarter the value in manufacturing and direct imports. All of these business communities fought hard to wrest some of the control over the commerce of the west from Winnipeg.

They were not alone. By the turn of the century, merchants and manufacturers on the Pacific Coast, initially interested in the booming mining regions of interior British Columbia, turned their sights to the rapidly expanding prairie communities as markets for products such as lumber and as a source of goods to be exported through their ports. Vancouver's business community barely managed to keep pace with the spectaculor growth in manufacturing and mercantile activity experienced by their prairie rivals and zealously sought to improve their competitive position. The Panama Canal, nearing completion in the years immediately prior to World War I, promised to make the city a more attractive importing and exporting centre by substantially reducing shipping time and costs between the Pacific Coast and Europe.[4]

Although by World War I, Winnipeg, Vancouver, Calgary, Edmonton, Regina, and Saskatoon would all emerge as the pre-eminent cities of the west, throughout the pre-war years, it was not always clear which western towns would be transformed into thriving urban centres. For example, Moose Jaw expanded far more quickly than nearby Regina prior to 1906, and had nearly the same population. Five years later, Regina had twice as many inhabitants as Moose Jaw. During the first decade of the twentieth century, then, western business communities actively competed with each other and their counterparts in eastern Canada for a share of western prosperity. Political and business leaders in prairie and Pacific communities anxiously enticed government institutions, manufacturers, and railway companies to establish operations in their towns.

Railway connections were critical to urban promoters. With the active encouragement of local boosters and national political leaders, the west became the centre of much of Canada's railway construction activity. Between 1905 and 1914, the Grand Trunk Pacific, a wholly owned subsidiary of the Grand Trunk Railway, built a main line northwest from Winnipeg via Saskatoon to Edmonton and beyond through the Rockies to a new northern Pacific Coast port, Prince Rupert. Canadian Northern officials extended their short Manitoba lines to create a main line running from Winnipeg to central Manitoba and across Saskatchewan just north of Saskatoon to Edmonton. Anxious to tap some of the Canadian Pacific's southern territory, Canadian Northern strategists also pieced together a loop-line from Brandon west to Regina and then north to Saskatoon and Prince Albert, and constructed a new line southwest from Saskatoon to Calgary. After 1910, work began on a line that paralleled the Grand Trunk Pacific from Edmonton through the Yellowhead Pass in the Rockies but then veered southwest through the Fraser Valley to Vancouver. Canadian Pacific officials countered these various incursions into their territory by expanding their prairie system northward. By taking firm control of the Calgary and Edmonton Railway and patching together branch lines, they created two direct lines running northwesterly to Edmonton from Moose Jaw as well as from Portage La Prairie via Saskatoon. Besides these larger projects, both the Canadian Northern and Canadian Pacific scrambled for control of the expanding prairie economy through the construction of a multitude of short feeder lines.[5]

By 1914, the three transcontinentals and a few smaller companies had added a total of over 9,000 miles to the 4,500 miles of track that had been operated in the prairie west and British Columbia at the turn of the century. Much of this expansion took place in Saskatchewan and, to a lesser extent, Alberta. Moreover, this enormous growth of the western railway network showed no signs of slowing: about 4,200 miles, almost half of the total expansion that took place between 1900 and 1914, came into operation after 1910; by the summer of 1914, a further 7,000 miles of track was under construction or had been contracted for, and another 10,000 miles had been surveyed. Much of this activity was taking place in or was projected for British Columbia and Alberta. If all of this mileage came into operation, it would more than double the network of rails in western Canada.[6]

In fixing western rates, therefore, railway freight officers had to consider the way in which their decisions might be affected by dramatic changes in the railway system and in the patterns of western

settlement and economic development. In the face of so much uncertainty, they clung to the basic outlines of a rate structure that had
been established in the nineteenth century. As was done in the
United States, they adopted a general merchandise tariff for prairie
traffic that was relatively higher than the one used in the east. An
even higher set of rates (known as the mountain scale) was applied
on internal and outgoing freight shipped from most parts of the
Pacific Coast region, including British Columbia. These standard
tariffs in turn shaped many of the special commodity and distributing rates within the region.

Two developments complicated this situation. First, as a result of
the Canadian Northern's 1901 agreement with the Manitoba government, the railway agreed to reduce its general rates 15 per cent
below the existing level in that province, and then made a voluntary
reduction of 7.5 per cent on rates in the remainder of the prairie
west. To remain competitive, the Canadian Pacific had little choice
but to follow suit. As a result, two general merchandise tariffs were
in use on the prairies, one applying to shipments within Manitoba,
and the other applying to all shipments within Saskatchewan and
Alberta, and to goods consigned from Manitoba to those provinces.[7]

The special rate advantages that Winnipeg's business community
had wrung from the railways during the nineteenth century further
complicated the rate situation. Under a special reduction on freight
carried between Winnipeg and the Lakehead, and low traders' tariffs
between the city and a specific list of merchants in other western
centres, Winnipeg jobbers could import goods from eastern Canada
and subsequently reship them at the same rate as their eastern competitors could send them directly, with the addition only of a small
handling charge. Although originally limited to freight carried from
eastern Canada via an all-Canadian route, it proved impossible to
identify those goods and the special low rates were gradually extended to all goods shipped out of Winnipeg, including those imported via the United States or manufactured in the city itself. Aside
from giving those merchants named on the tariff an advantage over
those in the same community who were not listed, the traders' rates
made it more difficult for other western business communities to
secure their own distributing trade.[8]

To establish their towns as important shipping centres, urban business and political leaders sought the kinds of freight rate advantages
that would, at minimum, ensure their control over their immediate
territory. In this struggle for a share of the expanding trade of the
prairies, all of the principle features of the traditional western rate
structure came under vigorous attack. Western business organiza-

tions accused railway officials of responding far too slowly to rapidly changing circumstances, and took their grievances to the Board of Railway Commissioners.

When the railway commission convened its first set of hearings throughout the west in 1904, merchant organizations in Brandon, Regina, Vancouver, and Victoria attacked the special rate advantages their rivals in Winnipeg enjoyed. Canadian Pacific and Canadian Northern officials were also anxious to cancel these rates and so actively encouraged such complaints. Since neither railway wanted to be viewed as the initiator of such a change and incur the political wrath of the influential Winnipeg business community, they hoped to have the commission declare the traders' tariffs illegal. In seeking to eliminate Winnipeg's rate advantages, however, railway officials soon found that they had opened a Pandora's Box. What began as an attack on the discriminatory features of a single tariff resulted in a series of challenges to the reasonableness of the entire structure of prairie west and British Columbia rates.

The railway commission did not respond to the general grievances in the prairies concerning Winnipeg's rate advantages until 1907, when first railway officials and then the board of trade of Portage La Prairie applied for a special hearing on the matter. Towards the conclusion of this brief proceeding, Chief Commissioner Killam made it abundantly clear that he would rule that the Winnipeg tariffs were discriminatory.[9] Railway officials, who already had received an informal opinion from the commission's chief traffic officer to that effect, soon introduced a new set of tolls that would become effective in November 1907. The new tariff prompted a storm of protest from the Winnipeg business community. The railway commissioners considered suspending the rates until they could hear these complaints, but a flood of telegrams from business organizations in other western centres convinced them otherwise.[10] At the subsequent hearing, Winnipeg merchants described the burden imposed by the new tariff, while their competitors from Moose Jaw, Regina, Brandon, and Portage La Prairie protested that, compared to other prairie centres, the Winnipeg business community was still receiving relatively lower rates on freight shipped from the Lakehead.[11] In the face of these competing claims, the board did not interfere with the compromise which railway officials had designed. In an attempt to stifle continued criticism of Winnipeg's advantages, railway freight officers voluntarily reduced the rate of fifth-class freight and on agricultural implements shipped from the Lakehead to a number of western centres in 1908. Within a year, however, the Regina, Moose Jaw, and Edmonton Boards of Trade, were complaining that the concessions were not significant enough, and turned to the railway commission with their grievances. They complained both of the lower rate between the Lakehead and Winnipeg and of the relatively lower merchandise tariff applied in Manitoba.[12]

Canadian Northern and Canadian Pacific management, joined by various Winnipeg shipping organizations, fought any further changes to the western rate structure. Counsel for the railways argued that the large quantity of traffic carried between the Lakehead and Winnipeg reduced the cost of operation, and therefore justified the lower tariff on that section. Moreover, they argued that because the special tariff from the Lakehead and the lower scale of rates in Manitoba had been "imposed" on the companies by the Manitoba agreement, they should not be made the basis of comparison with any others.[13] When the board rejected these arguments and ordered the elimination of the discrimination against Regina and other western centres, railway management delayed the implementation of new tariffs by applying for an appeal to the Supreme Court. Their lawyers contended that the railway commission had erred on a matter of law in refusing to consider the contractual nature of the rates as a defence against the charge of discrimination. The railway commission granted the appeal. The Supreme Court subsequently ruled that the significance and effect of matters such as rate agreements were a matter for the board, not for the court. The high court effectively upheld the broad discretion enjoyed by the commission.[14]

After failing in a final attempt to have the board reconsider the case, the railway companies finally introduced their revised tariffs in April 1912, to the immediate protests of the Regina business community. Freight officials now used the same formula to determine the rates from Fort William to Winnipeg and other western centres, but employed the relatively higher general tariffs to calculate the new rates to points in Alberta and Saskatchewan.[15] Therefore, instead of an anticipated reduction of eight cents per hundred pounds on the important fifth-class general merchandise rate, Regina merchants received only a five cent reduction. As Table 9 illustrates, they did not gain the kind of competitive advantage in the distributing trade that they had been seeking.[16]

The railway commissioners ignored the protests and approved the revised tariffs because they were just as anxious as railway freight agents to balance the interests of the feuding prairie communities. The solution devised by the railways, however, highlighted yet another anomaly in the western rate structure. While the freight tolls

Table 9
Prairie Distributing Rates per 30,000 Lbs of Fifth-Class Freight, Fort William to
Swift Current, Reshipped at Winnipeg and Regina

	Winnipeg	Regina	Benefit to Winnipeg
December 1907 (resulting from Portage La Prairie complaint)	$282	$312	$30
March 1908 (CPR, concession on fifth class rate)	$282	$297	$15
November 1909 (what Regina Board of Trade seeking)	$282	$273	(−$9)
April 1912 (resulting from Regina Board of Trade complaint)	$270	$282	$12
September 1914 (resulting from Western Rates inquiry)	$258	$264	$6

Sources: BRC Transcripts, vol. 92, file vol. 200, 118, 122, 133–4; NA, Records of the Canadian Transport Commission, RG 46, Board of Railway Commissioners, Central Registry Files, vol. 1441, file 12682, pt. 3, Report of Chief Traffic Officer, Discrimination in Favour of Winnipeg and Against Regina, 29 May 1912.

introduced in 1907 to replace the Winnipeg traders' tariffs on out-bound freight had called attention to the low inbound rates enjoyed by the city's merchants, the 1912 readjustment highlighted the fact that freight rates in Saskatchewan and Alberta were higher than those in Manitoba. Winnipeg merchants continued to try to minimize their advantages by pointing to the lower rates enjoyed by all eastern shippers, and spearheaded the campaign to equalize eastern and western rates. By 1912, therefore, the railway commission was no closer to a resolution of western rate grievances than it had been in 1904; each attempt at a compromise solution had only generated more questions about the western rate structure.

The railway commission's experience with British Columbia rate grievances followed a similar pattern. The complaints of the business communities of Vancouver and Victoria also had begun as an attack on Winnipeg's favoured position in the western rate structure, and offered all the complications that the prairie western battles over distributing territory had raised. Not surprisingly, the Winnipeg business community opposed any change in the existing rate structure, while merchants in interior trading centres, such as Nelson in British Columbia, and Calgary in Alberta, did not want "a quarrel between Winnipeg and Vancouver traders" to disrupt their own trading networks. Freight officials, knowing that whatever solution they adopted would be controversial, preferred to have the railway commission order and support any rate readjustment.[17] Railway managers nevertheless were anxious for a ruling on their own terms, since the allegations raised some regulatory issues of broader significance to them. The complaint largely rested on a comparison of rates carried in what railway officials regarded as two distinct operating districts – across the prairies and through the Rocky Mountains. They sought a strong and clear ruling that evidence of different levels of rates in different parts of the country did not constitute an allegation of discrimination.

At the outset of the first major hearing into the matter in 1906, counsel for the Canadian Pacific went so far as to ask the commission to rule on the principle and not to proceed any further with its inquiry. Chief Commissioner Killam rejected such a strict interpretation of the board's mandate under the Railway Act. He agreed that the Railway Act prohibited any difference in tolls on goods which were carried "under substantially similar circumstances and conditions in the same line", and any tolls which "unjustly" discriminated between different localities, but he rejected the lawyers' argument that these two clauses of the Railway Act should be read together. Instead he ruled that the board had no choice but to disallow all tolls which discriminated in the manner described in the first clause, but that the second clause permitted the railway commission to consider whether any other rate situations resulted in "unjust" discrimination. This interpretation preserved a wide regulatory discretion for the agency, and opened the door to a fuller analysis of the factors that shaped the construction of regional rates.[18]

Counsel for the Canadian Pacific then sought to ensure that the commission would rule that the charging of different rates in different regions was just. When Killam suggested that the whole matter be turned over to Hardwell for investigation, they insisted that the board should listen to more than one expert. The lawyers had the railway's freight traffic manager present a comparison showing that the rates from the Pacific compared favourably with those south of the border, and had the chief engineer describe the difficult and expensive service required to move trains through the Rocky Mountains. Because none of the shipping organizations were prepared to challenge this testimony, the commission decided to sponsored its own investigation, to "afford it all the information possible for the purpose of enabling it to arrive at a correct conclusion."[19]

Hardwell's report confirmed the Canadian Pacific's contention that the mountain sections were more expensive to operate. He concluded that the greater expense associated with clearing snow slides, the extra locomotive- and man-power needed to negotiate steeper grades, and the relatively higher wages paid in the district all made mountain operations more costly. Nevertheless, the chief traffic officer also felt that Pacific Coast merchants faced considerable obstacles in operating their businesses. As a concession to them, he suggested reducing the mountain scale so as to restore the original relationship between mountain and prairie freight tariffs, which had been disrupted by the Manitoba agreement reductions.[20]

When Hardwell's report was circulated among the interested parties, railway officials pointed out that the commission had no right to consider his recommendations. Because he confirmed that the costs of operation were higher in British Columbia, no case of discrimination existed. A majority of the commission agreed. The chief commissioner concluded that "it does not constitute discrimination – much less unjust discrimination – for a railway company to charge higher rates for shorter distances over a line having small business or expensive in construction, maintenance or operation, than over a line having a large business or comparatively inexpensive in construction, maintenance and operation." Both the testimony of railway officials and the board's independent investigation, he noted, confirmed that this represented an accurate description of the different portions of the Canadian Pacific being compared in this case. The commission therefore ruled that the extra expense associated with the railway's mountain operations should be reflected in the British Columbia rate structure. Typically, the board still found a way to offer some rate concessions. Killam ruled that there was some discrimination in favour of Winnipeg because, at the time of the adoption of the Crow's Nest Pass agreement, railway officials had granted Winnipeg merchants rate reductions similar to those received by eastern businesses, but had made no adjustment in the rates from the Pacific coast.[21]

In most cases, the railway commission avoided the complex issue of the relationship between freight rates and transportation costs. By ruling in 1906 that operating expenditures justified the higher scale of rates in British Columbia, the commission invited a more careful examination of that relationship. Although railway officials offered private concessions to the Vancouver Board of Trade fol-

Table 10
Vancouver and Winnipeg Fifth-Class Distributing Rates per 30,000 Lbs

	Calgary from Winnipeg (838 miles)	Calgary from Vancouver (646 miles)	Benefit to Winnipeg
1905 Prior to Pacific Coast Cities complaint	$225	$273	$48
1906 What Pacific Coast Cities seeking	$225	$225	$0
1906 Recommendation of Chief Traffic Officer Hardwell (rejected)	$225	$252	$27
1908 Concessions by Canadian Pacific to Pacific Coast Cities also readjustment prairie rates	$213	$261	$48
1914 Resulting from Western Rates Enquiry	$195	$252	$57

Sources: NA, Records of the Canadian Transport commission, RG 46, Board of Railway Commissioners, Transcripts of Hearings, vol. 92, file vol. 200, 118, 122, 133–4; RG 46, Board of Railway Commissioners, Hearing Exhibits, file 1992, Vancouver Board of Trade Rate Case, Exhibits 2 and 3.

lowing the 1906 case, they could not stave off further challenges to the mountain tariff.[22] Indeed, as Table 9 indicates, those concessions simply matched simultaneous reductions in the rates from Winnipeg, leaving the relative competitive position of Pacific Coast businesses unchanged.

In 1909, the Vancouver Board of Trade launched a case which zeroed in on the idea that the higher costs of operation in British Columbia justified a different scale of rates than existed elsewhere in the country. Although the Board of Trade distinguished the case from previous complaints in 1904 by comparing the rates from the Pacific Coast with those from central Canada, the central issue of discrimination was the same. This time, however, representatives of the Vancouver business community hoped to openly challenge the factual findings of the railways and of Hardwell by sponsoring their own investigation of the figures. Their strategy provoked a controversy over access to railway operating information. In 1909 and again in 1910, W.A. Macdonald, the board of trade's lawyer, asked for a breakdown of the operating, construction, maintenance, and other expenses for each regional division of the Canadian Pacific. Counsel for the railway objected that Macdonald should not be permitted to go on a "fishing inquiry into a great mass of facts to see if anything there will help him." Chief Commissioner Mabee preferred to follow the board's regular procedure in dealing with allegations of discrimination and allowed railway counsel to accept the onus of defending the discriminatory rates. Railway counsel then repeated the types of comparisons of operating conditions found in British Columbia and in the prairie west they had presented in 1906. In an effort to silence Macdonald's demands for more detailed cost information, an auditor with the railway calculated the cost of hauling 1,000 tons of freight one mile in different western divisions. According to his estimates, it cost 91 per cent more to carry freight through the mountains than in the region between Fort William and Winnipeg, whereas it cost only 26 per cent more to haul the same quantity through the prairie west.[23]

Macdonald lacked the technical support to challenge these conclusions. He continued to insist, however, that railway officials provide him with the relevant tariffs and operating statistics for central Canada. While Chief Commissioner Mabee did not want to frustrate Macdonald's inquiry, he also wanted to avoid entangling the hearings in reams of potentially meaningless figures. He suggested that the Canadian Pacific's statistician simply provide similar cost estimates for the railway's divisions east of Fort William, a proposition to which both Macdonald and railway lawyers agreed. Although Macdonald was undoubtedly just "fishing," as Canadian Pacific officials suspected, they seemed equally surprised by his catch. The statistician's estimates, presented the next day of the hearing, showed that it cost 46 per cent more to haul one thousand tons one mile in central Canada than it did between the Lakehead and Winnipeg. While these figures did confirm that operating costs were almost twice as high in British Columbia as in the east, they demonstrated what most prairie dwellers always suspected, that central Canadian shippers enjoyed lower rates in spite of the fact that the service they received cost from 20 per cent to 46 per cent more than that in the prairie west.[24]

Macdonald made the most of these statistics. He contended that the railway companies could not argue that operating costs justified higher rates in British Columbia, since there was no direct relationship between costs of operation and regional freight rate structures. Railway counsel insisted that the Vancouver Board of Trade alleged that the rates were discriminatory, not unreasonable: they had provided sufficient evidence of different conditions through the Rockies to counter the charge of discrimination. Chief Commissioner Mabee concluded that it would be futile to deny that the question of reasonableness had come to the fore during the hearings, and ruled that the entire case should become part of, and be considered within the context of, the general inquiry into western rates that the commission had launched early in 1912.[25]

The petition that prompted the western rates inquiry also invited an examination of railway costs and rates. Shortly after the election of a new Conservative government in Ottawa in September 1911, the Winnipeg Board of Trade spearheaded a western campaign for railway rate equalization. The city's business community succeeded in rallying diverse prairie interests around the question of western versus eastern rates. At least sixty town, village, and municipal councils or local boards of trade endorsed a standard-form petition demanding that the dominion government formally adopt a policy of rate equality for Canada, allowing only those regional variations that might be justified by higher costs of operation.[26]

Prairie business and political leaders may have hoped that Prime Minister Borden's administration would be anxious to compensate for the fact that it had come to power by opposing a reciprocity agreement with the United States, an issue popular in their region. Although the petitions demanded direct legislative action, Chief Commissioner Mabee told the party's chief western organizer, Robert Rogers, that the railway commission could better resolve the problem. Mabee assured Rogers, "I know that the western rates are high – possibly, in many instances, too high – and if the Winnipeg Board of Trade will formulate their plans, I will set on foot a diligent and active enquiry with reference to the whole rate situation in the three prairie provinces." After learning that the board of trade objected to developing their own case, Mabee announced in early January of 1912 that the railway commission would initiate its own inquiry into western rates.[27]

The government appointed two lawyers, H.W. Whitla of Winnipeg and James Bicknell of Toronto, to assist the commission in the investigation. In addition, J.P. Muller, a former statistical officer of the Interstate Commerce Commission who operated an independent railway accounting and consulting firm in Washington, DC, was hired to "reduce the [railway] figures to a point."[28] Other western interests did not trust the dominion team as the only representative of the "public interest." Business leaders in Saskatchewan and Alberta convinced their governments to join together and hire their own legal counsel, M.K. Cowan and J.F. Orde, to ensure that the questions of the differing tariffs within the prairies and distributing rates would not be forgotten. W.A. Macdonald, although now employed by the government of British Columbia, continued to represent the interests of those merchants and manufacturers in the province who were anxious to eliminate the mountain scale of rates. The city and board of trade of Winnipeg sought to defend their particular interests by retaining Isaac Pitblado as counsel.

The dominion government's team wanted to undertake the kind of detailed investigation of the financial affairs of the railway companies, or at least of the Canadian Pacific Railway, that so many thought would prove western rates to be unreasonable. It soon became clear that such a process would be time-consuming: the inquiry adjourned three times over the next three months because the railway companies were still collecting the detailed information that had been requested of them. As an alternative, Cowan, representing the Alberta and Saskatchewan governments, contended that the main issue was not reasonableness but discrimination and that the railway companies should be required to justify the existence of different rates in the regions of Canada. Mabee, anxious to make some progress in the case, accepted Cowan's suggestion without precluding the dominion lawyers from developing their case later.[29]

Railway managers believed their companies were "quickly reaching that point where further decreases in the rates cannot be met by increased efficiency of operation," and thus took a rather dim view of the western inquiry.[30] Contrary to their customary practice, they refused to accept the onus of justifying the allegedly discriminatory rates. Therefore, Cowan had to spend a day examining a few railway officers and presenting exhibits, including the estimate of costs that had been introduced in the Vancouver Board of Trade case. Because Cowan was able to show that rates in the prairie west were higher than in the east for a roughly similar service and in spite of lower costs, Chief Commissioner Mabee ruled that a *prima facie* case of rate discrimination existed. It now rested with the railway companies to justify those regional differences.[31]

The refusal of counsel for the railways to accept the onus was strictly tactical, for once the burden of proof was shifted to them, they effectively took control of the inquiry. They first secured a long adjournment to prepare their case, a delay prolonged by the sudden death of Chief Commissioner Mabee in late April 1912. In early September, one of the dominion government's lawyers warned Mabee's successor, Henry L. Drayton, that the progress of the case would be slowed if at the last moment the railways were allowed to "file a complicated and lengthy defence accompanied by intricate statements." He rightly anticipated the railway companies' strategy. Railway counsel ignored Drayton's request that they provide an outline of their arguments and evidence to the other lawyers in advance of the hearings. Instead, for four days in early October, officials of the Canadian Pacific, Canadian Northern, and Grand Trunk Pacific presented a massive amount of documentary material. The Canadian Pacific alone, Cowan calculated, filed 169 exhibits, covering 328 pages and comprising more than 23,000 comparisons from freight tariffs that were up to twenty-five years old.[32]

Through this strategic use of information, counsel for the railways overloaded the decision-making process and obscured the main issues. In order to allow counsel time to digest the material that had been presented, the railway commission had to permit two long adjournments. When the commission did finally meet again in January and in June 1913, the investigation became bogged down in a seemingly endless cross-examination and re-examination of railway officials concerning the accuracy and relevance of the exhibits. Cowan, Bicknell, and the other lawyers devoted their time and energy to discrediting material that provided, for example, a selective history of a wide number of western tolls and purportedly showed that western Canadians generally paid less in transportation charges than their counterparts south of the border. The result of this phase of the inquiry was best described by a frustrated Chief Commissioner Drayton as "rambling and destructive."[33]

Counsel for the dominion government complained that the railway officials were presenting "all sorts of figures, which instead of clarifying the issue, becloud it."[34] In contrast, they promised that J.P. Muller, their rate expert, would reduce the figures to a point and bring a more constructive approach to the inquiry. The hearings had to adjourn while Muller analyzed the massive array of statistical information he had collected from the railway companies. Finally on 25 November 1913, he began his testimony, having already submitted six volumes of documentation replete with technical financial calculations and extensive citations of American railway commission and judicial decisions. Muller offered the railway commission evidence of the unreasonableness of the western tariff structure and clear standards upon which future rates should be based. Here was the kind of major investigation of western rates and the operations of the Canadian Pacific Railway which so many had longed for and expected.

As a cost accountant, Muller concentrated on the relationship between rates and the cost of service. He boldly concluded that "A comparison of that portion of the CPR west of Fort William with the averages for the entire property certainly warrants the assertion that the western half of the property is from every viewpoint disproportionately productive of more net revenue than the average." By using what he regarded as a more accurate estimate of divisional operating expenses, Muller found that the Canadian Pacific expended less for each dollar of freight revenue in its operations west of the Lakehead than east of that point. To buttress his argument, he compared his figures with the average ratio of earnings-to-expenses on twenty-five eastern and twenty-five western railroads in the United States. He demonstrated that net revenues were lower in eastern Canada and higher in the west than in similar territory south of the border. He thus reached the conclusion that had been expected of him and of the inquiry, that western Canadians paid more in freight rates than the cost of operations justified.[35]

Muller proceeded to show how reasonable rates ought to be determined. Citing a number of American judgments, including the landmark 1898 Supreme Court ruling in *Smyth* v. *Ames*, he concluded that tariffs should allow the railways to recoup their costs and to earn a "fair rate of return" on the capital invested. Although he expressed considerable support for basing investment on a valuation of the cost of reproducing the property currently in use, the railway statistician proposed an alternative and much simpler method. Looking at the operating records of the Canadian Pacific and American railways, Muller asserted that what he called a "gross profit on operating costs" of 50 per cent, or better still 66 ⅔ per cent, had been sufficient to induce further expansion and investment. In the future, he suggested, railway regulation would involve reviewing these figures for five-year periods and adjusting rates to ensure the appropriate profit level. For the American cost accountant, rate-making and rate regulation were just a matter of figures.[36]

Muller formulated new tariffs for the prairie divisions of the Canadian Pacific and Canadian Northern railways by adding his estimates of the average basic cost of carrying one hundred pounds of freight 50 miles and the average associated expense of handling that freight at terminals, plus the appropriate percentage of "profit." His proposed new tariff for the Canadian Pacific advanced the rates for freight carried distances of less than 100 miles, but produced increasingly larger reductions for every 50 miles above the first 100 miles. While the Canadian Northern tariff followed a similar pattern, all rates were higher than those currently in effect and were significantly higher than those proposed for the Canadian Pacific. Through a series of meticulous calculations, the rate expert showed the Board of Railway Commissioners that a proper railway tariff based on cost could be established.[37]

Muller's bold conclusion and prescription withered when subjected to two and one-half days of cross-examination by railway officials and regulators. Railway officials quickly zeroed in on one key element in Muller's analysis as a weak link in his argument – the operating ratio. Both his conclusion concerning the reasonableness of western rates and his procedure for calculating a fair profit rested on the value of this statistic, which gives the proportion of expenses to earnings. In a lengthy written critique of Muller's proposals, Canadian Pacific officials demonstrated that, in averaging the operating ratio of twenty-five eastern and western American railways, Muller masked widely differing operations. They showed that only sixteen of the fifty companies enjoyed either a reasonable or exorbitant profit, as defined by Muller. At least one of the railways that earned the appropriate profit, it was pointed out, had not paid any interest on its common stock for a number of years. In cross-examination, Muller admitted that unless similar conditions of operations, volume, and type of traffic existed, a comparison of operating ratios could not provide a clear guide either to the rate level on a particular railway or its profitability. Pressed on this point by Commissioner McLean, Muller responded that he did not want to be understood as attaching too much importance to the statistic. It was a strange admission from an expert who based all of his conclusions on operating ratios.[38]

Counsel for the railways also had Muller assist them in discrediting the divisional estimates of expenses and earnings that they themselves had introduced in the Vancouver Board of Trade case. Although Muller had adopted a different system for calculating divisional expenditures, he used the revenue figures developed by the railways to calculate the regional operating ratios. Railway officials now argued that these statistics did not provide a particularly accurate portrait of divisional railway traffic and operating conditions, because no distinction was made between through and local traffic. As a result, divisions of the railway with a high proportion of through-to-local traffic, namely the prairie west system, the line between Winnipeg to Fort William, and the mileage north of Lake Superior, were bound to show a more favourable operating ratio. Muller agreed. For the purpose of accurately calculating divisional or regional operating ratios, he conceded, such estimates were "misleading" and "grossly incorrect."[39]

Even if a reasonably accurate estimate of expenses and profits could be made, it became apparent that the construction of tariffs based on cost still raised a number of thorny questions. How did one apply cost of service principles to fix rates on more than one railway? Muller designed different tariffs for each of the Canadian Pacific and Canadian Northern railways, but admitted that realistically, the Canadian Northern and Grand Trunk Pacific would have to adopt their rival's lower tariffs between most points. He defended the use of the Canadian Pacific as the rate-making standard since it was a relatively mature enterprise, playing down the fact that his rate proposals would produce an unfair rate of return on the other lines at a crucial stage in their development.[40]

Furthermore, how should the regulators separate the railways into units so as to calculate costs and fix rates? Muller designed separate tariffs for each of the Canadian Pacific's four western divisions, but contended elsewhere that tariffs in the region from the Lakehead to the mountains should be the same so as to prevent freight rates from inhibiting the development of the newer, less populated areas. Because Muller had admitted that his figures were misleading when applied to the ends of the railway system where less through traffic could be expected, his separation of British Columbia as an operating unit was no more or less justified than the decision of railway officials to do so.[41]

Muller also admitted that some developmental rates lower than his recommended tariff would be necessary on some key commodities and under certain circumstances. These would have to be made up for elsewhere in the tariff, although Muller agreed he had not dealt with this problem in his proposals. Commissioner McLean pointedly asked, "If we get the cost of service from your theory, in actual practice it is only one factor and we must then consider the nature of the commodity and the development of traffic, so that it is a matter of judgment to ascertain what rate should be, in other words what the commodity will stand?" In short, McLean continued, railway officials and regulators could only consider costs as one factor in fixing most rates. Muller conceded the commissioner's point reluctantly, still insisting that the cost of service should be considered as the "basic factor."[42]

The clashes between Muller and McLean reflected differing conceptions of science, expertise, and, therefore, regulation. Muller's "science" was decidedly mathematical and deductive; his experts were statisticians and accountants. His ideal regulators, having plugged the best available numbers into the proper formulas, would recreate the whole rate structure. The "science" of McLean, as well as the railway commission in general, was inductive and highly empirical; its experts had acquired an intimate understanding of the factors shaping the existing rate structure. In the commission's view, ideal regulators developed some general principles as they responded to specific complaints, but continued to examine the precise circumstances surrounding each grievance. Regulation involved a respect for the rate-making decisions reached by those most directly engaged in the matter – railway freight officers, but it also involved a willingness to assess and make incremental adjustments to those decisions.

Muller's presentation appeared to vindicate the views of McLean and his colleagues by demonstrating just how difficult it would be to fix freight rates in a manner that related equally to cost and to the production of a certain level of profits. In fact, some of the general problems raised during the hearing (for example, what railway should serve as the standard and how other tariffs could be adjusted when lower developmental rates seemed necessary) forced the Interstate Commerce Commission to abandon its attempt to guarantee American railway companies a fixed rate of return during the 1920s. Rate regulation could not readily be reduced to mathematical formulas.[43]

The board's findings in the western rates inquiry, announced less than four months after the hearing adjourned, demonstrated how inexact a science regulation could be. In a 200-page judgment released on 7 April 1914, Chief Commissioner Drayton discussed and assessed the various arguments and alternatives that had been offered to the commission, and ordered a number of important changes in the rate structure. The commission agreed with the lawyers appointed by the Winnipeg business community and the Saskatchewan and Alberta governments that the case had involved a matter of discrimination. Adopting the controversial divisional statistics as a rough guide, "subject undoubtedly to very considerable percentage of error and variation," the board concluded that the rates in western Canada did produce much more favourable financial returns than those collected by eastern lines. They also agreed with railway counsel that the product of the low rates in eastern Canada were the product of competition. Given the dismal financial results of the Grand Trunk, it was apparent that eastern freight tariffs were barely even remunerative. To conclude that officials on the largest eastern railway adopted those tariffs voluntarily, Chief Commissioner Drayton observed, "the Board would in effect find that the management of the Grand Trunk instead of desiring to make as much money as possible for its shareholders was a philanthropic association engaged in business for the benefit of its shippers."[44]

Did the distinct competitive situation in eastern Canada justify the discrimination in rates between the region and western Canada? Although previous regulatory judgments suggested that it did, Drayton did not want it thought that the commission was tied to precedent. He noted that "broad equity" would justify intervention "had any injustice been done to or wrong practised on the West by rates said to be based on water competition." Here the chief commissioner returned to a theme that dominated much of the decision. The notion that any real division of interest existed between the users of the railway network was rejected. Just as easterners would benefit if there was a general reduction in western rates as was requested, so the lower scale of rates now in effect east of the Lakehead enabled westerners to ship their grain and other products to compete in the markets of the world. "In every Province," the Chief Commissioner declared in one of several statesmanlike pronouncements, "the [Canadian Pacific] line is performing the functions of a National not a Provincial undertaking, and its continued activities are necessary in the interests of the country as a whole." Therefore, the different rate structures in eastern and western Canada, justified by very distinct conditions and not injurious to any particular region, could not be said to constitute unjust discrimination.[45]

If western rates were not discriminatory, were they unreasonable? The board lacked few guidelines for dealing with this question, but rejected the proposal that was suggested by the expert and lawyers representing the dominion government, that reasonable rates should be based on actual operating costs. The chief commissioner excerpted a number of Muller's own admissions concerning the meaningless nature of the operating ratio as a standard for determining a fair rate of return, and the unreliability of many of the statistical estimates. In a somewhat cruel touch, Drayton noted that the American railway commission, having considered a very careful analysis undertaken, "if I remember rightly, by Mr. Muller himself," had concluded that estimates of costs "are mere approximations, especially when applied to a specific branch of the traffic, which are interesting and to a certain extent useful as general guides, but which cannot be relied upon as decisive factors."[46] Freight rate regulation was too complex a matter to be a mere exercise in accounting.

How, then, could the commission determine whether rates were "reasonable"? While Drayton clearly asserted that "railway rates should be of such a character as to attract investment and to render railway securities marketable," he did not indicate how the board would apply that relatively well-accepted principle in practice. He did conclude that the board should not consider, as railway counsel had argued, the demand for future railway extensions and expansion of service, or, that they should contemplate further duplication in the existing rail system. Nor could the commission adopt the position of many of the shippers' lawyers that rates be fixed according to the needs of the Canadian Pacific alone. The warnings by officials from the Canadian Northern and Grand Trunk Pacific as to the impact of rate reductions on their struggling and still incomplete lines could not be ignored. In considering all of these issues, the commission managed to describe the broad environment in which the railways were operating, while deftly avoiding any fixed standards of reasonableness. The decision, thus, did not offer a clear ruling as to whether western rates were reasonable.[47]

Despite this, the judgment did order a number of rate reductions. Strangely, there seemed little logical connection between the substantive recommendations for reductions and the detailed discussion of the issues that had preceded them. The freight tariff for the Manitoba division remained unchanged, implying that the board concluded that those rates were reasonable. Counsel for Alberta and Saskatchewan, who had been careful not to ignore the other issues of interest to shippers in their provinces, did convince the board to make the Manitoba scale of rates the standard for all the prairie provinces. As well, to further clarify and equalize the conditions between prairie communities, the board reduced both the rates on freight brought in from the Lakehead, and the tolls on goods distributed out of major western centres. As Table 9 helps illustrate, these adjustments reduced freight rates generally for western businesses, but more significantly, substantially diminished the rate advantages that Winnipeg's business community had enjoyed in western Canada.

Counsel for British Columbia were less successful in advancing the interests of shippers on the Pacific Coast. Because railway officials had admitted that divisional cost estimates were unreliable, they had tried to argue that the commission lacked the kind of evidence that would permit the singling out of a small portion of its line, the British Columbia section, for differential treatment. The commission continued to accept that higher costs of operation justified the relatively higher rates through the mountains, although it did accept a compromise worked out by Hardwell which lowered the mountain tariff by from 15 to 30 per cent. The judgment offered no evidence either to justify the continued differential treatment, or to support the reductions that were granted. The concession on the mountain tariff did not improve the competitive situation of the Vancouver business community. In working out new special tariffs from Vancouver and from Fort William to interior British Columbia and prairie points, the commission deliberately sought to preserve existing "powers of distribution."[48] In fact, as Table 10 shows, Vancouver merchants and manufacturers ended up worse off in shipping freight to points such as Calgary, relative to their competitors in Winnipeg.

In ruling that higher rates in the prairie west and British Columbia were not discriminatory, the railway commission rejected the demand that rates in western and eastern Canada should be equalized. The commission did consider the reduction of the disparity in regional rates to be a desirable objective, but one to be achieved when circumstances permitted the implementation of increases in eastern freight tariffs. By refusing to accept any fixed measure of reasonableness, the commission continued to use the discretion provided by a vague standard to order a number of rate adjustments. Those changes were not insignificant: the adjustment in the distributing rates, the extension of the Manitoba scale throughout the prairie west, the concession on the British Columbia mountain tariff and reductions in a number of local commodity rates, on items such as grain and coal, produced some real savings in freight charges for western business communities.[49]

"The conclusions which have been arrived at," the Chief Commissioner wrote towards the end of the decision, "represent what the Board considers a just and reasonable mean between the extremes; and it is of the opinion that the results, having regard to the railway situation in the west, are fair not only to the people but to the railway companies.[50] In handling the complex questions raised by western rate grievances, the board avoided mathematical calculations in favour of "a just and reasonable mean."

At the outset of the western rates inquiry, counsel appointed by the dominion government insisted that it would be "just a matter of figures." The figures proved more elusive, ambiguous, and controversial than he or other proponents of the investigation might have expected. Still, the government's lawyer retained his belief that the railway commission could adopt a more cost-oriented approach, that the proper statistics could be found on which to base such decisions. He accused railway officials, with some justification, of deliberately using their access to critical information to overload the commission with detail, and to obscure rather than clarify the main issues. He harboured the fairly popular suspicion that railway officials knew more than they let on, and were covering up the real facts.[51]

The blundering introduction of the controversial divisional estimates in the Vancouver Board of Trade case and the trouble railway officials had in defending many features of the rate structure suggest otherwise. Railway officials simply did not know all that much about costs because tradition, intuition, and bargaining, rather than clear principles or accurate statistics, governed the making of rates. As Commissioner McLean later explained to an audience of mathematically-oriented engineers, "Railway rates are shot through with compromises. They have not a monopoly in this respect. Business, the British constitution, life itself are all built up on compromises. The test is how they work."[52]

Regulation, McLean might have added, was also built on compromise. The western rates inquiry confirmed that the railway commission had no intention of disrupting the web of compromises contained in the rate structure, but instead would itself resort to compromise as a regulatory strategy. "A just and reasonable mean," epitomized the commission's approach to freight rate regulation in the years prior to World War I. The board's broad administrative discretion, uninhibited by constitutional strictures such as existed in the United States, enabled it to avoid many of the problems associated with basing rates on costs. It continued to accept existing rate-making practices and to try to conciliate and balance contending interests. Administrative regulation remained a political art, not a mathematical science.

The test of compromise, McLean argued, was in how well it worked. Could the board's strategy of conciliation resolve western freight rate grievances? The *Manitoba Free Press* offered a less charitable headline for describing the western rates decision, not "a just and reasonable mean" but "Sops Instead of Justice." Canadian Pacific president Thomas Shaugnessy agreed, although he did not share the view that "justice" meant rate equalization. The commission, in his view, had gone far beyond the facts and ordered reductions that "cannot but be regarded as unnecessarily and unjustifiably drastic in character." The results of the inquiry received much more favourable press in Saskatchewan and Alberta, further underlining the important divisions of interest within the prairie west. Nevertheless, the critical reactions captured the intensity of freight rate issues in western Canada. That intensity always had made compromise difficult to achieve.[53]

Shortly after the judgment in the western rates investigation, the government and railway commission received a new set of resolutions from western communities. While welcoming the reductions ordered, the petitions stated that no rate structure could be deemed fair, just, and equitable to the people of the west that permitted higher rates in the west than in the east, except insofar as the cost of performing the service was greater. Regional rate grievances could not be resolved so easily. Underlying the disputes were not questions of figures, or of law, but of regional development policy: "the question of ending this injustice is a national question, and will not be settled until it is settled right."[54] Before the Board of Railway Commissioners and the dominion government returned to this "national question," however, World War I dramatically altered the regulatory environment.

CHAPTER EIGHT

Casualties of War

The railway commission rendered its decision on the western rates inquiry on 6 April 1914. Within four months, Canada was at war. Neither the commissioners nor any of the parties to the western investigation anticipated the enormous changes World War I would produce in the Canadian railway situation. The war created substantial operating demands on the railway network, increased the costs of labour and materials, and dried up crucial sources of investment capital. This was not the type of economic growth on which railway promoters had been counting. The financial position of the Grand Trunk and Canadian Northern railway systems went from precarious to near bankrupt.

In 1915 Senator W.C. Edwards explained to the railway commission that "Canada got drunk with prosperity unfortunately and had enormous ideas about her future development." In the overall national interest, he and many others observed, it was now time to dispense with much of Canada's duplicate railway service.[1] Railway promoters, anxious to avoid such a grim fate, turned to Canadian politicians and regulators for assistance in the form of subsidies, loans, and freight rate advances. Between 1914 and 1921, the dominion government and the Board of Railway Commissioners were required to make fundamental decisions about the immediate financial condition and the future development of the Canadian railway industry. In the end, neither the government, the railway commission, or the railway companies emerged unscathed. They could all be counted among the casualties of war.

Even before the outbreak of the war, the financial strategy adopted by the promoters of the Canadian Northern and Grand Trunk Pacific transcontinentals placed their projects in a precarious position. In the first decade of the twentieth century, capital was readily available in London, the world's financial centre, but the promoters of the transcontinentals had to compete with a host of other "overseas" investment opportunities. To do so, they relied on bonds rather than on more flexible securities to finance the construction of their lines.[2] From a very early stage, the companies therefore needed to begin earning enough money from operations to cover large fixed debts. Increased operating earnings, it was generally agreed, depended on the early completion of the transcontinental lines. It was at this point that the strategy began to unravel. Construction costs increased and expenditures outran original estimates on both projects, with the result that new infusions of capital were needed to complete them. Canadian Northern officials oversaw the construction of an extensive system of branch lines throughout the prairie west, but, on the eve of the war, estimated that they needed an additional $42 million to complete their main line. Grand Trunk Pacific promoters succeeded in joining the rails of their main line in April 1914, but lacked any kind of branch line infrastructure and required an immediate $20 million to finish the mountain section. As early as 1912, an international financial recession made the chances of finding this further capital investment unlikely.[3]

A general depression in the Canadian economy beginning in the fall of 1913 heightened the crisis facing the transcontinentals by cutting cash revenues from operations. The railways were already being operated on the margin – even in the year of unprecedented business and railway prosperity ending June 1913, operating expenses and fixed charges had swallowed 97 per cent of the Canadian Northern's gross railway earnings. The Grand Trunk Pacific did not have to pay any fixed charges in that year, but expenses alone accounted for 89 per cent of its earnings; in the next year expenditures and interest on the debt practically equalled the revenue from its railway operations.[4] Officials from both transcontinentals turned to the government to stave off bankruptcy. Since the dominion and provincial governments had already provided enormous amounts of assistance and staked their credit on the two railways, they had a vested interest in keeping them solvent. In the years immediately prior to the war, the dominion government had agreed to provide the Canadian Northern with further financial subsidies totaling $15.5 million and a bond guarantee of $45 million to allow it to continue construction. Similarly, in 1913, the government loaned the Grand Trunk Pacific $15 million, and the following year guaranteed the principal and interest on $16 million in bonds.[5]

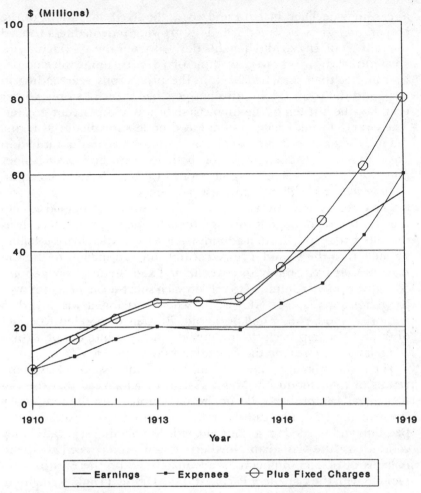

Figure 4
Canadian Northern Railway, Earnings, Expenses, and Fixed Charges, 1910–21
Source: Appendix B, Table B.8.

Just as the financial recession appeared to be lifting in 1914, the outbreak of the war dried up London's money markets. Throughout 1914 and 1915, promoters of the Canadian Northern and the Grand Trunk Pacific were forced to use their government-guaranteed bonds as collateral to negotiate short-term, high-interest loans from New York financiers. These loans covered immediate needs but only added to the burden of the companies' debt. The results of this policy on the Canadian Northern can be observed in Figure 4. Although Canadian Northern officials reduced operating expenditures as earnings declined in 1914 and 1915, the fixed obligations of the corporation grew by one-third. This growing indebtedness robbed the railway of any of the benefits derived from the spectacular increase in traffic after 1915. By June of 1917, earnings were 60 per cent higher than they had been in the prosperous year ending in 1913 and the cost of doing this business had grown by only 56 per cent, but the burden of the financial debt was 168 per cent greater. The Grand Trunk Pacific system was even less fortunate; its traffic did not increase so that it earned little more in 1917 than it had in 1913. Operating expenditures on both its main and branch lines outstripped earnings, leaving no money to cover fixed charges, including over $8 million in interest payments.

The Conservative government of Robert Borden struggled to help the new transcontinentals through their financial straits. As early as the fall of 1914, the Borden administration forwarded loans totalling $6 million to the Grand Trunk Pacific, and $10 million to the Canadian Northern simply to cover their fixed financial obligations. The government continued to rely on such short-term measures over the following years. In May 1916, when Parliament was asked to authorize another $23 million in aid, Borden responded to critics of this ad hoc approach by announcing the appointment of a royal commission to examine the Canadian railway problem.[6]

The three men appointed to the Royal Commission released the results of their inquiry in May 1917. They all agreed that the Canadian railway problem did not result simply from the temporary stress of the war. The railway system suffered from excessive duplication and needed to be consolidated. "Remaining separate," they concluded, "the Canadian Northern system would need to spend millions of dollars to obtain an adequate hold on the East in competition with the Canadian Pacific and the Grand Trunk. Remaining separate, the Grand Trunk and Grand Trunk Pacific system would need to spend millions of dollars on new branches in the West, in order to hold its own with the Canadian Pacific and the Canadian Northern." Moreover, each system needed the money immediately. Canada, they concluded, neither required nor could afford three competitive systems.[7]

The three commissioners did not agree on a solution to the problem. Commissioner A.M. Smith, president of the New York Central Railway, recommended that the ailing railways remain in private hands, but be consolidated on a regional basis – the Grand Trunk in the east and the Canadian Northern in the west. In the majority report, Chief Commissioner Drayton of the Board of Railway Commissioners joined a British railway economist, W.M. Acworth, in recommending the amalgamation of all Canadian railways except the prosperous Canadian Pacific into a single publicly-owned company, managed by an independent board of trustees. The Drayton-Acworth recommendations shaped and legitimated the subsequent railway policy of Prime Minister Borden, who regarded Smith's proposals as "wholly impracticable."[8]

After 1917, the Borden government abandoned short-term assistance in favour of a policy of public acquisition and consolidation. It cobbled together and began to operate what became known in 1919 as Canadian National Railways. In September 1917, Parliament approved the acquisition of the Canadian Northern Railways system and within a year an independent board of management was operating the Canadian Northern, as well as fifteen lines the government already had been operating, including the National Transcontinental and Intercolonial railways. Officials with Canada's oldest system, the Grand Trunk, did not prove as co-operative as their counterparts at the Canadian Northern, and actively obstructed efforts to nationalize either their railway or the Grand Trunk Pacific. The practical bankruptcy of the western transcontinental and the serious operating problems encountered on the Grand Trunk's eastern system, particularly after 1917, considerably weakened such resistance. In October 1919, after a protracted struggle and negotiation, the dominion government succeeded in purchasing the Grand Trunk, having already placed the company's western subsidiary into receivership. With the acquisition of the Grand Trunk, the government ensured that the publicly owned Canadian National Railways would at least have an opportunity to be something more than a collection of bankrupt railways; the managers of the railway would have a system with the ability to compete for traffic in all regions with the Canadian Pacific, which was to remain a private operation.[9]

Through the creation of Canadian National, the Borden government acknowledged that the problems in the railway industry were structural, and were not simply a product of difficult war-time operations. The war highlighted and aggravated two problems that seriously undermined the long-term survival of the Canadian Northern and Grand Trunk companies as transcontinental systems – high fixed financial commitments and the provision of rail service far in excess of foreseeable demand. At the same time, the war created some short-term operating problems for the Canadian railway industry. Beginning in 1916, shortages dramatically increased the costs of fuel, particularly coal, for all Canadian railways. Although fuel consumption grew slightly, the cost of fuel used for every 100 locomotive miles in the freight service increased by 55 per cent between 1917 and 1919. The scarcity of manpower created by the war allowed

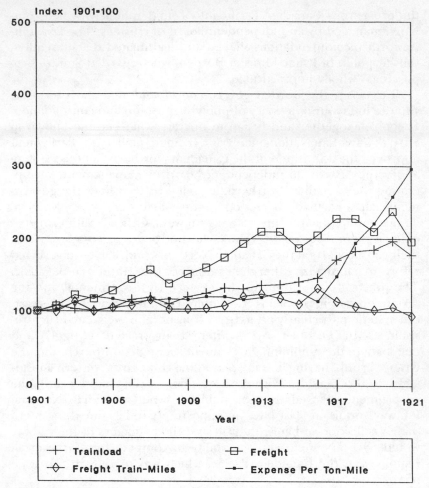

Figure 5
Grand Trunk Railway Freight Operations, 1901–21
Source: Appendix B, Table B.2.

American railway unions and subsequently their Canadian affiliates
to win significant improvements in wages and other benefits, assisting
their members to cope with the spiralling cost of living. The average
annual amount spent per railway employee increased 37 per cent
between 1913 and 1917, although an 18 per cent reduction in the
work-force ensured that the total wage bill grew by only 12 per cent.
By the end of 1919, that wage bill was 80 per cent greater than it
had been 1917, the combined result of a 52 per cent growth in wages
per employee and the expansion of the work-force back almost to
its pre-war level.[10]

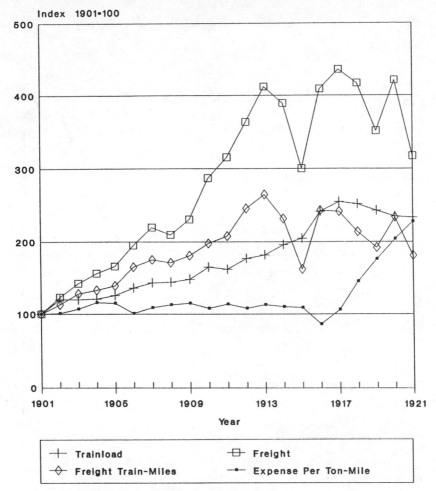

Figure 6
Canadian Pacific Railway Freight Operations, 1901–21
Source: Appendix B, Table B.2.

Because wages and fuel accounted for approximately 60 per cent and 15 per cent respectively of the total cost of operating the railways, these developments had a significant effect on their overall performance, as Figures 4–8 illustrate. Beginning in 1917, Grand Trunk and Canadian Pacific managers lost control of the expenses associated with the cost of moving one ton of freight one mile, which they had reduced in the nineteenth century and kept stable throughout the early twentieth century. As a result, after 1917, overall operating expenses absorbed an increasing proportion of railway earnings. For Grand Trunk officials, who were already grappling with the crisis

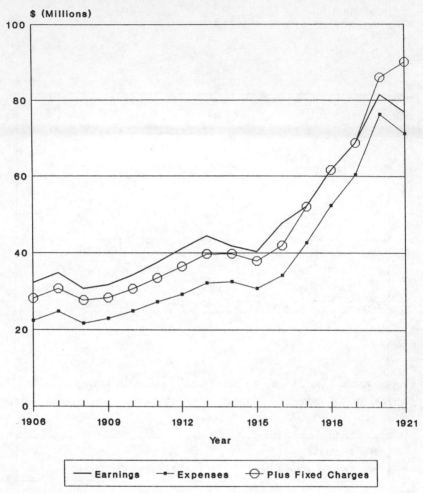

Figure 7
Grand Trunk Railway, Earnings, Expenses, and Fixed Charges, 1906–21
Source: Appendix B, Table B.6.

on the Grand Trunk Pacific, and whose railway carried relatively higher fixed charges than did the rival Canadian Pacific, this development was particularly ominous.

In the context of both the arduous operating environment and the scarcity of external sources of investment, revenues generated from operations acquired an unprecedented significance in railway corporate strategies.[11] Railway managers adopted two sets of policies to deal with the operating problems they faced. First, they sought to minimize expenditures, both co-operatively and independently.

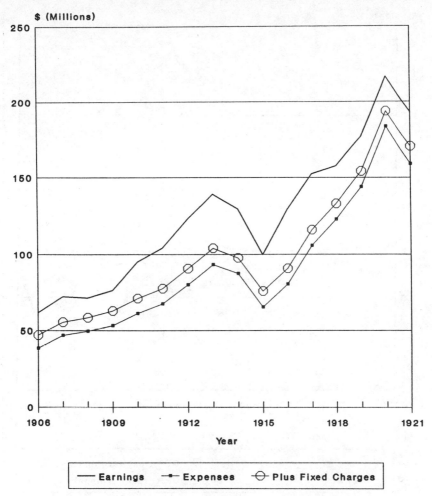

$ (Millions)

Figure 8
Canadian Pacific Railway, Earnings, Expenses, and Fixed Charges, 1906–21
Source: Appendix B, Table B.7.

On 23 October 1917, they organized the Canadian Railway Association for National Defence, later known as the Canadian Railway War Board, largely to deal with serious car shortages. In the wartime atmosphere, the railways were able to co-operate with each other as well as with government agencies and shippers to improve the amount of freight loaded in each car, an activity most companies had been engaging in independently. Greater loading reduced the movement of trains and resulted in some savings. The war also permitted the railways to cancel duplicate and "unnecessarily fre-

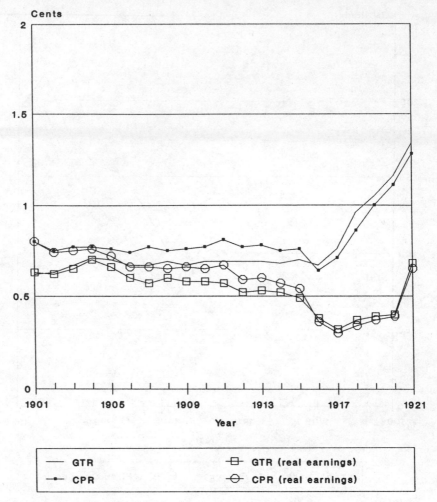

Figure 9
Grand Trunk / Canadian Pacific Freight Earnings per Ton-mile, 1901–21
Source: Appendix B, Table B.5.

quent passenger train service."[12] Finally, some companies simply put off maintenance expenditures that were not immediately required. All of these temporary expedients helped the railways to minimize expenditures.

Second, railway officials applied for freight rate increases to help them keep pace with advancing costs. As Figure 9 demonstrates, they could point to the fact that freight rates, which continued to be quite stable prior to the war, had failed to keep pace with the cost of living. Real earnings per ton-mile gradually declined after 1904, but in the years following 1916, they really plummeted. In response, railway executives turned to the Board of Railway Commissioners for assistance, and, for the first time in the history of the commission, applied for general advances in freight rates.

The war, therefore, altered the terms of the regulatory debate. Prior to 1914, regulation had largely involved the adjustment of rates between shipping communities; the commissioners were sensitive to, but rarely confronted, the direct impact of those adjustments on the railway industry. As railway companies sought rate advances, the state of their industry became the focus of regulation. Moreover, as the Borden government became increasingly committed to the survival of the railway system, to the point of ownership, the railway commission's political masters acquired a greater stake in the outcome of freight rate regulation.

As early as 1909, Chief Commissioner Mabee had indicated that the board appreciated that traffic, wage, and other costs were increasing, and that "where we are presented with any sort of material that one can distort into evidence, we will endeavour to deal just as generously with the railway companies as with the shippers." When the railway companies presented general evidence of increased costs and some specific facts concerning the increased value of the traffic in question, the commission approved a number of freight rate advances on lumber in 1910, and a general increase in the charge for carrying pulpwood in 1914.[13]

In spite of the commission's apparent sympathy for the railway industry's operating situation, Canadian railways did not apply for a general rate advance until February 1915. It was no coincidence that the application followed by two months an Interstate Commerce Commission decision to grant a large number of increases averaging 5 per cent to railways operating in the eastern United States. The Canadian application closely resembled the American one, proposing advances in both class rates and alterations in a wide variety of commodity rates on eastern lines only. Canadian railways operated a North American industry: American rail competition determined many features of the Canadian rate structure and the American labour situation shaped developments north of the border. It was not surprising then that applications for increases in Canadian rates often followed those made in the United States. The American railway situation rather than Canadian regulators had the effect of restraining freight rate increases in Canada.[14]

In support of their application for an advance in eastern rates, railway officials pointed to the thorough investigation already undertaken by the American railway commission and presented evidence to show that the Canadian situation was no different. Major shipping organizations, including the Canadian Manufacturers' Association, the Montreal and Toronto Boards of Trade, the Dominion Millers' Association, the Canadian Lumbermen's Association and the Canadian Pulp and Paper Association, did not challenge the railway companies' claims that costs were advancing. While some shippers argued that their industries could not afford any increase no matter how justifiable it might be, most agreed that they would accept a "properly adjusted" advance, if the railway commissioners agreed it was necessary.[15]

Business leaders did insist, however, that the board first consider a number of important factors, one of which was the burden such an advance would impose on shippers. Leading organizations arranged for the board to listen to over thirty witnesses estimate the extra transportation costs their industries would have to absorb. In the course of that testimony, several shippers underlined the fact that any rate advance would disrupt business already disturbed by the war situation. The lawyer appointed by the dominion government to represent the "public interest" expressed shock that the railways should apply for an increase "during this time of stress."[16] The board was also asked to determine whether "the real remedy for the troubles of the railways is higher freight rates." In particular, it was noted that two quite different railways operated in eastern Canada, "one which stands for absolute prosperity and self-sufficiency throughout the world," the other pleading abject poverty. It was contended that the Canadian Pacific, which began paying regular dividends of 10 per cent in 1912, demonstrated that a properly managed railway could earn a substantial profit under existing rates; the problems of the Grand Trunk, it was argued, should not be attributed to low freight rates.[16]

Throughout the hearings, the commissioners remained sceptical of the hardship that an advance would impose on the business sector. They prodded a number of shippers into admitting that the burden that would be imposed by the increase was slight in relation to the volume and value of their business. It became apparent, for example, that a dramatic 16 to 20 per cent advance in the rate for unrolled leather amounted to only an extra $15 on a carload valued at between $7500 and $9000. At the same time, the commissioners sought to demonstrate that they were willing to undertake the kind of independent investigation the shipping community was demanding, and that they intended to concentrate on one company, the Grand Trunk. This railway provided a useful standard for the region, since it represented a rough mean between its two main eastern competitors, the prosperous Canadian Pacific, and the near-bankrupt Canadian Northern. The commissioners therefore pressed Grand Trunk officials to provide details regarding the railway's stock and bond issues, capital expenditures, and depreciation accounts. After meeting in conference with the chief traffic officer of the board, Grand Trunk officials also agreed to a detailed estimate of the impact of the increases on their earnings, a formidable task that involved the examination of some 270,000 traffic receipts from four selected weeks in 1913 and 1914.[17]

As a result of these investigations, the board concluded that an increase in freight rates was justified, and reaffirmed its statement made in the western rates decision that "railway rates should be rates of such a character as to attract investment and to render securities marketable." In translating that definition of "reasonable" rates into a workable decision, however, the commissioners refused to be tied to any kind of precise formula based, for example, on the capital cost of the railways. While suggesting that railways should be allowed to earn 6 per cent on the physical value of the railway, they did not undertake or even propose the type of elaborate valuations of property undertaken on American railways. Some crude estimates showing that the Grand Trunk did not receive such a rate of return were included in the judgment. The commissioners emphasized that many other factors determined their decision to grant the rate advance, particularly a considerable increase in the cost of wages and materials, evidence of efficient operations, and poor financial returns. Chief Commissioner Drayton warned that maintaining current rates represented a false economy, since Grand Trunk managers were being forced to economize on bridge and track renewals, engine and car repairs, and other maintenance expenses, cutbacks which "cannot continue indefinitely without great loss and inconvenience to the shipping and travelling public."[18]

Having concluded that an advance in rates was justified, the railway commission still had to consider the specific means of granting the increase. The railway companies did not apply for a general horizontal advance, but instead offered specific rate proposals that covered general merchandise tariffs as well as special rates on some 150 commodities, including key products such as grain, livestock, and steel as well as relatively minor freight items. The commissioners accepted the judgment of railway officials with respect to the general merchandise tariffs, although they did modify a proposed increase in rates between the Maritimes and central Canada.[19] The board also readily dealt with about one-third of the specific proposals since the shippers either agreed to the change or registered no objection with the board or any of the business organizations represented at the hearings. Where disputes did arise, the commissioners first encouraged private settlements, and, failing that, would determine whether the proposed change placed rates on a more logical basis, or imposed any burden on the shipper when assessed against the value of the freight. In the end, they sanctioned another one-third of the proposals, and modified or rejected the remainder.[20]

Consideration of this extensive list of commodity rates was time-consuming. To further complicate matters, railway officials encountered difficulties in developing an alternative to their original proposal for increased grain rates, which had been rejected by the board. The commission accepted the view of a number of grain shippers that a proposal that had not been approved by two railways which were about to begin operating in the east (the National Transcontinental and the Canadian Northern) would be unworkable. If any change was to be approved, the board and the grain shippers wanted a more permanent solution. Unable to reach agreement among themselves, railway officials finally withdrew the proposed increase in May 1916. The board then delivered its judgment on the remainder of the rate case within a month, almost one and one-half years after the original application.[21]

The railway commissioners handled with caution this first application for a general increase in rates. Although sympathetic to the increased costs facing the railway companies, they were equally concerned with the comments of some shippers that the application represented a perversion of the regulatory process, that the railways were "seeking the assistance of the Board to advance freight rates on the public whom they were really appointed to protect."[22] The commissioners sought to make their final decision more authoritative and acceptable to shippers by giving them a chance to participate fully in the regulatory process, by responding to their demands for an investigation of the railways, and by modifying some of the original proposals. While railway company officials chafed at the lengthy hearings, and at constantly being required to defend their proposals, the railway commission had to consider its own interests. In attempting to avoid a confrontation with any of its major clients, it tried to give the impression of behaving fairly and weighing every party's concern, even though the process might be cumbersome.

Railway officials hoped to circumvent this regulatory process when they next applied for a rate advance in March 1917. As operating costs rapidly escalated, and as American railway executives asked the Interstate Commerce Commission to approve a 15 per cent advance, F.H. Phippen of the ailing Canadian Northern arranged a conference between the directors of Canada's three major railways and the railway commission. At the meeting, the commissioners rejected the railways' proposal for an immediate but temporary percentage advance on selected commodities. Railway officials, anxious for a quick decision, then sought another way to avoid regulatory hearings. They asked the Board to request an immediate 15 per cent advance from the government under the emergency powers of the War Measures Act.[23]

The railway commission refused to make the request, but did, however, expedite the holding of public hearings on the application. In June 1917, Assistant Chief Commissioner D'Arcy Scott and Commissioner Goodeve convened sessions in Montreal and Toronto, while Chief Commissioner Drayton and Commissioner McLean attended parallel hearings in nine western Canadian communities. For the most part, the presentations of shipping organizations in the hearings followed the lines established in the previous eastern case. While some shippers pleaded that their industry could not survive any increase, many others, including the Canadian Manufacturers' Association and the boards of trade of Montreal, Toronto, Hamilton, Fort William, Saskatoon, Calgary, and Edmonton, indicated that they would accept the 15 per cent increase as an emergency measure, but only if the board determined that it was absolutely necessary. The most vigorous opposition to the application came from the boards of trade of Vancouver, Winnipeg, and Kitchener, from farm organizations in Manitoba and Ontario, and from the government of Manitoba. They questioned the wisdom of a rate increase that would increase the revenues of the prosperous Canadian Pacific by $29 million, simply to provide the ailing Grand Trunk and Canadian Northern companies with some $11 million in assistance. "My trouble in this application," the Canadian Northern's F.H. Phippen sighed, "appears to be that I have a partner who is altogether too rich."[24]

The debate was not just over Phippen's rich partner; it represented a dispute over the appropriate policy response to the Canadian railway problem. Opponents of the advance insisted that Chief Commissioner Drayton, who had just completed his work as a member of the Royal Commission on Railways, had already recommended the real solution to the Canadian railway problem – public ownership. Increasing freight rates, the Manitoba government's lawyer Isaac Pitblado observed, was "like treating a man with an incurable inward disease by putting plasters on him outside."[25] He and other opponents of the advance contended that the board should reject the application and instead, acting in its capacity as the government's expert authority on railway matters, urge the government to adopt the recommendations of the royal commission. Drayton and his colleagues on the railway commission refused to be drawn into this policy debate. "The incorporation of railway companies and the determination of their routes – the question of private or public ownership of railways," Drayton observed in the board's judgment on the application, "are matters entirely for Parliament." On the other hand, the railway commission's duties did include allowing "fair and just rates to the carriers for the service they perform." Citing rapidly escalating costs and declining net earnings on all railways, including the Canadian Pacific, and again warning of the possible breakdown of the system should railway officials be forced to continue reducing maintenance expenditures, the board approved the railway companies' application.[26]

As the railways proposed, freight rates in most of Canada would be advanced 15 per cent, and coal rates would increase fifteen cents a ton. The board made two important modifications. First, the commission limited the increase to 10 per cent in British Columbia, without offering any explanation or regulatory principle in support of this special treatment. Second, those commodities covered by the Crow's Nest Pass agreement – eastbound western grain and westbound eastern freight such as fruit, coal oil, and agricultural implements – would only be advanced 10 per cent. In reaching this second conclusion, Drayton ruled that the rate-making authority delegated to the commission in the Railway Act had been restricted by all "Special Acts" that were in existence prior to 1904. While the dominion legislation confirming the agreement between the Canadian Northern and the Manitoba government specifically preserved the regulatory authority of the railway commission, the Crow's Nest Pass legislation of 1897 did not. Therefore, Drayton concluded, rates might be advanced over those established in the Manitoba Agreement, but not beyond the reductions secured under the Crow's Nest Pass agreement, "no matter how great the shortage may be in railway revenue." A contractual arrangement that Van Horne had proclaimed as a good deal for the Canadian Pacific in 1897, acquired an unanticipated significance nearly twenty years later.[27]

Although the railway commission otherwise approved the application, its ruling hardly represented the kind of immediate emergency relief railway officials had first sought. The board held back its decision until 26 December 1917, while the railways worked out some complications involving the relation between new rates from

Detroit and in Ontario, and while the commission considered a separate but related application for an advance in the rates on freight carried between eastern and western Canada. The rate advance was further delayed when the governments of Manitoba, Saskatchewan, and Alberta, the Winnipeg Board of Trade, the Canadian Council of Agriculture, the United Farmers of Ontario, and a coalition of livestock associations, asked Prime Minister Borden's newly formed Union government to overturn the board's judgment. These opponents of the rate increase told the government that the railway commission had entered the policy-making realm and improperly tried to resolve the Canadian railway problem through a freight rate advance. H.J. Symington, now representing the Manitoba government, observed, "We have been relying on the medicine man when we need a surgeon." The government should perform the surgery, not by granting a rate increase, but by taking over the management of Canada's railways for the remainder of the war. Alternatively, should the government believe that some increase in railway revenues was required, it should apply a war tax on shippers that would be allocated to those railways that most needed higher revenues. For the most part, Symington and others discussed the rate advance in the context of the government's overall railway policy.[28]

Counsel for the railways objected to such a broad policy debate being interjected into the hearing of an appeal from a railway commission judgment. They contended that, in view of the board's "technical knowledge" and its "long and careful investigation" of the matter, "your Council should be slow to interfere with its findings unless they are shown clearly to be wrong or based upon some misconception of the merits or of its functions under the statute." Otherwise, the cabinet would be forced to "sit as a Board of Review" every time any member of the public opposed an order of the railway commission. While the Supreme Court considered whether the board made errors in law, the railway lawyers argued, the cabinet should limit its role to reviewing the board's judgments on questions of fact.[29]

The Borden administration could not so easily separate its railway policy from the board's decision. By 1 March 1918, when it heard the final arguments in the appeal, the government was itself responsible for financing and operating a good portion of the railway system. The minister of finance, Thomas White, projected serious post-war deficits should the government deny the 15 per cent advance. "Freight must bear the cost, or public taxation provide the deficit," Trade and Commerce Minister George Foster noted in his diary, "There is no question as to which alternative is to be chosen."[30]

The rest of the cabinet shared Foster's view, and upheld the rate advance. In an attempt to appease critics, the government amended the board's order so that the advance would lapse one year after the war ended, and, in a separate cabinet order, imposed a special wartime tax on the Canadian Pacific to ensure that the company did not profit from an increase the other railways needed. The Canadian Pacific was expected to pay one-half of its net earnings from railway operations that exceeded a 7 per cent return on its common stock after the payment of fixed charges, pension fund contributions, and dividends on preferrcd stock. Earnings from other operations were subject to the Income War Tax Act. The government tried to preserve the railway commission's regulatory authority while appeasing critics of the decision, by supplementing the original decision, rather than by overturning or substantially amending it.[31]

The new rates became effective 15 March 1918. Although the board had done what it could to expedite the regulatory process, the public hearings, the investigations, and the appeals had so delayed the regulatory response to their needs that the relief afforded by the new rates was no longer adequate to meet spiralling operating costs. Within a few months of the 15 per cent decision, railway officials returned to the commission for yet another rate advance, and again sought to avoid the regulatory process.

This time, railway officials were in a stronger position to press for an emergency advance. In May 1918, the United States Railroad Administration, now in control of American railways, agreed to grant railway employees south of the border a significant increase in their scale of wages in order to keep pace with the cost of living. To cover the enlarged wage bill, the Railroad Administration ordered an advance in freight rates of around 28 per cent.[32] Canadian railway workers threatened to strike if they did not get a matching increase. As a result, the managers of the largest railways in Canada approached Chief Commissioner Drayton to see what could be done about granting them a similar advance in freight rates. Drayton agreed to bypass the usual regulatory process because, as he explained to the acting prime minister, a formal application to the board would inevitably mean delays, "and the labour situation appears to be one which permits of no delay." Moreover, he noted that the railway commission was powerless to order rates in excess of the Crow's Nest Pass Agreement "and other rate-making agreements." Although the board had ruled it could override the Manitoba agreement, the government of that province intended appealing thc ruling to the Supreme Court. In view of these circumstances, Drayton urged the government to order increases in freight rates similar to those that had been made by the United States Railroad Administration. The threat of a disruptive national rail strike at a crucial point in the war ensured that the government would approve the advance.[33]

On the recommendation of the chief commissioner, the Borden administration left the details of the increase to the expertise of the railway commission, sanctioning the specific changes on 27 July 1918. In eastern Canada, class and many commodity rates were advanced 25 per cent. The change in western Canada was less dramatic – the new tariffs were to represent a 25 per cent increase on the freight rates that had been in effect prior to the March 1918 15 per cent advance. The commission also limited the increase on a number of specific commodities, including gravel, livestock, and western grain. Rather than have the new rates expire at the end of the war, the terms were that both the government and the railway commission would receive and monitor monthly financial statements from all major railway companies, and order reductions whenever earnings exceeded the amount required "to meet increased costs and permit transportation to be properly and efficiently carried on."[34]

In the 25 per cent advance granted July 1918, the government and the railway commission avoided a repetition of their experience in the previous rate application. While the railway commission retained its authority as rate expert, the government took the responsibility for the decision to assist the railways. The decision to have both the government and railway commission monitor the railway companies' financial returns confirmed their shared responsibility for the extraordinary regulatory decisions that the war and the financial crisis of the railways required. Both politicians and independent regulators acknowledged that some rate questions could and did involve general issues of public policy best addressed by those directly responsible to the electorate.

Railway company officials expected a similar approach would be taken to their next request for a rate advance, also spurred by labour developments south of the border. Between 1918 and 1920, railway workers continued to use the bargaining leverage offered by the war and its immediate aftermath to keep pace with the inflationary spiral. In the spring of 1920, American railway unions went on strike to seek further wage increases, and the dispute was referred to the newly created United States Railroad Labor Board. On 6 July 1920, three railway executives, two from the government-owned Canadian National and one from the Canadian Pacific, met with Prime Minister

Borden and the cabinet to discuss the railway labour situation. The government, fearful of a national railway strike, indicated that the Canadian railway workers would have to receive the same increase their American counterparts were awarded. The railway executives left the meeting believing that, while the government would not directly grant a corresponding rate increase as it had in July 1918, it would support their application to the railway commission.[35]

One member of the cabinet – Arthur Meighen – who was not present for this meeting succeeded Sir Robert Borden as prime minister just four days later. When approached by the railway companies for the promised support, the new prime minister responded that wage settlements were a matter for the railways, and rate increases should be dealt with by the railway commission. Meighen, who inherited a crumbling coalition government, chose to distance the government from any unpopular decisions. The CPR and CNR officials thus had to proceed on their own to ask the board to sanction a 35 per cent horizontal advance, which was later increased to 40 per cent when the outcome of the United States Railroad Labor Board award became known.[36]

The railway commission that heard this application was headed by a dynamic new chief commissioner, Frank Broadstreet Carvell. As minister of public works in Borden's coalition government, Carvell had prompted a storm of controversy by his policy of retrenchment, and the "straight-flung, frank expressions of opinion" with which he responded to critics. Anxious to leave the Union government, in 1919 the New Brunswick Liberal traded places with Drayton, who accepted a position in the cabinet as minister of finance. Although Carvell had been a member of the important cabinet committee which oversaw the nationalization of the railways, he was an outspoken opponent of public ownership and operation of the railways. As a former director of the New Brunswick Telephone Company, he believed he understood the financial problems facing private utility corporations. "Fighting Frank Carvell" brought strong views and a pugnacious personality to the railway commission.[37]

The new chief commissioner shaped the board's response to the 40 per cent application. At the first hearing convened on 10 August 1920, Carvell made it abundantly clear that the board was not going to "sit here hearing the application for three months, for that is not necessary." He asked the parties to co-ordinate their presentations, and bluntly rejected appeals to have the board travel to hear testimony. Although some twenty business organizations and industries, as well as the governments of New Brunswick, Manitoba, and Saskatchewan sent representatives to the hearings, Carvell adjourned the hearings on 21 August, after having listened to arguments for only seven days. Within two and one-half weeks, the commission delivered its judgment, largely in favour of the railway companies' application.[38]

During the brief public hearings, opponents of the advance argued that the commission should only consider the needs of the prosperous Canadian Pacific. The government-owned Canadian National system, they contended, could not be considered a proper business enterprise, because it included many unprofitable colonization roads and had not had a chance to consolidate its operations. A number of shipping representatives also cited the remarks of Railways Minister John Reid, who in March 1920 had invited Parliament to consider whether rates should be raised on the Canadian National or its deficits shouldered by the country through taxes. Carvell bristled at these comments. During the hearings and in his subsequent decision, he observed that, since Parliament had not responded to Reid's invitation in the months following his statement, the board must assume that government ownership did not exclude the Canadian National system from the normal regulatory process.[39]

Nevertheless, in spite of these comments, Carvell's own decision concentrated on the financial position of the Canadian Pacific. No one could really deny that even the private railway faced significantly increased costs. Before the war, operating expenses generally absorbed about 66 per cent of the railway's earnings; the operating ratio in 1919 was 81 per cent and for the first six months of 1920 it reached 87 per cent. The chief commissioner rejected the critics' contention that the company should draw on its reserves, estimated at $317 million, to overcome its temporary economic difficulties. Canadian Pacific officials, he noted, demonstrated that about half of the reserve fund was contingent on land sales, and that only $53 million represented readily available cash. Carvell argued that without some cash reserves, the company would have been forced to increase its fixed charges in order to finance the construction of some $8 million worth of branch lines in western Canada over the previous year. "I consider it a national necessity," Carvell concluded, "that the Canadian Pacific Railway at least be kept in a healthy financial condition, with the hope that, as a result the other great railway system may be benefited in a corresponding degree."[40]

The railway commission approved an immediate 40 per cent advance in eastern freight tariffs, and a 35 per cent increase in western rates for the remainder of 1920. As of 1 January 1921, all of the new tariffs would be reduced by 5 per cent. The differing treatment of the regions was based on a cursory examination of western rates, which "forced" the chief commissioner to the conclusion that "the rates in western Canada average considerably greater than in the east, possibly around 15 per cent to 18 per cent." Coal and fuel wood did not receive the full advance so as not to aggravate continuing shortages and, as an incentive towards the improvement of the highways, the board left the freight tariff on crushed stone, gravel, and sand unchanged.[41] Chief Commissioner Carvell's "rough-shod methods," his refusal to travel to western Canada, and the general haste with which he conducted the hearings and rendered the decision provoked as much controversy as the increase itself. Within a week of the judgment, the premier of Manitoba, the government of Saskatchewan, the city of Toronto, the Canadian Wholesale Grocers' Association, and the Toronto, Winnipeg, Edmonton, and Halifax boards of trade demanded that the government overturn the board's decision, or at least suspend it pending the hearing of a formal appeal to the cabinet. Meighen would only agree to facilitate an early hearing of the appeal.[42]

When the cabinet convened that hearing, opponents of the advance complained that the railway commission should not have granted such an enormous advance without a full investigation. They again argued that the reserves of the Canadian Pacific were sufficient to tide it over its temporary financial problems, and that the financial position of the CNR should not be used as the basis for rate adjustments. Furthermore, Carvell's remark concerning "the national necessity" of advancing rates was attacked as showing that the board was once again engaged in policy-making rather than determining whether rates were reasonable. On behalf of the Manitoba government, H.J. Symington also protested that although Carvell had concluded that western rates were 15 to 18 per cent higher than eastern rates, he only differentiated the rate increase by 5 per cent. After a two-day hearing, Prime Minister Meighen confided to Hugh Armstrong that although he thought "no more than substantial justice" had been done by the railway commission, "I do not think the hearing was very diplomatically conducted nor the judgment well worded."[43]

In the resulting cabinet decision, Meighen attempted to placate the opponents of the advance without actually altering the board's judgment. After noting the railway commission's superior experience and ability in determining "the more or less technical matters" brought before it, the decision outlined the role of the cabinet in the regulatory process. If the railway commission failed to consider important evidence or for some other reason erred so as to produce "a substantial miscarriage of justice," the government should intervene. In this particular case, Meighen and his cabinet colleagues ruled that the board had not erred in estimating the amount the Canadian Pacific would receive from the rate advance.[44]

There was, however, a second ground for government intervention. If, in reaching its decision, the regulatory commission applied "principles which the Committee of the Privy Council consider not in consonance with public policy, such appropriate action should be taken as will lead to a finding in which only correct principles will be applied." In this instance, the cabinet ruled that, as a matter of policy, the board should not consider the requirements of the Canadian National Railways system in determining the reasonableness of rates. Therefore, the decision was referred back to the board to see if any correction was necessary. The cabinet also asked the board to consider whether the extra 5 per cent advance granted until the end of 1920 could be eliminated or, "if absolutely necessary," could be reduced and extended over a longer period. On another matter of policy, the government, "strongly impressed" with the need to equalize eastern and western rates "with the least possible delay," ordered the commission to determine whether conditions had changed since the 1914 rate inquiry.[45]

The decision that Meighen drafted set out for the first time some clear principles governing cabinet review of board decisions. The cabinet, in his view, should not be a court of appeal on questions of fact only, but should consider the board's decisions in light of the government's general railway policy. The ruling that the financial needs of the Canadian National system should not be considered by the railway commission was a clear response to Carvell's complaint that the regulatory status of the public system had never been defined. In asking the board to review its judgment in the context of this ruling, rather than in following the Railway Act and having the cabinet "amend, vary or rescind" the board's order, Meighen left the application of the policy to the railway commission. This novel approach appeared to emphasize the commission's role as the expert body in the regulatory process.

The emphasis on first principles in the cabinet order fits well with the image of Meighen as a politician of conviction. Nevertheless, both Meighen's refusal to support the railway company's original application, his language in the order, and his decision to refer many matters back to the commission reveals an equivocation and opportunism more frequently associated with his Liberal opponent, William Lyon Mackenzie King. The Conservative leader simply sought to avoid any association with a tough decision. It involved considerable sleight of hand, for example, to ask the board to reconsider the rate advance. The decision had not been based on the

Canadian National's financial needs: the board's estimates, which the government defended, demonstrated that the new rates would even the balance sheet of the Canadian Pacific in 1920 and allow a reasonable surplus in 1921, but would leave the public system with a substantial operating deficit. Moreover, Meighen and his cabinet colleagues received a new financial estimate specially prepared for them by a Canadian Pacific official and the Manitoba government's railway expert, which showed that the railway commission had been too optimistic! The prime minister clearly understood, but did not enunciate, that the policy statement concerning the Canadian National would not alter the conclusions reached by the railway commission.[46]

By referring the question of western rates back to the board, the Meighen administration also tried to champion an attractive political issue, without actually doing anything. It did not amend, or ask the railway commission to amend, the rate increase so as to produce greater parity between eastern and western tariffs. It did not even state that the rates must be equalized. The cabinet simply restated the policy already adopted by the railway commission that it was desirable to make eastern and western rates as equal as circumstances allowed. While this was a potentially useful and harmless statement for the government, in the context of the rest of the cabinet decision and the controversy surrounding Carvell's behaviour, it helped to reinforce the view that the railway commission was insensitive to regional concerns.

The cabinet's decision irritated a number of the railway commissioners. When the Manitoba and Saskatchewan governments demanded that the board suspend the increases or reduce western rates in light of the government's decision, the commissioners responded that the cabinet had exceeded its statutory authority, which was limited to amending, rescinding or varying the board's orders. They therefore interpreted the government's comments as mere suggestions for the board's consideration, rather than as an order. In a brief statement on behalf of the board, Commissioner J.G. Rutherford, a Manitoban with an active interest in agriculture, vigorously defended the original decision. Admitting that some of the language used in the judgment might have conveyed certain wrong impressions, the commissioner clarified the reasons for the decision and emphasized that the increase would not cover the deficits of the Canadian National system.[47]

In the case of the 40 per cent advance, the government and railway commission abandoned the model that had been provided by the 25 per cent advance approved in 1918. Although in both instances the rate increase was prompted by the settlement of railway labour difficulties, a matter of national importance, in 1920 the Meighen government refused to grant, or even support, the railway companies' corresponding demand for a rate advance. Instead of encouraging the government to act or leaving it to face the political consequences, the railway commission then claimed responsibility for making what might more appropriately have been termed a policy decision. In the subsequent appeal to cabinet, the government distanced itself from the decision, and tried to leave the entire matter to the railway commission. Both governing institutions proved uncooperative in their approach to an extraordinary and controversial regulatory demand.

Chief Commissioner Carvell's "rough-shod methods" aggravated an already difficult situation. The commission granted a 40 per cent advance in rates without allowing shipping organizations to present their concerns, as they had been able to when the board considered lesser increases of 5 per cent and 15 per cent. In the commissioners' haste to respond to the immediate needs of the railway companies, they overlooked the importance of the regulatory process, and in the process alienated a considerable number of their other clients. By denying full participation to all interested parties, the "efficient" handling of the case undermined the effectiveness of the board. Instead, it guaranteed that the process, and therefore the decision, would be seen as unfair.

If the outspoken views and constant interventions of "Fighting Frank Carvell" on one side of the issue during the hearings personalized an allegedly impersonal, quasi-judicial process, his subsequent behaviour fanned the flames of controversy. In response to the cabinet request that the board consider the issue of rate equalization, he and Commissioner A.C. Boyce travelled throughout western Canada in the spring of 1921. At these hearings, Carvell interrupted witnesses who appeared to be wandering off-topic, or badgered them when they were discussing the issue at hand. Outside the hearings, he delivered public speeches in defence of the board's unpopular 1920 decision and lectured westerners on their exaggeration of the influence of freight rates and on the serious financial problems facing the Canadian National Railways system. At the conclusion of this tour, Carvell acknowledged the unpopular course he had taken. "I may have to some extent overstepped the bounds of propriety as a man occupying the position of a judge," he observed, but added, "I have stated a good many times that I not only occupied the position of a judge, but that we are administrators as well, and as administrators we have been trying to give to the people some idea of the true situation and some of the reasons why we had to adopt the course we adopted." While the chief commissioner appeared to believe that he had done some good, his various patronizing and "injudicious" comments further undermined the credibility of the railway commission.[48]

Carvell's further efforts to bring about a reduction in rates did little to alleviate matters. Following a decline in the price of materials and a controversial wage cut by the Canadian Pacific in July 1921, the chief commissioner initiated a number of informal conferences with railway officials to discuss rates. Although the freight officers agreed to reduce rates on livestock voluntarily, the chief commissioner eventually ordered them to reduce most of their other freight tariffs to a level 10 per cent below what they had been following the 1920 40 per cent advance. Unfortunately for Carvell, a majority of his colleagues refused to join the decision, pending the investigation of the disputed wage cut by a government-appointed board of conciliation and investigation. They only agreed to the reductions following the completion of that investigation, and therefore delayed the introduction of the new rates from early September until late November.[49] The events surrounding the decision simply reinforced the public perception that the railway commission had become more concerned with the financial needs of the railway companies and their workers than with the conditions facing the shipping community.

"It seems to me the railways have no friends whatever," a Montreal industrialist remarked to the railway commission early in 1922, "Everybody is taking a hack out of them." Carvell interjected, "There are a good many people who seem to think this Board are their friends." "Yes, and they are taking a hack out of us," quipped McLean.[50]

As Carvell and McLean acknowledged, by 1921 the Board of Railway Commissioners was under siege. In December 1921 the Canadian Council of Agriculture asked the newly elected government of Mackenzie King to use "its undoubted authority to override and if necessary re-organize the personnel of the Railway Commission in order that relief from the crushing burden of freight rates may be secured." During the same month, an editorial cartoon in the Grain Growers' Guide showed a hard-working railway commissioner turning the handle of a "freight rate separator," which provided the lion's share of the profits from an honest farmer's produce to a rotund, well-dressed, and, of course, cigar-smoking railway magnate. The railway commissioner proclaimed, "She's working fine now."[51]

Table 11
Freight Rates and the Railway Commission, 1914–22
(Index, 1914 = 100)

	Ontario	Prairies	Canadian Pacific Railway	
			Freight Earnings per Ton-mile	Real Freight Earnings per Ton-mile
1914	100	100	100	100
1915	100	100	101	93
December 1916	105	100	85	63
1917	105	100	94	53
March 1918	121	115	114	60
August 1918	151	125	114	60
1919	151	125	133	65
September 1920	211	169	148	69
January 1921	204	162		
December 1921	190	152	170	114

Sources: Calculations based on material from Appendix B, Table B.5; CNR, vol. 8546, Grand Trunk Railway, History of Freight Rates in the provinces of Ontario and Quebec (Montreal, 1912), and railway commission decisions cited in this chapter.

The cartoon portrayed the regulatory agency as a captive of the industry that it was intended to regulate. Such a notion was not new, and undoubtedly some observers always believed it to be true of the board. Nevertheless, it is arguable that the image of Canada's railway commission as a "captive" of the railway industry took firm historical root between 1914 and 1921. That image has persisted. In fact, a number of scholars regard the wartime experience as a demonstration of the true nature of regulation – to protect the profits of private industry.

The railway commissioners did become increasingly concerned with the fortunes of the industry whose pricing policies it supervised, and agreed to a number of unprecedented rate advances. If a shipper paid $100 for a shipment in 1914, Table 11 shows that even after two sets of reductions, the shipment would still cost $90 and $50 more in eastern and western Canada respectively in 1921. These increases must be set against changes in the cost of living, however. Table 11 and Figure 9 both indicate that when considered in terms of constant dollars, the increases really only restored rates to their pre-war levels.

It would certainly have been difficult to convince officials of the Grand Trunk and Canadian Northern that regulators ensured their continued profitability. In fact, the collapse of those railways and the simultaneous breakdown of the American rail system during the war has given rise to a quite different view of regulation. It is now argued that the railway commissions in both countries were far too protective of the interests of shippers and starved the railways of necessary revenues. Regulators failed to acknowledge the impact of escalating operating costs and, by also failing to respond to railway demands for increased rates, helped undermine a viable industry.[52]

Railway revenues on the Canadian Northern and the Grand Trunk and its western extension certainly fell short of what was required during the war. Any improvement in revenues, therefore, would have made some sort of difference to the economic performance of those railways, but such advances would not have solved the financial problems facing the projects. The corporations depended heavily on bonds and guaranteed securities of one type or another, and therefore carried a large debt load into the war crisis. Even had freight rates kept pace with spiralling prices, those high fixed charges would have overwhelmed the earning power of the railways.[53] The Canadian Pacific survived the wartime financial crisis, not only because it was a complete and fully developed transcontinental, but because its managers had consciously kept fixed charges low and maintained substantial cash reserves.

The financial crisis on Canada's transcontinentals preceded the railway industry's wartime operating problems. In the latter half of 1916, rapidly increasing costs had begun to get out of control, and real earning per ton-mile declined dramatically. In response to these developments and to a similar application by their American counterparts, Canadian railway officials turned to the railway commission to ask for increased freight rates. By the time the board received the first application for a general rate advance, therefore, the Canadian Northern and the Grand Trunk Pacific already were virtually bankrupt. Regulation did not undermine Canada's railway corporations. On the other hand, only one major company survived the wartime crisis. Administrative regulation did not guarantee the profits of an otherwise unstable industry, help reverse the fortunes of ailing companies, or preclude the nationalization of a significant part of Canada's industry, as some proponents of the "capture" thesis would argue.

The railway commissioners, like the industry it regulated and its political masters in Parliament, fumbled in the dark, grappling with the unprecedented and largely unanticipated problems generated by the outbreak of war. The demands produced by wartime inflation and by the financial crisis facing the railways raised, and were seen as involving, broader policy questions than routine regulatory cases. The 1918 25 per cent advance provided one possible response to these demands – shared government and commission responsibility for extraordinary regulatory decisions. Such an approach was abandoned by both the government and the railway commission in 1920, at considerable cost to the latter. The railway commission did not provide authority and legitimacy to the rate increases the industry sought. Instead, by appearing to bow to the demands of the railway industry too readily, the regulatory agency sacrificed its own authority and legitimacy. The Board of Railway Commissioners, like much of the private railway system it regulated, was a casualty of war.

CHAPTER NINE

"An Equilator [?] Rather Than a Mathematical Equality"

Chief Commissioner Carvell's controversial western tour in the spring of 1921 represented the first phase of a new inquiry into the equalization of eastern and western tariffs. In asking the board to undertake the investigation, Prime Minister Meighen hoped to overcome his government's other liabilities in western Canada by championing a long-standing and widely shared regional grievance. Liberal leader William Lyon Mackenzie King, who succeeded Meighen in December 1921 and served as prime minister for most of the 1920s, also championed the cause of freight rate "equality." Regional rate grievances, embodied in a quest for equality, dominated the regulatory agenda for the next decade.

What precisely did rate equalization mean? Prime Minister King reportedly told Canadian Pacific President E.W. Beatty that it was "an equilator [?] rather than a mathematical equality I had in mind, something that wd. recognize geographical considerations, but in interests of country as a whole and people as a whole." Although this obscure phrase might seem appropriate to the prime minister who "skilfully avoided what was wrong / Without saying what was right," in fact King was capturing the essence of the movement for freight rate equalization in the 1920s. It was not the "mathematical" calculation of a nation-wide uniform rate schedule but rather the promotion of equal economic opportunities among Canada's regions that became the objective of the proponents of freight rate equalization. [1]

King also told Beatty that "we should aim at this [equalization] thro Commission Control," that the Board of Railway Commissioners "shld. be given a free hand" in the matter of freight rates. [2] Such a policy proved difficult to sustain. By 1921, the government, not private corporations, operated much of the Canadian railway system. In addition, the government, not the railway commission, had temporarily set aside the rates fixed by the Crow's Nest Pass and Manitoba agreements during the war. Many groups now looked to the government to determine the fate of those agreements, and to use the publicly-owned Canadian National Railways to provide leadership during rate-making disputes. Throughout the early 1920s, the government, the railway companies, and the Board of Railway Commissioners each struggled to respond to demands for equality. Freight rate equalization, bound up with questions of regional economic development, tested the boundaries between public and private spheres, and between politics and administration.

It is not surprising that Prime Ministers Meighen and King were anxious to be seen as favouring freight-rate "equality." The formation of the Union government during the war disrupted traditional party affiliations and created a political opportunity for various movements that promised to deliver to Canadians the wartime ideals of justice, equality, and freedom. The inflationary spiral prior to 1921, followed by the severe recession that lasted well into 1924, contributed to the success of those political movements which translated broad ideals into specific economic goals. New business and political organizations made freight rate demands part of broader campaigns against regional disparities in the prairie west, the Maritimes, and British Columbia.

World War I proved to be a mixed blessing for prairie agriculture, as historian John Thompson has demonstrated. In an effort to profit from extremely favourable grain prices, farmers mined their soil, avoided diversifying their crops, and invested in land and equipment on credit despite high interest rates. Between 1918 and 1924, near-drought conditions in the southern prairies and the return of grain prices to pre-war levels created serious hardship for prairie farmers, particularly those carrying high levels of debt. The price collapse was particularly devastating, and was made more dramatic by the end of government control over the marketing of wheat prior to the 1920 crop season. In the fall of 1920, the average price for a bushel of wheat peaked at about $3.50, then dropped below $2.00 for the first time since 1917, before continuing its slide into 1921. Other farmers also faced greatly reduced incomes: between the spring of 1920 and 1921, for example, the price paid for good quality steers delivered at Winnipeg dropped by half, from nearly $14 to $7 a head.[3]

Between 1919 and 1921, economic conditions also deteriorated in the Maritimes. The price on salt cod dropped by one-half, to the detriment of the Atlantic fishery, and conditions in the mining and manufacturing sectors proved worrisome. It was becoming apparent that coal-mining operations were being undermined by a declining demand for coal as alternative sources of fuel and energy were adopted, and competition from new and more accessible mines. Nor could local industry be counted upon to purchase the coal. Pig-iron production declined to almost one-half of its pre-war levels, and by 1925, there were nearly 10,000 fewer people working in iron- and steel-related industries than there had been in 1921. When financiers consolidated both of Nova Scotia's steel companies into the giant British Empire Steel and Coal Company in 1920, it was seen as a desperate bid to overcome the serious crisis facing a key sector of the Maritime economy. The following year there was more bad news for the region when the Maritime Nail Company of Saint John, and the Canadian Car and Foundry Company of Amherst, once a national leader in the production of railway cars, transferred their manufacturing operations to Montreal.[4]

On the Pacific Coast, the return to a peace-time economy and the collapse of commodity prices buffeted the British Columbia economy as well. The industrial work-force in Vancouver and in the province as a whole plummeted nearly 50 per cent between 1919 and 1921. In contrast to the Maritimes, however, conditions there recovered more quickly and showed fewer signs of long-term decay. With the conclusion of the war, the province could finally take advantage of the Panama Canal to export grain, lumber, and other products to Europe. After a poor year in 1920, the value of goods exported through Vancouver expanded rapidly, doubling in the five years between 1921 and 1926. By 1925, there were nearly as many British Columbia workers engaged in manufacturing as in 1919. While the work-force in Vancouver did not rebound to the same extent, during the early 1920s the city nevertheless surpassed Winnipeg to become Canada's fourth largest manufacturing centre. After an initial shock, the economy of British Columbia emerged from the post-war period relatively unscathed, with only the import trade remaining stagnant.[5]

New political movements were built upon both the economic disruption and utopianism generated by the conclusion of "The War to End all Wars." Between 1919 and 1922, the United Farmers helped form provincial governments in Ontario, Alberta, and Manitoba. Farm, labour, and other independent candidates also challenged the traditional parties in Nova Scotia, Saskatchewan, and British Columbia, attracting at least 30 per cent of the electorate in those provinces. The new administrations, as well as those governments whose power had been threatened, sought to appeal to these new farm- and labour-based movements without alienating local business interests. They looked for broad issues that could unite diverse political coalitions. In the prairie west, these were the traditional regional issues: the tariff, the regulation of the grain trade, the construction of an alternate railway to Hudson Bay, and freight rates. In British Columbia, the government of Premier "Honest John" Oliver sought to retain power by waging a battle against the dominion government over old-age pensions, the return of the railway lands to the province, and freight rates. In the Maritimes, business and professional interests championed a politically potent campaign on behalf of "Maritime Rights," calling for larger annual provincial subsidies, protection for the steel and coal industries, various initiatives to develop the ports of Halifax and Saint John, and freight rates that would assist the development of the region. Under the banner of "Maritime Rights," the conservative party swept into power in 1925, demolishing an eight-year-old Liberal government in New Brunswick and a Liberal dynasty of forty-four years in Nova Scotia.[6] Throughout the 1920s, then, provincial governments across the country posed as defenders of regional interests.

Provincial political and business leaders saw real advantages in championing freight rate grievances. Freight rate issues could be formulated so as to appeal to the specific economic ambitions of local business leaders while at the same time tapping the broader anti-Canadian Pacific or anti-Ontario sentiment of other members of the society. Commercial, industrial and farm leaders looked to the issue as one popular enough to attract new members to their organizations, while at the same time they sought to have the expense of presenting their grievances to the railway commission and the dominion government covered by governments. Provincial political leaders saw rate grievances as one part of a broader campaign against regional disparities, campaigns which promised to divert attention from conflicts within their provinces and to unite a divided and volatile electorate. Provincial governments readily agreed to appoint railway experts and special counsel to formulate and present rate grievances, and thereby acquired an important stake in the regulatory response to those demands.

Provincial governments were not alone in their interest in regional freight rate questions: the dominion government also faced pressures from within. In the election of 1921, the newly-created Progressive party of Canada captured sixty-four seats running on the Farmers' Platform, a policy statement developed by the Canadian Council of Agriculture. This gave the Progressive party fourteen more seats than Meighen's "National Liberal and Conservative Party," and provided the votes that King's Liberals would need in order to govern. In spite of its attempt at a national orientation (and some moderate success in Ontario), over one-half of the national Progressive members were from the prairie west. With thirty-seven of the forty-three prairie representatives in the House of Commons, they were virtually the only voice representing that region. As a result, the Progressive movement became a significant vehicle for prairie grievances.[7]

Liberal candidates in the 1921 general election won all but six seats in Nova Scotia and New Brunswick, promising "to advocate and stand by Maritime rights first, last and all the time." The understandable preoccupation of the minority King government with the Progressives, however, allowed the Conservative party to become the champion of the Maritimes. "Maritime Rights" clearly helped the national Conservatives win two local by-elections in 1923, and two years later, all but four of twenty-one Liberals were defeated by Conservative proponents of the region's interests. The Conservatives, whose parliamentary caucus had a strong contingent from British Columbia, championed some of those province's causes as well, although the evidence of their hold on the province would not be apparent until the elections of 1925 and 1926.[8]

Both provincial and national politicians, therefore, soon realized that regional economic issues appealed to a volatile electorate. Although the members of the Board of Railway Commissioners were insulated from such immediate political considerations, they could not ignore, nor would politicians allow them to ignore, the role that freight rate decisions played in shaping regional development. In this highly charged atmosphere, regulators grappled with the question of rate equalization.

The 1921 inquiry by the Board of Railway Commissioners highlighted both the sources and the intensity of freight rate grievances. Although the commissioners' initial mandate was to examine the relative level of tariffs in central Canada and the prairie west, they subsequently expanded their inquiry to consider allegations of territorial discrimination against British Columbia and the Maritimes. As they travelled across the country, they encountered a similar concern everywhere: freight rates should be adjusted so as to recognize the unique geographical and economic nature of Canada's different regions.

"In my opinion," observed H.J. Symington, the lawyer appointed by the Manitoba and Saskatchewan governments, "the equal treatment of unequal things is just as bad as the unequal treatment of equal things." The west, a predominantly agricultural community dependent on the carriage of goods over long distances, had needs quite different from the east. In view of this fact and the testimony the commissioners heard concerning the burden that freight rates imposed on western agriculture, Symington recommended that rates on grain should be cut immediately, and that other reductions should be applied to the shipment of cattle, coal, agricultural implements, and other basic agricultural commodities.[9] To emphasize the need for grain rate reductions, he produced an array of statistical exhibits, including a controversial estimate showing substantial earnings on a trainload of grain carried from western Canada to the Lakehead, which purported to show that the grain traffic generated great profits to the railways. In spite of serious criticism of this estimate from railway officials and the commissioners, Symington insisted that of all the freight being carried in Canada, western grain contributed more than its fair share to the financing of railway operations. He concluded that this disproportionate burden placed on western Canada's principal product, grain, was contrary to a genuine policy of rate equality.[10]

Noticeably absent from Symington's presentation and from the testimony of various other witnesses from the prairie west was the very issue the railway commission had been asked to study: the equalization of the general merchandise tariffs in the west with those in central Canada. Although that traditional question had been at the heart of the earlier western rates case in 1914, it was now largely a dead issue. The reason for this lay in the fact that the railway commission had consistently imposed higher horizontal advances in the east: a 34 per cent pre-war difference between central and western Canadian rates on fifth-class freight (the most common classification of merchandise distributed in carloads) had been subsequently narrowed to 14 per cent. Western merchants now saw little to gain in a further narrowing of that gap. Indeed, they feared that a genuine equalization would require them to accept eastern classification structures and traffic rules, thereby disrupting existing distribution networks in the prairie west.[11]

In contrast, the principal rate demand of business and political leaders from British Columbia continued to be the elimination of the higher general tariff relative to the rest of Canada applied in British Columbia. John Oliver, the premier of British Columbia, personally appeared before the commission to demonstrate that the higher rates were contrary to the spirit of the province's pact with the dominion government at the time of its entrance into Confederation. The province's counsel, Gerry G. McGeer, supplemented this constitutional argument by attacking the notion that higher costs justified the rates. He cited the opinion of one engineer that the Canadian National's line through the province practically eliminated the mountains as a cost factor. British Columbia's shippers, he alleged, should not continue to pay for the Canadian Pacific's decision to construct and operate, at great expense, its line through the Kicking Horse Pass. In any event, McGeer noted that officials from the private railway could not prove that the operating performance on the mountain section was any worse than elsewhere, since they no longer kept the divisional revenue statistics that had proven so embarrassing in the western rates case.[12]

While McGeer sought the adoption of a uniform tariff for all of western Canada, he shared Symington's view that freight rates should be adjusted to meet the diverse needs of Canada's regions. He arranged to have more than twenty businessmen, primarily manufacturers, make presentations describing how the high mountain scale of rates prevented the expansion of their business by restricting their access to prairie markets. This focus on manufacturing was deliberate: McGeer hoped to counter the allegation of many business leaders from Winnipeg and other Western communities that rate reductions would simply give Vancouver merchants a greater competitive advantage in distributing goods throughout the prairie west, without any benefit to the consumer. A true policy of freight rate equalization, McGeer concluded, would remove the barriers to, and support, the industrial development of all of British Columbia.[13]

The commission heard similar arguments when they travelled to the Maritimes. Lawyers Robert E. Finn and Ivan C. Rand, representing Nova Scotia and New Brunswick respectively, also sought a policy of freight rate equalization that would encourage their region's industrial development. Like McGeer, Finn and Rand orchestrated the testimony of regional manufacturers, who sought to show that their very survival depended on their ability to compete in the large consumer markets in central Canada and the prairie west. Although Finn and Rand admitted that on a distance basis, rates from the Maritimes were already lower than elsewhere in Canada, they nevertheless called for further reductions. Given the Maritime provinces' geographical position, "projected into the Atlantic as an eastern extremity of the Dominion," Rand asked whether it was reasonable "to formulate a rate that will isolate that portion of the country from the rest of it?" According to Finn and Rand, a true policy of freight rate equalization did not mean uniformity; it meant that Maritime shippers should enjoy lower rates than those that existed elsewhere in Canada so as to sustain the region's industrial development.[14]

Towards the conclusion of the equalization hearing, Commissioner Rutherford observed that "There is not one of these different phases of this somewhat complex question that is before us today in which that geographical element does not play a very large part."[15] Although each lawyer offered some historical or statistical evidence to support his recommendations, each one ultimately argued that a policy of freight rate equalization should recognize the particular geographical and industrial condition of the regions. Such an argument challenged the regulatory role that the commission had defined for itself. The board had ruled previously that although it might sanction rates if railway officials adjusted them to compensate industries for geographical or other competitive disadvantages, it could not *order* them to adopt these developmental rates. While that regulatory principle might have been modified in some particular cases, a number of the commissioners were uncomfortable with a definition of equalization that asked them to abandon the principle altogether. "Where will it lead us?" Assistant Chief Commissioner McLean asked when the prairie west's lawyer, H.J. Symington, asserted that the board could even order the railways to carry the traffic of certain industries at a loss if it was in the public interest. The railway commission would become a "sort of industrial development body," McLean continued in response to his own question, and "I don't think Parliament has given us that power."[16]

As McLean and his colleagues considered their dilemma, the uncertain status of the Crow's Nest Pass agreement provided the catalyst for a consideration of regional rate demands by the elected politicians. The 1918 25 per cent horizontal advance adopted by order-in-council had been made "notwithstanding the provisions of any legislation heretofore passed, or of any rate-limiting agreement heretofore made." The resulting increase had marked the first time that the rates on eastbound grain and a variety of westbound commodities had exceeded those agreed to by the Canadian Pacific in 1897. In 1919, Parliament had adopted a measure which had had the effect of further suspending the traditional rates until 6 July 1922.[17] The Progressive party, upon which the Liberal minority government depended for support, had made the restoration of the historic rates a key policy demand. Because Prime Minister King's own party was divided over the issue, he preferred to have a special parliamentary committee study the question. On 5 May 1922, such a committee was appointed to study "the question of railway transportation costs ... with particular regard to the effect of the rates established by the Crows Nest Pass Agreement upon Canadian National Railways and other lines, as well as upon agricultural development and Canadian industry generally."[18]

Although ostensibly concerned with the Crow's Nest Pass agreement, members of the Special Committee to Consider Railway Transportation Costs listened to Premier John Oliver and G.G. McGeer discuss the mountain differential in British Columbia, to R.E. Finn and a number of Maritime producers outline the problems facing their region, as well as to H.J. Symington describe the favourable financial returns of western railway operations, and the profitability of grain traffic in particular. In short, the committee reheard all the arguments that had recently been presented to the Board of Railway Commissioners during its inquiry. There was one important difference. Whereas during the commission inquiry railway officials had simply challenged the factual evidence presented in support of each region's grievances, before the parliamentary committee, they went on the offensive. E.W. Beatty of the Canadian Pacific and D.B. Hanna of the Canadian National first described how their financial position would have been altered in 1921 had the low Crow rates been in effect then: a deficit of $14 million would have been the result on the otherwise profitable private railway, and a shortfall of $25 million instead of $16 million would have occurred on the public railway. The railway executives shrewdly proposed an alternative to the restoration of the Crow rates. They noted that the reinstatement of the Crow rates would only reduce rates on western grain bound for eastern points, and on a limited number of farm-related commodities produced in the east and bound for western communities, including coal oil, fruit, livestock, agricultural implements, binder twine, hardware and household furniture. Instead, they offered reductions that when combined with reductions already in effect would have restored pre-1920 rates on a wide variety of commodities carried in all parts of Canada, including forest products, building materials, potatoes, fertilizers, ores, pig-iron, a number of semi-fabricated iron and steel commodities, most types of coal, and even western grain. Railway officials offered rate changes which would appear to benefit all parts of the country instead of restoring the Crow rates, which they argued only would benefit prairie shippers. They clearly hoped to isolate those political, business and farm leaders who were championing the Crow rates.[19]

The strategy very nearly succeeded. The committee defeated by a single vote Progressive leader T.A. Crerar's proposal to reinstate the eastbound grain rates but suspend the rates on westbound commodities for another year. Instead, in what was to be its final report, the committee recommended that all the Crow rates be suspended for another year and that the government be allowed to extend the suspension for a second year, if "then existing conditions justify the same." This "final" report, however, never saw the light of day.

Crerar planned to reintroduce his proposal when Parliament considered the report, and Prime Minister King learned that enough members of his own party might vote with the Progressives to carry it. Rumours even circulated that the Conservative party might introduce a similar proposal.[20] King faced a political crisis.

It would thus seem to be more than just a coincidence that the Special Committee on Transportation Costs reconvened two days after approving its "final" report. Ostensibly, a Canadian National Railways official wished to present new figures on the impact of the Crow's Nest Pass agreement. Naturally, of course, the final product of the meeting was a new report, which was adopted after all of the Conservative and some of the Liberal members had left the proceedings in disgust, and which altered the original version in several respects. Although now "impressed" instead of "perhaps impressed" by the arguments concerning British Columbia and Maritime rates, the committee still reported that such matters lay outside its mandate. It continued to emphasize the complexity of estimating the impact of the restoration of the Crow rates, agreed that "fixing rates by legislation is no doubt generally a bad principle," and concluded that rate questions should be dealt with by the railway commission. Nevertheless, the "Committee has reached the conclusion that an immediate reduction of freight rates on grain and flour is in the national interest" and recommended that the Crow rates on grain and flour should be reinstated. As Crerar had suggested, the other Crow rates on westbound commodities were to be suspended for a period of up to two years. The committee also recommended that "Basic commodities which may be afforded reductions should have the earliest possible consideration by the Board of Railway Commissioners." This report was duly approved by Parliament, and the government subsequently drafted legislation consistent with the committee's recommendations concerning the Crow's Nest Pass rates. The result, as Table 12 illustrates, was the restoration of the grain rates of 1899 for most shippers in western Canada.[21]

With the exception of rates on western grain, Parliament deferred to the technical expertise of the railway commission, "the only body in Canada equipped for the determination of the intricate matters relative to railway rate making."[22] The board's judgment on the remaining regional grievances, released shortly after Parliament determined the immediate future of the Crow's Nest Pass rates, revealed how far the "intricacies" of freight rates were from being technical matters.

Before touching on the regional issues, the commissioners responded to the suggestion concerning rate reductions on basic commodities made by the Special Committee on Transportation Costs.

Table 12
Freight Rates on Western Grain to Fort William and Port Arthur
(Cents per 100 Lbs), 1886 – 1927

	From Winnipeg	From Calgary	From Saskatoon
September 1886	28	33	–
September 1887	24	33	–
October 1888 (Northern Pacific sets rates)	21	33	–
September 1893	17	29	–
August 1898 (Crow's Nest Pass agreement)	15.5	27.5	27.5
September 1899 (Crow's Nest Pass agreement)	14	26	26
October 1903 (Manitoba agreement)	10	24	24
March 1918 (BRC advance)	12	26	24
August 1918 (Order-in-Council advance)	14	30	28
September 1920 (BRC advance)	19	40.5	38
January 1921 (BRC reduction)	18	39	36.5
December 1921 (BRC reduction)	17	36	33.5
July 1922 (Parliament reinstates Crow rates)	14	26	24
September 1927 (BRC adjusts Crow rates)	14	26	22

Sources: J.A. Argo, "Historical Review of Canadian Railway Freight Rate Structure, 1876–1938,", in R.A.C. Henry & Associates, *Railway Freight Rates in Canada* (Ottawa, 1939), 139; Dominion Bureau of Statistics, *Grain Statistics* (Ottawa, 1930), Table 127, 173.

Although they emphasized that such a recommendation was not legally binding, the commissioners agreed to treat the opinion of a parliamentary committee with respect. Pointing to depressed industrial conditions, they concluded that "as a matter of emergency action," rates on basic commodities should be adjusted on the basis of the voluntary reductions offered by railway officials during the parliamentary hearings. Using the Canadian Pacific's own estimates, the board calculated that, even after the reintroduction of the Crow's

Nest Pass grain rates, the private railway could still afford to reduce its tariffs on the other commodities mentioned in its offer by 7.5 per cent, and to adopt its original proposal with respect to coal rates. The implication was clear – in consequence of Parliament's decision decision on grain rates, a number of other Canadian producers would not receive the full reductions that had been proposed by the railways on their own initiative.[23]

In dealing with the regional questions, the commissioners studiously ignored the definition of "equalization" that had been offered by counsel for the provincial governments. They did cite Symington's observations on the differences in traffic conditions between the prairie west and the east as supporting the board's traditional view that the mere existence of different regional rate structures did not constitute an unjust discrimination under "the inhibitions of the Railway Act."[24] They rejected as irrelevant any special claims either British Columbia or the Maritimes might have arising out of Confederation, and did not acknowledge any of the contentions concerning the geographical disadvantages under which the regions' industries operated.

This harsh treatment of the arguments did not, however, preclude some favourable concessions. Without providing any evidence as to changed operating conditions or offering any other regulatory principle, the board ordered that the British Columbia mountain tariff be reduced from 1.5 to 1.25 times the prairie scale. This order, as Table 13 illustrates, greatly diminished the difference in the freight paid by shippers of general merchandise in British Columbia and the prairie west. In the case of the Maritimes, the commissioners concluded that the formula used to construct through rates to the prairie west did not recognize the fundamental principle of lower rates for longer hauls. As a result, they introduced a new tariff that had the effect of reducing, for example, the difference between the fifth-class rate paid by a Saint John and a Montreal business both shipping to Winnipeg, from twenty cents to twelve cents. Without committing the board to a specific regional rate policy or principle of equalization, the commissioners thus sought to accommodate regional grievances by offering some rate relief to shippers in British Columbia and the Maritimes.[25]

The final judgment in the equalization case represented not the end but the beginning of the regional rate controversies of the 1920s. Representatives of each region had defined and presented their basic positions and arguments during the course of the commission inquiry and the parliamentary debate. Shipping interests, governments, and their legal representatives could all be encouraged by

Table 13
British Columbia and Prairie Fifth-Class Rates per 30,000 Lbs/200 Miles, 1912–23

	British Columbia	Alberta Saskatchewan	Difference
April 1912	$168	$99	$69
July 1915			
(Western Rates Case)	$117	$93	$24
March 1918			
(BRC advance)	$129	$102	$27
August 1918			
(Order-in-council advance)	$145.50	$115.50	$30
September 1920			
(BRC advance)	$196.50	$156	$40.50
January 1921			
(BRC reduction)	$189	$150	$39
December 1921			
(BRC reduction)	$177	$141	$36
August 1922			
(BRC reduction "equalization")	$159	$141	$18

Sources: J.A. Argo, "Historical Review of Canadian Railway Freight Rate Structure, 1876 – 1938," in R.A.C. Henry & Associates, Railway Freight Rates in Canada (Ottawa, 1939), Schedule 23; railway commission cases cited in chapters 7 and 8.

the outcome. The grain rate legislation offered a potential precedent for other government-directed initiatives with respect to fundamental rate matters. As significantly, it seemed clear that the parliamentary debate produced political signals to which the railway commission had responded. Although the commissioners had not recognized the basic principle of "equalization," they had offered some significant concessions. With such encouraging signs, the advocates of regional rate grievances looked for ways to increase the pressure on the elected politicians in Parliament and their unelected counterparts on the railway commission.

Champions of regional rate issues followed diverse routes. British Columbia pressed for direct concessions from the government and eventually launched a formal appeal of the board's equalization judgment to cabinet. Another debate over the Crow's Nest Pass agreement afforded the prairie west the opportunity to acquire further legislative reductions in basic commodity rates. The Maritimes, whose rate demands represented part of a broader debate over the restructuring of the management of the Intercolonial Railway, pressed both Canadian National officials and that railway's political masters for special consideration. The regional rate controversies represented separate but intertwined strands of the equalization web, which continued to entangle politicians, railway officials, and regulators.

As a result of the government's action on the Crow rates, and even before the railway commission rendered its equalization judgment, Premier Oliver had pressed the King government to appoint a royal commission to consider British Columbia's case for equality of rates. The railway commission's subsequent concession on British Columbia's rates did not dampen Oliver's enthusiasm, and only encouraged him to continue pressing for the complete elimination of the mountain scale. When no royal commission was forthcoming, the premier pressed his demands by appealing the equalization judgment to cabinet. At a special hearing in February 1923, Oliver personally delivered what Mackenzie King described as an "earnest and powerful appeal" for freight rate justice based on British Columbia's agreement to enter Confederation in 1871. At a later hearing in August, G.G. McGeer, counsel for British Columbia, repeated the other arguments that had previously been presented to the Board of Railway Commissioners concerning the construction, improvements, and financial returns of the rail lines running through British Columbia.[26]

McGeer now added a new item to his list of rate demands. He asked that low transcontinental rates, an advantage already enjoyed by merchants in Victoria and Vancouver, be extended inland to business leaders in Edmonton and Calgary. This new rate demand did not represent an unselfish gesture; it represented the price paid by the government of British Columbia to Herbert Greenfield's new United Farmers government in Alberta for their support in the battle for the elimination of the mountain scale. Greenfield was already engaged in freight rate diplomacy within his own province: he had originally seen reduced rates through the mountains as a way to reduce the costs of exports and imports to farmers and rural merchants in Alberta, but that policy ran afoul of the business communities in Edmonton and Calgary, who feared increased competition from Vancouver. In an attempt to balance these interests, the Alberta premier made his support of the elimination of the mountain scale contingent on the equalization of the rates to Edmonton and Calgary from eastern Canada with the low transcontinental rates enjoyed by Vancouver. To retain its new ally in the fight over the mountain scale, the government of British Columbia agreed to support this objective.[27]

Neither this new rate demand nor much of the statistical material McGeer presented had been brought to the attention of the Board of Railway Commissioners during the equalization hearings. Lawyers for the railways questioned the right of parties to introduce completely new evidence in a procedure that ostensibly represented an appeal of the board's decision. Prime Minister Mackenzie King responded by quoting approvingly a description of the appeal process given by the Speaker of the House of Commons:

It [British Columbia's case] is being considered by the Government under the administrative powers which the Governor-in-Council did not delegate or alienate when the Railway Board was created. The fact that the Cabinet hears Counsel representing both sides of the issue does not constitute it a tribunal. The ministers are at liberty to take all the information required before arriving at a decision upon which they will base the advice to be tendered to His Excellency the Governor-General. They may be guided by considerations of public policy quite foreign to the brief.[28]

Such a broad definition of the cabinet's role in appeals did not go uncontested. Several lawyers representing the railways and other shipping interests opposed to British Columbia's case warned that if the cabinet began to weigh evidence and substitute its own judgment on questions of fact, it would destroy the effectiveness of the railway commission and only "encourage the clamour and insistence of disappointed applicants."[29]

While the members of the government did not allow these arguments to interfere with the appeal proceedings, they had to be concerned about the impact of their decision on the regulatory process. They also had to be concerned with its impact on the political process. The opposition Conservatives had championed British Columbia's freight rate grievances during the previous session of Parliament, and there had been some concern that the Progressive party might support the Conservative efforts. The dominion Liberal administration in Ottawa also hoped to avoid a direct confrontation with its provincial counterpart. At the same time, both the board and cabinet hearings revealed that there was considerable opposition in the prairie west to British Columbia's claims.[30]

During the course of the cabinet appeal, McGeer had raised yet another issue, the question of western grain rates to the Pacific Coast. He had contended that it was a "startling thing" that the board did not adjust grain rates to the Pacific Coast following the reinstatement of the eastbound Crow rates. As Table 14 illustrates, the Crow rates threatened to undermine Vancouver's rate advantages in the western prairie provinces. In responding to British Columbia's demands, the King government focused on this issue, since it appealed to a broader coalition of interests than did the question of the mountain scale,

Table 14
Export Grain Rates per 30,000 Lbs Shipped from Calgary, 1908–27

	Vancouver (646 miles)	Fort William (1242 miles)	Benefit to Vancouver
December 1908	$67.50	$72	$4.50
December 1909	$58.50	$72	$13.50
June 1920 (BRC advance)	$78	$90	$12
September 1920 (BRC advance)	$105	$121.50	$16.50
January 1921 (BRC reduction)	$102	$117	$15
December 1921 (BRC reduction)	$93	$108	$15
August 1922 (Crow's Nest Pass Agreement and Railway concession to Vancouver)	$75	$78	$3
October 1923 (BRC reduction)	$67.50	$78	$10.50
September 1925 (BRC Order 36769)	$63	$78	$15
September 1927 (BRC general investigation)	$60	$78	$18

Sources: J.A. Argo, "Historical Review of Canadian Railway Freight Rate Structure, 1876–1938," in R.A.C. Henry & Associates, *Railway Freight Rates in Canada* (Ottawa, 1939), 139; Dominion Bureau of Statistics, *Grain Statistics* (Ottawa, 1930), Tables 141, 181.

and involved less interference in the regulatory process. On 12 September, the King government ordered that the subject "should be referred to said Board for immediate consideration" and that "an inquiry as to the said rates on grain should be made by the said Board." The railway commissioners interpreted the original order simply as a request for an inquiry, but the government came under considerable pressure to have the issue completely resolved before the peak of the grain harvest. On 2 October, a second order-in-council amended the first one, referring the question of grain rates to the board "for immediate determination."[31]

The board responded quickly to the second order-in-council. On 10 October, it ordered a 10 per cent reduction in westbound export grain rates. As Table 14 shows, the concession was significant, for it followed a 20 per cent voluntary reduction the railway commission had already convinced the railways to adopt. It helped to restore the attractiveness of Vancouver, at least in terms of freight rates, to shippers in the western prairie provinces. The board, however, refused to accept the argument that the rates should be adjusted in relation to the eastbound Crow rates and deliberately arrived at its concession by a different calculation. All but one commissioner ruled "that the rates adopted by Parliament established for particular reasons, and under special conditions, were not to be taken as the basis or standard of other rates." The decision reflected a degree of hostility towards Parliament's interference with the board's jurisdiction over freight rates, and signalled that such legislative interference would be interpreted strictly.[32]

The ruling on grain rates represented the extent of British Columbia's success in appealing the board's equalization judgment. On 24 October, the government decided that the remainder of the appeal related "wholly to questions of fact and the principles in regard to the Regulation of Railway Rates in Canada under the jurisdiction of the Board." It simply referred all the matters back to the board, and added the opinion "that in the future, should transportation and traffic conditions so change as to render practicable a nearer approach to equalization of rates as between Prairie and Pacific Territory, the Board should in the exercise of its discretion take such action as may be necessary to bring about this result." The government upheld the railway commission's regulatory authority, and through its "opinion," gave tacit support to the commission's ruling on the mountain differential.[33] Neither the cabinet decisions nor the board's order concerning export grain ended British Columbia's rate crusade. Premier Oliver, anticipating a provincial election in 1924, demanded to know why the government had ignored British Columbia's special claims based on the terms of Confederation. In an effort to defuse the issue, Prime Minister King suggested to the British Columbia premier that those constitutional arguments might be referred to the Supreme Court. While not rejecting such a reference outright, Oliver made it clear that he was not anxious to adopt such a course, admitting that "With us the question at issue is not so much a legal question as one of equity and justice." Having essentially exhausted the regulatory process, representatives of British Columbia continued to press politicians for "equitable consideration" of their grievances, and looked for other opportunities to achieve their goals.[34]

Unlike their counterparts from British Columbia, business and political leaders from the Maritimes concentrated instead on lobbying the management and political masters of the government-owned Canadian National Railways. The reasons were simple. The Intercolonial and Prince Edward Island Railways, which had been operated directly by the Department of Railways and Canals following their construction in the 1870s, always had been exempt from the rulings of the Board of Railway Commissioners. It was 1923 before these lines were officially incorporated into the Canadian National system and placed under the authority of the regulatory agency. Furthermore, since the Maritimes had always been served by government-owned railways, community leaders were accustomed to pressuring both local management and political leaders for freight rate concessions.[35]

The incorporation of the Intercolonial and Prince Edward Island Railways into the Canadian National system, and a number of subsequent decisions by the new public railway managers aggravated and complicated Maritime freight rate grievances. Many local operations were moved out of the Maritimes, and an attempt was made to establish an eastern division of the national system that did not respect the territory once covered by the Intercolonial. As well, the new managers continued an unpopular policy of rate equalization that the Intercolonial's managers had begun prior to the war. While local merchandise tariffs traditionally were lower than in central Canada, in 1913 and 1915 rates on freight shipped less than 500 miles had been raised to the central Canadian level. In 1923, Canadian National managers completed the process by equalizing the rates on freight shipped over 500 miles within the Maritimes. Maritime leaders took their grievances directly to the politicians. Shortly after the equalization judgment in 1922, Nova Scotia's R.E. Finn met with Prime Minister King to present some of the Maritime grievances. Finn capitalized upon the government's decision to reinstate the Crow. While western producers were benefiting to the extent of $30 million, Finn argued, the Maritimes "were handicapped to a degree of almost industrial destruction." For the most part, the prime minister and his government proved unreceptive to such pleas.[36]

Maritime community leaders had more success when they took their grievances directly to Henry Thornton, who was appointed president of the Canadian National Railways system in 1922. Like any good railway manager, Thornton tried to appease the complainants without surrendering to their demands. He appointed a regional freight agent who had the support of Maritime community leaders, an appointment which the prime minister actively "encouraged." Canadian National officials reduced local tariffs on potatoes and grain, cut rates between Prince Edward Island and the mainland, and resolved a long-standing grievance by agreeing to charge the lower Saint John rate on grain exported through Halifax. Thornton also agreed to reduce the critical through rates between the Mari-

Table 15
Maritime Fifth-Class Freight Rates per 30,000 Lbs Shipped between Saint John
and Toronto, 1898 – 1927

	Westbound from Saint John	Eastbound to Saint John
September 1898 Intercolonial Direct Service to Montreal	$105	$105
May 1900	$96	$105
February 1908	$96	$96
December 1916 BRC Eastern Rates advance	$105	$105
March 1918 BRC advance	$120	$120
August 1918 Order-in-council advance	$150	$150
January 1921 BRC advance	$204	$204
December 1921 BRC reduction	$189	$189
April 1924 Canadian National voluntary concession	$174	$174
July 1927 Maritime Freight Rates Act	$156	$174

Sources: NA, Department of Railways and Canals, RG 43, vol. 372, file 6946, pt 162, Appendix 1.

times and western Ontario. As Table 15 indicates, this concession cut by about $15 the price of shipping a 30,000 lb carload of fifth-class merchandise between the regions, in the process restoring rates to a level somewhat higher than they had been after the 1918 rate advance.[37]

These concessions did not bring an end to Maritime grievances, any more than the concessions in the mountain scale and export grain rates ended the claims of British Columbia. Under pressure from business organizations, the governments of Nova Scotia, New Brunswick, and Prince Edward Island agreed to follow the example of other provinces and appoint a freight rate expert to represent their collective interests. While they did not immediately follow through with their promise, this action demonstrated their continued commitment to redressing regional rate grievances.[38] Like their counterparts in British Columbia, Maritime leaders organized and looked for opportunities to forward their demands. The renewal of the debate over the Crow's Nest Pass agreement in 1924 offered both Maritime and British Columbia leaders just such an opportunity.

The advocates of regional rate issues in the prairie west had a number of bargaining advantages over their counterparts in other regions. Although the Progressives were no longer the political force they had been in 1922, members of the Liberal government remained concerned about their ability to recapture their western supporters in the next election which was expected sometime in 1925.[39] Moreover, under the terms of the arrangement adopted in 1922, unless the government acted by 6 July 1924, the low rates on westbound commodities contained in the Crow agreement would come into effect automatically. Those reductions would provide western merchants with a competitive advantage over their eastern counterparts in distributing such goods as agricultural implements, binder twine, fruit, and various types of hardware. As consumers of these products, western farmers could see that the reinstatement of the Crow might produce lower prices. Community leaders in the prairie west could acquire these benefits simply by preventing the government from taking any action.

Because the rates would automatically be reinstated, railway officials had to take the offensive. On 15 May 1924, Thornton and Beatty sent a memorandum to the King government asking that "the Crow's Nest Act, as it relates to commodities other than grain and grain products, should be repealed and that the whole question of what are just and reasonable rates should be left to the Board of Railway Commissioners to determine." The railway executives adopted a different strategy than that taken in 1922: they indicated that the low Crow rates would be applied only to those points originally covered by the 1897 agreement, which would create serious distortions and disparities between commodities and between communities.[40]

The King government responded to the railway memo, and to pressures from other organizations, by convening a special hearing of the cabinet just over a week before the Crow rates would come into effect. In spite of the change of venue from the parliamentary committee of 1922, the arguments largely remained the same. H.J. Symington, appearing on behalf of all three prairie governments, promised that the reinstatement of the Crow rates would create traffic for the railways and produce general prosperity for the nation. Hurriedly organized delegations from British Columbia and the Maritimes appeared to ask the government not to allow the restoration of the Crow to affect their regional demands. It should not be the national policy of the government, one Maritime politician noted, to give the prairies "certain things by legal enactment, while we must take pot luck and go before the Railway Commission."[41]

In the end, the administration of Mackenzie King chose the path of least resistance and did nothing. By adopting this course, the prime minister tried to play both sides of the issue. To supporters of the Crow rates, the government presented itself as the opponent of the railway corporations and the champion of western interests. To those such as Premier John Oliver of British Columbia who opposed the restoration of the rates, the prime minister argued that, "The coming into full force of the Crow's Nest Pass Agreement was not a matter which it was within the power of Administration to control at this last session of Parliament." In his response to the complaints of Premier Oliver, however, King suggested that the government's decision was not just politically convenient, but also was strategic. He wrote:

It is practically certain that, as a consequence of the revival in toto of the Crow's Nest Pass Agreement, discriminations in rail rates will become increasingly apparent, not only as regards British Columbia, but as respects many parts of Canada. This cannot fail to bring the whole matter to the attention of the Railway Commission and of Parliament. As you may know, it sometimes requires a surgical operation to remedy an abnormal condition. It may well be that the restoration of the Crow's Nest Pass Agreement, under conditions as they have changed owing to and since the war, will prove the operation necessary to benefit the commercial and industrial structure of the entire Dominion.[42]

In sum, King contended, and genuinely may have believed, that as the problems associated with the restoration of the Crow became apparent, the Progressives would be blamed, and support for a more effective readjustment of the entire freight rate structure would grow. Just who King expected would be responsible for this adjustment, and how he thought it would be achieved, remained unclear.

By 6 July 1924, the eve of the restoration of the Crow agreement in its entirety, "equality of rates," had become not only the "shibboleth" of Prime Minister King's Liberal party but of business and political leaders in British Columbia, the prairie west, and the Maritimes. Representatives of each region rallied a variety of interests and organized a number of specific freight rate grievances around the policy of equalization. They did not seek equal freight rates, but equality of treatment.

The Board of Railway Commissioners resisted the idea that a regulatory agency should adjust rates to serve the particular geographical and productive needs of Canada's regions. They offered concessions on specific rate grievances, but refused to recognize the principle of "equalization" upon which the rate demands were based. Whether the board ever enjoyed the kind of prestige which would have allowed it to resolve these regional rate grievances, by the early 1920s it certainly lacked the image of an impartial arbiter that might have given its judgments some authority.

Regional interests readily turned from the commission to the government in order to settle their grievances. In the early 1920s, a number of avenues were open to those unhappy with the board's decisions. British Columbia leaders utilized the appeal process incorporated in the Railway Act, a process whose potential already had been proven in the appeal of the 1920 horizontal advance. Maritime interests directly pressured the government and the management of the publicly-owned Canadian National to consider their special industrial needs. For western merchants and farmers, the dominion government's 1897 agreement with the Canadian Pacific Railway provided the means for a direct appeal to Parliament on certain freight rate issues. The dependence of the Liberal government on western Progressive support provided the leverage to turn the uncertain status of the Crow's Nest Pass agreement into an extremely effective political weapon.

Representatives of each region first turned to the railway commission, and then used the "political" route to win further concessions, with considerable success. Advocates of lower Maritime rates had reduced the cost of shipping various goods to the prairie west, and within their own region. A long-standing grievance of the city of Halifax had finally been resolved. On behalf of British Columbia businesses, Premier John Oliver and Gerry McGeer won significant reductions in the mountain freight tariff and in the export rates on western grain shipped through Vancouver. The most significant achievement prior to 1924 was the 1922 western grain legislation. In establishing a special rate on eastbound grain "in the national interest," Parliament followed what several of the railway commissioners implied was the proper course. Politicians, not the regulators, accepted the responsibility for setting freight rates designed to promote economic development. Here again, as with the 25 per cent increase in 1918, was a glimmer of recognition that some rate questions raised such broad policy issues that they properly belonged in the political realm, and could not be treated as technical, administrative matters.

Once again, the idea failed to take hold. The rate controversy which began on 7 July 1924, when the railway companies introduced new tariffs based on the Crow's Nest Pass agreement, would demonstrate that some "political" intervention was far less damaging to the credibility of the regulatory system than was the politicians' willingness to avoid confronting vexing policy questions by constantly referring them back to their independent commission of "experts."

CHAPTER TEN

Regions of Regulation

On 7 July 1924, officials of the Canadian Pacific and Canadian National railways introduced tariffs consistent with their legal interpretation of the Crow's Nest Pass agreement. As they had warned, they applied the low commodity rates only from points in eastern Canada to points in western Canada that had been covered in the original agreement. The tariffs produced the intended effect – chaos. Manufacturers of agricultural implements, binder twine, paints, paper, and bar-iron in Brantford, Welland, Sarnia, Vancouver, Winnipeg, and Sydney continued to pay 1924 rates while their competitors in Hamilton and Montreal received reductions of as much as fifty cents per hundred pounds in the price of shipping their products to western markets. The limited application of the westbound Crow rates gave eastern wholesale houses a new competitive advantage over their counterparts in Winnipeg, and offered distributors in Calgary and Regina a chance to capture the territory of their rivals in Edmonton and Saskatoon. While the freight rate reductions might never have been translated into lower retail prices, the uncertainty created by the chaotic application of the Crow rates ensured that few, if any, of the savings were passed on to consumers.[1]

As a result of the disruption and confusion created by the railway companies' action on 7 July, the railway commission and government were deluged with complaints from both opponents and supporters of the Crow's Nest Pass rates. The chaotic situation provided an opportunity for another debate about the Crow agreement, as well as regional rate structures in general. All of the issues and problems surrounding the question of "equalization" resurfaced to confront the railway commissioners and the politicians to whom they were ultimately responsible.

Regional rate demands prompted a debate over the "regions" of regulation. While politicians continued to avoid the issue by leaving as much responsibility with the railway commission as possible, they did begin to direct the board towards certain broader policy goals. Faced with regional demands and political directives, the railway commissioners openly disagreed about their role in the rate-making process and about the legitimate boundaries of their jurisdiction. On the eve of the Great Depression, as the railway era drew to a close, commission regulation faced a serious crisis, and politicians became increasingly involved in resolving rate grievances. The controversies related to "equalization" revealed that at critical moments, the separation of "politics" and "administration" into autonomous regions of regulation could not be sustained.

The railway commission took the initiative in responding to the outcry over the restoration of the westbound Crow rates. Before it was able to begin its investigation, however, Chief Commissioner Carvell, who had served as such a lightning rod for regional discontent, died. The King government chose to overlook the obvious choice as Carvell's successor, Simon McLean. McLean, a commissioner since 1908 and assistant chief commissioner since 1918, was generally acknowledged as the freight rate expert on the board, but had two major liabilities – a central Canadian background, and an association with the unpopular decisions of Carvell's board. Instead, the King government selected H.A. McKeown, the chief justice of New Brunswick's King's Bench, who had earned the prime minister's respect for his handling of the investigation into the collapse of the Home Bank.[2] McKeown faced the unenviable task of rebuilding the railway commission's reputation while resolving a complex and explosive question – the proper place of the Crow's Nest Pass rates in the Canadian freight rate structure.

For seven days in late September, the Board of Railway Commissioners listened to arguments largely concerning their jurisdiction with respect to the Crow's Nest Pass agreement and the proper interpretation of the rates within the agreement. Counsel presented two rather stark alternatives. Representatives of the four western and three Maritime provincial governments, as well as the Canadian Manufacturers' Association, joined in asking the commission to maintain its historic position: to respect the low rates created by legislators, and to eliminate any discrimination that they produced. Although ideally they believed that the commission should construct a new rate structure that was fair and equitable to all parts of Canada, they also called for the immediate application of the Crow rates to all points in Canada.[3]

For their part, railway counsel warned of the ominous financial burden the restoration and extension of the Crow rates would impose on the Canadian Pacific and the struggling Canadian National systems. They argued that the commission's previous respect for the Crow rates had simply been based on the legal uncertainty surrounding them. The board must now resolve that uncertainty by asserting their unquestioned jurisdiction over all rates in Canada, returning the railway tariffs to the just and reasonable ones in existence prior to 7 July, and continuing to balance the needs of the railway industry and the shippers of Canada alike. And that is precisely what the railway commission did. Within weeks of the conclusion of the hearings, a majority of the board unravelled the tangle of legal arguments, and ruled that the Crow's Nest Pass agreement did not restrict its regulatory authority and that all tariffs in existence on 6 July should be restored within fifteen days.[4]

The new chief commissioner allowed a more experienced member of the commission, A.C. Boyce, to write the decision on behalf of four of the six members of the board. Boyce agreed with counsel for the railway companies that the original Crow's Nest Pass Subsidy Act simply authorized the Canadian Pacific and dominion government to enter into an agreement, and that the subsequent agreement was a rate contract just like others that the railway commission had set aside in the past. He also concluded that the legislation did not constitute what was known as a "Special Act," so that even if the agreement was read as part of the legislation, its terms did not override conflicting provisions in the Railway Act. Although the commissioner acknowledged that the board had treated the Crow agreement as if it did have some kind of special status, he observed that the commission had never heard all of the legal arguments before, nor given the matter the grave consideration now required by the "condition of chaos ... without any parallel in the history of freight rate making in Canada."[5]

Boyce's legal interpretation flowed from his perception of the proper role of the railway commission. As a result of the restoration of the Crow rates, he warned, "the general jurisdiction conferred upon the Board by the Railway Act is threatened with paralysis." To be effective, the commission must disregard any special legislation that interfered with the board's power to "fix, determine and enforce just and reasonable rates," including the 1922 statute that permanently reinstated Crow rates on grain. Although the actual order of the board would not affect the Crow grain rates (it declared all freight tariffs in existence on 6 July 1924 to be just and reasonable), Boyce concluded that the board had the right to alter them in the future. His decision challenged and precluded direct legislative interference with respect to freight rates.[6]

Not surprisingly, within a week of the judgment, the premiers of Alberta, Saskatchewan, and Manitoba, as well as a number of other interests, demanded the suspension of the board's order and prepared appeals to both the cabinet and the Supreme Court. The controversy came at a particularly awkward time for the dominion government. While Prime Minister King, on his first official tour of western Canada, was busily portraying the Liberals as the champions of western interests, his party, engaged in by-elections in British Columbia and Ontario, was fending off Conservative charges that the government had become a captive of prairie interests. The King administration sought to avoid offending anyone by asking the Supreme Court to expedite a hearing of the legal issues and by refusing to interfere with the board's order until the cabinet heard an appeal on the matter.[7]

Opponents of the board's decision told the cabinet that the unelected and unaccountable members of the railway commission had flagrantly disregarded the "expressed will and intention of Parliament." Whatever legal interpretation the Supreme Court might reach, they contended, the government was free to reassert parliamentary supremacy and responsible government by restoring the Crow rates and extending them throughout Canada without discrimination. "I am here on the basis that I understood what the policy of the government was," H.J. Symington concluded, "If I am wrong, then I am through."[8] Symington was wrong. From the outset, Prime Minister King had deliberately avoided dividing his own party and losing the support of the Progressive party by refusing to adopt any policy. While King had hoped that the rate chaos might eventually generate some kind of consensus, several stormy cabinet meetings following the hearing convinced him to continue procrastinating. On Christmas Day of 1924, the government overruled the order of the railway commission, but postponed any further readjustment of rates pending the Supreme Court's decision. By remaining silent on the question of discrimination, the King government simply restored chaos.[9]

Two months later, on 25 February 1925, the Supreme Court knocked the legal foundation out from under the railway commission's order. While recognizing "the wide character of the control over rates vested in the Board of Railway Commissioners," the court rejected Boyce's attempt to extend the commission's jurisdiction to "the authorization of tolls in excess of maxima which Parliament had seen, or should see, fit to fix by Special Acts," including the Crow's Nest Pass Act. At the same time, the court upheld the legality of the chaotic rate structure: the railway companies had interpreted their obligations correctly on 7 July, and were not legally obliged under either the Crow agreement or the Railway Act to extend the statutory rates throughout Canada. Under the existing law, Chief Justice Anglin concluded, neither the railway commission nor the court had the legal authority to bring to an end the resulting chaos – "the remedy lies with the High Court of Parliament."[10]

In spite of this clear call for action, the government of Mackenzie King did nothing for several months. Finally, on 5 June 1925, the government attempted to diffuse the Crow's Nest Pass and other regional rate grievances with Order-in-council PC 886. The government promised legislation that would more clearly define the Crow rates on grain in order to encourage "one of the chief assets of the Dominion." The other Crow rates on westbound commodities were cancelled. The government sought to appease western and other regional interests by directing the railway commission to undertake a comprehensive review of the rate structure "so as to permit of the freest possible interchange of commodities between the various provinces and territories of the Dominion and the expansion of its trade, both foreign and domestic, having due regard to the needs of its agricultural and other basic industries." The board was, in effect, asked to adopt the definition of rate equalization championed by advocates of regional issues. So as to assure British Columbia, Maritime, and other interests that they would not be forgotten, PC 886 specifically ordered the commission to consider the effect of increased traffic westward and eastward through Pacific Coast ports, to examine the claim that the Maritimes "are entitled to the restoration of the rate basis which they enjoyed prior to 1919," and to look at measures that would encourage the movement of traffic through Canadian ports.[11]

The government's attempt to diffuse the rate issue appears to have worked. Although the *Manitoba Free Press* described the cancellation of the westbound rates as "a complete defeat for the West," the King administration did not face the same barrage of protests from western business and farm organizations as it had just one year earlier. In spite of the fears of some western Liberals, the Crow debate did not help reunite the increasingly factious Progressive party.[12] The absence of serious opposition from the Progressives, a revival of the prairie economy, the promise of a general rate investigation, and, perhaps even as King had predicted, the chaotic rate situation of the previous year, permitted the government to do something it had not dared to do in 1922, 1923, or 1924 – cancel the westbound Crow rates.

The government, not the railway commission, ultimately determined the future of the Crow's Nest Pass agreement. The board did try to assert exclusive jurisdiction over rate regulation, even over western grain tariffs, in order to separate clearly the regulatory commission from the political realm. The provisions in the Railway Act requiring the board to respect special acts, and allowing for appeals to cabinet, provided the particular means to thwart the board's efforts. Even in the absence of these provisions, however, the independence of the regulatory commission would not have been assured. The Crow debate was not a technical debate over freight rates; it was an impassioned debate over the government's regional and industrial development policy. The railway commissioners could not prevent politicians from responding to these broad freight rate grievances any more than railway officials had been able to in the nineteenth century.

Had there been an open recognition on the part of both the commissioners and the politicians of the political nature of the decisions the board was being asked to make, the government might have at least been expected to offer the commission a clearer policy directive than PC 886. Since decisions were portrayed as technical and administrative, however, politicians could evade their responsibilities by using the vague and even contradictory language contained in the order-in-council. On the one hand, PC 886 simply reiterated the language of the Railway Act in calling for a "fair and reasonable rate structure," equal in its application to all persons and localities "under substantially similar circumstances and conditions." On the other hand, the government asked the commission to establish rates in accordance with the geographical and productive needs of regional industries – which the board consistently had ruled was beyond its jurisdiction under the very same Railway Act. The contradictory nature of PC 886 aggravated a growing controversy between members of the railway commission over their regulatory authority and responsibility.

Chief Commissioner McKeown ignited the smouldering controversy among his colleagues through his unusual handling of British Columbia's demand that grain rates from the prairies to the Pacific Coast should be based on the Crow rates. Shortly after his appointment to the board in the fall of 1924, McKeown travelled to Vancouver with Commissioner Frank Oliver and agreed to hear the issue again, just one year after the commission had rejected the claim. Frank Oliver, a former Liberal politician and owner of the *Edmonton Bulletin*, had become the champion of regional interests on the board. In 1923, Oliver ignored the fact that he had not been a member of the commission at the time it heard British Columbia's case, and authored a dissenting judgment in support of its claims with respect to westbound grain rates. He also indicated that he favoured the elimination of the mountain scale.[13] British Columbia's rate advocate, Gerry McGeer, clearly hoped to convince the new chief commissioner to adopt his colleague's opinions.

Railway officials protested McKeown's surprise decision to reopen the case, but to no avail. They then insisted that the entire railway commission should hear their response to the four days of testimony McGeer had orchestrated. The chief commissioner refused; he gave them three weeks to send their written arguments to the board. Although the debate over the future of the Crow rates delayed a formal decision, McKeown infuriated both railway officials and some of his colleagues by publicly endorsing British Columbia's position on westbound grain rates.[14]

In spite of McKeown's views, Premier John Oliver still pressed Prime Minister King to include a specific reference to westbound rates in the statutory grain legislation. King remained evasive, but promised that the statute would be interpreted in light of the government's policy on equalization, as set forth in PC 886. The prime minister did encourage the president of Canadian National, Henry Thornton, to base the public railway's grain rates to the Pacific Coast on the eastbound Crow rate. Thornton supported the lowering of the rates. He believed that the resulting increase in traffic would strain the Canadian Pacific's mountain facilities, at which point the Canadian National could allow the private railway to use its two mountain routes "on terms," the terms to include "good behaviour." Nevertheless, Thornton did not want to antagonize Canadian Pacific officials by voluntarily reducing the rates; he wanted the railway commission to order the change.[15] Thornton's refusal underlined the degree to which the independent status of the Canadian National, and the continued existence of a private competitor, limited the government's ability to use the public railway to achieve its regulatory objectives.

The prime minister was under considerable pressure to have the British Columbia grain rates adjusted before the harvest, and an anticipated fall election. When Thornton proved unresponsive, King turned to Chief Commissioner Mckeown. During several meetings,

McKeown assured the prime minister that he had already prepared a decision "which will settle matters." There was one problem. The three commissioners whose names were attached to the 1923 judgment, Assistant Chief Commissioner McLean and Commissioners Boyce and Calvin Lawrence, remained opposed to any further concessions. They saw nothing in the statutory grain legislation that affected their previous ruling, and argued that in any event, the westbound grain case could and should be considered only as part of the general rate investigation. With one vacancy on the commission, McKeown and Oliver were outnumbered.[16]

Pressed by King for a favourable decision, the chief commissioner adopted a course of action with grave consequences for the railway commission. On 2 September, following a meeting of the full board, McKeown and Frank Oliver signed Order 36769, which required the railways to apply the Crow rates on grain bound for the Pacific Coast for export. Because the order was signed by the chief commissioner and one of his colleagues, it constituted an official judgment of the board, even though it excluded and overruled the views of a majority of the commissioners. Within a day, Commissioner Boyce prepared an angry dissenting judgment. Boyce "refrained from commenting on the ethics involved," but nevertheless referred to "the deplorable celerity and secrecy with which the judgment and order of the minority of the Board were issued," and demanded that it be rescinded. The following day Commissioner Lawrence joined his voice to that of Boyce. McLean avoided an open confrontation for the moment.[17]

Order 36769 did not resolve the grain rate issue. Within a month, the railway commission convened in response to protests from the Canadian Pacific, a host of business organizations outside of Alberta and British Columbia, and the governments of Nova Scotia, New Brunswick, and Manitoba. Shippers who opposed the elimination of the mountain scale were alarmed by the precedent the decision set. Others feared the order would complicate the board's ability to respond to other regional rate grievances. The protests hardened the positions of the commissioners. McKeown and Oliver stood by their decision; McLean, Boyce, and Lawrence wanted to cancel the new rates as soon as possible. The final determination of the matter rested with Thomas Vien, who became deputy chief commissioner of the board on 5 September, in the midst of the crisis. Not surprisingly, the prime minister's new appointment intended to side with McKeown and Oliver. When the other three commissioners threatened to announce publicly that "politics" had influenced the judgment, however, Vien sought a less embarrassing compromise. Claiming that he needed to familiarize himself with the case, Vien stalled until mid-December, after the dominion election and after the lower rates had been in place for the major part of the shipping season. His tactic worked. By December, Commissioners Boyce and Lawrence were unwilling to see "innocent parties" suffer, or traffic moving under the rates "impeded or embarrassed." They agreed that the new rates should stand, so long as Vien, Oliver, and McKeown agreed to reopen the issue during the board's general rate inquiry. Vien confidently and, as it turned out, correctly predicted to Mackenzie King that the new rates would not be altered as a result of the general investigation.[18] Table 14 shows how the decision and its subsequent adjustment in the general investigation significantly strengthened the competitive freight rate position of the port of Vancouver.

The compromise barely papered over the cracks in the railway commission. Although Boyce agreed not to change the rates, he refused to join Vien in upholding McKeown and Oliver's actions. He and McLean wrote separate judgments, in which they both described various irregularities in the decision-making process, including the failure to give due notice to all parties of the original November 1924 hearing, and the failure to hold any hearing to consider the impact of the 1925 grain legislation on the grain rates. In a thinly veiled reference to political interference, Boyce angrily observed that "There were, apparently, in his [the Chief Commissioner's] opinion, more pressing exigencies to be respected than the contention that the rights of property were being dealt with by him, as was contended, without due notice or process of law, and in the face of protest from the majority of the Board, he signed the order in question."[19]

The conflict on the railway commission involved more than a disagreement over regulatory procedure. Both McLean and Boyce attacked an identical section of the chief commissioner's September judgment. McKeown had argued that "The different sections of the country must be enabled to trade, to ship, to carry on business, and a series of schedules must be elaborated which will not fetter the country's industrial activity, but under which it can breathe and flourish." The board, McLean contended, did not have the authority to assist business by reducing freight rates. Boyce expressed considerable dismay that the chief commissioner should "try to exhume and galvanize into life and apparently set up as sound, a contention ... so emphatically rejected by this and other rate regulating tribunals as palpably unsound and inequitable."[20]

On the eve of the general investigation of the Canadian rate structure, the debate concerning westbound grain rates revealed ominous divisions of opinion among members of the board. McKeown's handling of the case raised serious questions about his credibility as chairman of the railway commission, and about the separation of the board's decision-making process from the formulation of government policy. The problem was not simply one of leadership or political interference, however, for the disagreement over the westbound grain rates revealed divergent visions over the legitimate powers of the regulatory agency. In the general rate investigation, the railway commissioners continued to debate the extent to which they might fix rates in order to encourage economic development.

One railway official observed that "Gabriel's horn was a poor instrument ... for raising dead ones" compared to the announcement of a general inquiry into the Canadian rate structure. Shippers all across Canada saw in the language of PC 886 and in the regulatory views expressed by the chief commissioner an opportunity to revive claims that the board had considered and rejected in the past. By the time the commissioners completed a tour from Saint John to Prince Rupert in the spring of 1926, they had been swamped by eighty separate submissions from representatives of individual industries, trade organizations, and provincial governments. Although the board tried to respond to all of the individual grievances they heard, they identified and paid considerable attention to nine major "regional" rate questions.

All of the issues had a familiar ring to them. The Maritime Transportation Rights Committee organized by the three provincial governments asked the commission to restore the relatively low local freight tariffs and eastbound rates from their region to the rest of Canada that had been enjoyed at some point in the past. British Columbia's Gerry McGeer tried to persuade the board to sustain the controversial westbound grain rate order, and to take the next logical step by eliminating the high mountain freight tariff on all goods. Both the Maritime committee and McGeer also supported the application of Quebec City's business and political leaders, who asked the board to alter a previous adverse ruling and reduce the rate on grain carried over the National Transcontinental portion of the Canadian National system from the west to their city, and possibly to Saint John and Halifax.[21]

The three lawyers representing each of the prairie western governments added four more issues to the commission's agenda. They all sought a broader and more generous interpretation of the statutory grain legislation than was reflected in the tariffs the railway companies had introduced. In addition, each lawyer addressed the question of "equalization." In view of the higher earning power of western over eastern traffic, they contended that the board should reduce the rates on commodities of particular importance to the west, particularly livestock, dairy products, and a number of items that had been part of the original Crow agreement. "Equalization," however, no longer provided an issue of sufficient importance to submerge the diverse interests of western communities. Alberta's representative reintroduced the issue of extending to Calgary and Edmonton the same low transcontinental rates that were offered on goods shipped from eastern Canada to Vancouver. He also joined with counsel for Saskatchewan in attacking one of the few remaining rate advantages enjoyed by the Winnipeg's business community – the low mileage rate applied between Fort William and Winnipeg.[22]

Because all of these issues had been considered previously by the railway commission, most of the lawyers found some way of bringing their request within the language of PC 886. Each region's representative argued that the specific reductions they requested would promote the "freest possible interchange of commodities" between the regions of Canada, or encourage the routing of traffic through Canadian ports. In spite of fifty-three days of testimony by railway officials and other experts, the introduction of 200 statistical exhibits, and a further twenty days of final legal arguments, the resolution of the majority of the issues hinged on an interpretation of the railway commission's mandate and jurisdiction. The various advocates of regional interests contended that PC 886 represented, in Gerry McGeer's words, "a direction for a new national policy." It was argued that the government had ordered the board, in clear and specific language, to consider issues of "semi-public policy" in determining the reasonableness of regional rates. Its normal regulatory mandate had been enlarged for the purposes of this enquiry "to embrace the field of trade development generally for the Dominion." In short, an unsympathetic Assistant Chief Commissioner McLean concluded, "we should become an all round fairy godmother."[23]

During the various discussions of the effect of PC 886, McLean and several of his colleagues insisted that the Railway Act circumscribed their jurisdiction. "There is one way to amend the Railway Act," McLean remarked, "and that is not by Order-in-Council."[24] The special legislative consideration received by one set of regional demands seemed to confirm that view. Maritime business and political leaders doubted that the railway commission would consider their claim that governments had maintained relatively low rates on the Intercolonial Railway prior to World War I in fulfilment of pledges made at the time of Confederation. In pressing for direct government intervention, Maritime leaders could point to two precedents: the formal exemption of the Intercolonial Railway from the jurisdiction of the railway commission prior to 1923, and the statutory recognition of special regional freight rate problems reflected in the government's 1925 grain rate legislation.[25]

The defeat of all but six of twenty-nine Liberal candidates in the Maritimes during the dominion election of October 1925 brought the region's grievances forcefully to the attention of Prime Minister King. As his second minority Liberal government clung to power, King appointed Sir Andrew Duncan, a British official who had just completed an investigation of the coal-mining industry for the Nova Scotia government, to head up a Royal Commission on Maritime Claims. Regional freight rate policy represented one of the leading issues considered by the commission. Shippers and their political representatives concentrated on three main issues: the restoration of rates that were lower westbound to Montreal and points beyond than eastbound, the reduction of local tariffs, and the fixing of rates that would encourage the routing of traffic through Maritime ports. In its report, the Duncan commission cited with approval the historic and geographic arguments that supported these demands.[26]

The solution to the rate problem recommended to and largely adopted by the King government involved statutory recognition of the particular developmental needs of the three eastern provinces. Citing evidence that rates in the Maritimes had been increased more than those in any other region since the opening decade of the century, it was determined that local tariffs and westbound rates on the Canadian National should be reduced 20 per cent. The rates were not fixed permanently but were to provide the basis for any subsequent adjustment by the railway commission in relation to increases or reductions in the cost of operation, or "as new industrial conditions arise." Perhaps most significantly, as Table 15 illustrates, the new rates on goods shipped from the Maritimes to central Canada were lower than those goods shipped from central Canada to the Maritimes. Advocates of Maritime rights had argued that this differential in rates, which had been part of the Intercolonial rate structure at various points in its history prior to 1908, had enabled Maritime businesses to survive by giving them access to the large central Canadian market while at the same time protecting them from competition in their own markets. The legislation provided that the Canadian National, and any competitor that voluntarily chose to reduce its rates, would be reimbursed through a direct government subsidy for any resulting losses in revenues. The idea of offering financial compensation for rates fixed "where national welfare demands" had been bandied about for some time and approved by the president of the Canadian National system.[27] The idea, and the resulting legislation, offered a new twist to the old nineteenth-century regulatory strategy of exchanging public assistance for rate concessions.

The King government ignored another set of recommendations contained in the Duncan report that reflected the controversy on the railway commission. As a result of an extensive interview with Chief Commissioner McKeown, the Duncan commission had recommended changes in the Railway Act to clarify and extend the authority of the railway commission so that there might be "a responsible review" of railway rate policy "in its relation to the natural basic products of the country, and the development of these products and associated enterprises." In particular, the Act should be amended so that "if from public policy they [the railway commissioners] felt that an experimental rate should be conceded, they should be free to constitute that rate, even although it might not, at the time, or of itself, give reasonable compensation to the railway company."[28] Chief Commissioner McKeown undoubtedly sought these amendments to break the stalemate on the railway commission, for the changes would have helped support those members of the board, such as himself and Oliver, who sought a more vigorous role for the regulators.

With no further direction of this kind from the government, the railway commission remained, according to Canadian Pacific president Edward Beatty, "hopelessly divided." Beatty warned Prime Minister King that the government would be seriously embarrassed if "this condition of stalemate" continued. King urged the members of the board to compromise their divergent views.[29] Whether as a result of King's minor intervention or whether, as is more likely, out of a sense of institutional and personal self-preservation, the members of the board did manage to cobble together a compromise.

Not all of the issues before the board produced serious divisions. For example, the commissioners were agreed on refusals to adjust the terminal rates between Fort William and Winnipeg, to apply the competitive transcontinental rates to Alberta points, or to make any other adjustments or reductions in western freight tariffs, with the exception of those relating to grain. They took issue with part of the way the railway companies had interpreted the statutory grain legislation, and ordered the rates extended to branch lines and to all of the Canadian National's western lines. Only Commissioner

Oliver supported an even more liberal interpretation of the legislation proposed by western interests, which would have altered quite
dramatically the traditional method for constructing grain rates.[30]
But difficulties did arise between them over Quebec City's application for a reduced rate on grain.

The intense disagreement engendered by this submission threatened to produce an even division of the commission. McKeown, Vien
and Oliver all applauded this "thoroughly Canadian policy" that
promised to reroute a portion of the large volume of Canadian grain
currently being carried over American routes to the Atlantic seaboard. On the other hand, McLean, Boyce, and Lawrence regarded
the application as a dangerous attempt to have the board go beyond
its proper jurisdiction and order "pioneer" rates in the hope of stimulating traffic. Commissioner Boyce broke the deadlock. Although
he rejected all of the arguments in support of this "drastic" rate
reduction, although he did not believe PC 886 expanded the board's
jurisdiction, and although he was not even convinced that the change
would produce the benefits its advocates expected, he nevertheless
felt "constrained to accept" the application, "though with some mis-
givings." Commissioner Lawrence, whose absence from much of the
general investigation had provoked considerable controversy, followed Boyce's lead, "though with a great deal of hesitation." Both
commissioners insisted that the special export rate be limited to
Quebec City only, and not extended either to Saint John or Halifax.[31]

Boyce evidently found compelling the political support for the
reduction, indirectly expressed not only in PC 886 but in a subsequent
order-in-council as well. He may also have been thinking about his
own career: he was already seeking reappointment to the board as
his first term drew to a close.[32] Deputy Commissioner Thomas Vien,
a former Quebec City politician, may have been instrumental in
getting Boyce to compromise. In spite of his enthusiastic support
for the rate reduction, Vien refused to extend it to Saint John and
Halifax, albeit on the technical ground that all Maritime applications
had been withdrawn after the passage of the Maritime Freight Rates
Act. In addition, Vien may have agreed to alter or moderate his
position on the two other main subjects facing the commission –
British Columbia grain rates and the mountain scale – in exchange
for Boyce's and Lawrence's movement on the Quebec City issue.
While the deputy chief commissioner continued to uphold the con-
troversial grain order, he rejected the position of McKeown and
Oliver who argued that the railway companies had not complied
with the order and reduced the rates as much as had been intended.
On this basis, McLean and Lawrence reluctantly agreed to uphold

the original order.[33] Vien also sided with McLean, Boyce, and Lawrence over the mountain scale. The four commissioners refused to join Chief Commissioner McKeown in ordering the elimination of the mountain scale. In spite of the fact that McKeown went to considerable trouble to base his conclusions on a conventional assessment of the operating results in the mountain section rather than on his more controversial views of the board's regulatory authority, Boyce and McLean found his statistical analysis unconvincing.[34]

In the general rate inquiry, the railway commissioners did avoid the kind of embarrassing and confusing division that had resulted from the controversial grain decision, but the fact that each commissioner authored a separate judgment in the inquiry was more indicative of the state of the board. The language and arguments used in support of the final conclusions revealed radically divergent views over the nature and role of regulation. In his judgment, Chief Commissioner McKeown reproduced the very comments from his controversial grain decision that Boyce and McLean already had contemptuously dismissed. McKeown agreed with his colleagues that the board must consider the financial requirements of the railway industry, but that the needs of industry and commerce should be the first priority of the board. In any event, both he, Oliver, and to some extent Vien noted that railway officials did not always recognize their own best interests: the previous reduction in grain rates had promoted traffic through Vancouver without impairing railway revenues. They saw no reason why the railway commission should not play a more active role in setting the rate policies of the railway companies. McLean and Boyce defended the board's traditional regulatory role. Throughout their judgments, they constantly returned to the principle "that the Board's functions do not extend to the removal, by adjustment of freight rates, of the natural geographic disadvantages which, in a country of such enormous extent and widely covered area, must naturally exist."[35]

The commitment of McLean and Boyce to this latter principle rested on two different, but easily confused, beliefs about the separation of public and private, and political and administrative, spheres. In their view, railway freight officials were in the best position to decide what kinds of rates would best develop the industries and communities they served; governments and their agencies only should supervise those decisions to make sure that they did not create unjust discriminations or result in excessive rates being charged to some shippers. Once public authorities started to set aside rates that were neither unreasonable nor discriminatory, in an attempt to achieve some other objective, the fine line between rate-regulating and rate-making had been crossed. This view could circumscribe the degree of control that all public authorities, including Parliament, should exercise over railway companies. Boyce's attempt to assert the board's exclusive jurisdiction over rate regulation during the Crow debate and the strict interpretation he and other commissioners offered of the 1922 and 1925 grain rate legislation reflected a general suspicion of direct interference in the rate-making process. The separation of the making and regulating of rates could, and on occasion did, serve a different purpose – to mark the boundaries between politics and administration. In this view, the railway commission's political masters could join private officials in making rates; administrators should prevent undue discrimination, excessive rates, and enforce any rates fixed by legislators. These definitions widened the scope of legitimate public intervention by the legislature, while sustaining the notion that the railway commission did not engage in policy-making.

Regional rate issues prompted a serious controversy over the legitimate regions of the railway commission's regulatory authority during the 1920s. Whatever consensus on the nature of regulation existed on the commission broke down amidst efforts by members of the board to shake the image of the commission as a captive client of the railway companies, and in the face of persistent pressure from regional interests and confusing signals from the commission's political masters. The statutory grain legislation, the machinations behind the westbound grain order, the Maritime Freight Rates Act, and PC 886 obscured the boundaries between politics and administration, and contributed to a debilitating conflict on the railway commission.

Given the divided views of the commissioners on many of the issues, it is not surprising that a number of interests appealed various aspects of the decision. Canadian National officials reserved the right to appeal the question of grain rates to Quebec City to the Supreme Court. Maritime interests asked that those lower grain rates be extended to Halifax and Saint John, and disputed the interpretation the railways gave to the Maritime rate legislation. Representatives of the provinces of Saskatchewan, Alberta, and British Columbia took to cabinet the various issues of interest to their province. Neither the commission, the Supreme Court, or the cabinet supported any of these efforts to extend or alter the decision that had been patched together in 1927.[36]

The last of these appeals was denied in 1933. By that time, the government, railway officials, and shippers were all grappling with a serious financial and industrial crisis. The Depression marked the conclusion of the age of the railway. Even as the regional freight rate controversies of the 1920s raged, a new form of overland transportation was coming into use that was to rival railway shipping capabilities in many areas – the motor truck. This new competitor and the serious financial crisis facing the Canadian National Railways system created new challenges. The Duff Royal Commission on Transportation of 1931, the Canadian Pacific-Canadian National Act of 1933, and the reorganization of the Board of Railway Commissioners into a Board of Transport Commissioners in 1937 reflected a new policy orientation, looking to the co-ordination as much as to the regulation of the transportation network.[37] Freight rate grievances would resurface, but within a dramatically different context.

The railway commission survived the debacle of the 1920s and the railway age, but not without suffering a considerable loss of authority and prestige. The attempt to define all freight rate conflicts as administrative problems proved futile, and undermined the railway commission's quest for legitimacy. Regulation by independent commission had not failed; politicians and commissioners simply had been forced to acknowledge, however reluctantly, the limits of regulation.

CHAPTER ELEVEN

Conclusion: The Limits of Regulation

"Wherever a railway breaks in upon the gloom of a depressed and secluded district," the promoter-engineer T.C. Keefer told a Montreal audience in 1853, "new life and vigour are infused into the native torpor – the long desired market is obtained – labour now reaps her own reward – the hitherto useless waterfall now turns the labouring wheel, now drives the merrier spindle, the cold and hungry are now nourished; and thus are made susceptible converts to a system the value of which they are not slow to appreciate." Bold prophecies of industrial progress and social order accompanied the coming of the steam locomotive in the nineteenth century.[1]

Canadians clung to the belief that the railway possessed the power to fulfill these prophecies. The exercise of such power by private railway corporations, however, was viewed with increasing suspicion and concern. The close ties between governments and railways offered merchants, manufacturers, and farmers a number of opportunities to reconcile private corporate behaviour with their own social and economic ambitions. Between 1850 and 1930, these business leaders tied the railway industry ever closer to government by convincing politicians to sponsor competitive rail lines, enter into contractual arrangements, create a special administrative agency, and fix freight rates by statute. In each of the ensuing regulatory struggles, community leaders, railway managers, politicians, and government officials encountered and then sought to re-define the limits of public and private power.

Those community leaders who challenged the railway rate-making process were themselves active participants in the market economy and did not readily abandon it. They reasoned that their grievances were a result of the monopoly of power enjoyed by railway corporations, a monopoly which was a product of an underdeveloped transportation network. They therefore used their influence with local governments to enhance competition and to promote financially the construction of competing rail lines. In this way, they transformed the most common and acceptable form of government activity in the nineteenth century – direct promotion of economic development – into a form of regulation.

Promoters of new and independent railways eagerly promised to provide communities with the benefits that would result from competition. Nevertheless, these same entrepreneurs were often subsequently tempted to abandon the independence of their railways in exchange for the immediate financial rewards or greater security offered by amalgamations with larger, established companies. In response, local governments began to offer their financial resources conditionally: railway entrepreneurs had to agree to remain independent and to adopt specific freight rate policies in exchange for public assistance. This regulatory strategy as it evolved at the local level provided the model for subsequent provincial and national initiatives. Both the Manitoba and dominion governments negotiated rate concessions with the Canadian Northern and Canadian Pacific railways in exchange for public subsidies that were critically important to those railways. Through such contractual agreements, government promotion of railways acquired a finer regulatory edge.

In spite of the longer term significance of the Manitoba and Crow's Nest Pass agreements, the market-based regulatory strategy of competition and contract proved limited in its effectiveness. While railway entrepreneurs might require public assistance, those governments providing the support also urgently needed the railways. Because of the importance of these projects to the development of broader government policies and to the overall health of the economy, railway promoters came to enjoy considerable influence and bargaining leverage with political leaders. Executives of major railways convinced the provincial and dominion governments to override local contracts in the wider regional or national interest, and when negotiating were often successful in exchanging minimal rate concessions for substantial public subsidies. Nor were the courts willing to enforce or respect local regulatory contracts. In the absence of strong legislative signals, and in the face of frequently vague contractual language, judges preferred to respect the rights of property and to protect the investments of shareholders rather than provide local communities with the uncertain benefits railway competition offered.

When shipping communities became dissatisfied with these initiatives, the market offered alternative regulatory solutions. Railway corporations tried to accommodate freight rate grievances by creating their own private forum for resolving disputes. Their self-regulating body, the Canadian Freight Association, expanded its range of concerns in the 1890s to include the setting of freight rates. While shippers could use this vehicle to air their complaints and request rate adjustments, they could not appeal the decisions of railway freight officials, who sat as judge, jury, and defendants. Railway officials had their own objectives; they were anxious to co-operate with one another in an effort to eliminate many special rates.

The courts represented another potential arena for resolving conflicts between railways and their clients. The earliest railway laws adopted in Canada, strongly influenced by the common and statutory law of England, outlawed discriminatory freight rates. However, English courts had sanctioned a wide range of rate practices as non-discriminatory, and those rulings were confirmed in an 1871 Canadian judgment (*Scott* v. *Midland Railway*). Furthermore, aggrieved shippers could not use the courts to present their collective grievances. The individual costs of mounting a legal challenge to the railways, both financially and in terms of continuing good business relations with railway officials, outweighed the benefits a single firm might acquire from a successful ruling on a particular business transaction.

Merchants, manufacturers, and farmers thus found that competition, contracts, railway self-regulation, and the existing legal system did not allow them to assert effective control over private rate-making. While these regulatory instruments were never fully abandoned, from the 1880s onward various business communities called for the creation of a new public agency – a railway commission. They appeared to have in mind some government institution less like the formal courts and more like the private boards of arbitration which business leaders often established to resolve disputes within their own communities. However, most shippers thought little about the specific nature of the institution; they simply turned to any new means of resolving freight rate disputes.

Railway officials saw few advantages in government regulation. They resisted efforts to enhance public control, first by directly opposing the proposal to create a railway commission and subsequently by seeking to restrict the powers such a tribunal would enjoy. In the 1880s, they used their influence with both the dominion government and with larger shippers to deflect the commission proposal: successfully, it would appear, since the government chose instead to enhance the powers of an existing cabinet committee, the Railway Committee of the Privy Council, rather than create a railway commission. However, railway officials never managed to eradicate completely from the political agenda the proposal for a regulatory commission. By the early 1900s, they recognized that the demand for the commission was too widespread for the government to ignore, and therefore concentrated on weakening the powers that the new institution would exercise. In this they failed, in spite of the economic importance of their industry and their favourable access to the legislative process. In the case of the Board of Railway Commissioners, the regulated industry definitely did not succeed in sponsoring or designing the law in its own interest.

The passage of the Railway Act of 1903 demonstrated the shifting influence of the railway corporations and their clients within the Canadian political system. Throughout much of the nineteenth century, disparate and locally based groups of shippers confronted a relatively concentrated and nationally organized railway industry. In response to increased competition, the tariff issue, and labour unionization drives, business communities began to develop more coherent organizations to represent their interests, although they remained quite regionally fragmented. The railway commission proposal represented one issue around which these organizations could rally support, and their lobbying did play a role in the passage of the 1903 legislation. While corporate influence remained significant, the general prosperity at the turn of the century made the large railway corporations appear less economically vulnerable to governments. A railway commission seemed less likely to provoke a flight of capital from the Canadian economy – with unpleasant political repercussions – than it had in the 1880s. Just as significantly, the opposition that the railways mounted to the 1903 legislation was constrained by their own interest in acquiring other financial favours from the government of far more significance to their transcontinental corporate strategies.

Neither shipping organizations nor railway managers designed the legislation that created the Board of Railway Commissioners; government officials designed the legislation. Those studies that analyse the origins of regulation and that focus only on the effective organization of interest-group pressures or the vote-getting behaviour of politicians as a means of achieving regulation overlook other potentially important influences on the specific policy that is adopted. The "relative autonomy" of state officials from interest-group pressures is extremely important in understanding the creation of the Board of Railway Commissioners. The regulatory experience of Railways Minister A.G. Blair and the ideas of a Progressive intellectual, Simon McLean, shaped the precise nature of the railway commission created by Parliament in 1903.[2]

McLean's Progressive conception of expertise and of "administration" as a unique governing function ensured that the railway commission would not be just a special court, as D'Alton McCarthy had conceived of it in the 1880s. The commission received wide powers of investigation and broad discretion that would make possible compromise and arbitration, rather than just adjudication. McLean, who was familiar with the problems facing the United States and English railway commissions, also took steps to protect the new regulatory agency from judicial interference. He found a receptive audience in Railways Minister Blair. Blair understood, and had been frustrated by, the limited impact of legal restrictions on railway behaviour. He resisted the efforts of railway officials to restrict the jurisdiction of the new regulatory agency. Thus, the extensive powers and general mandate granted to the Board of Railway Commissioners in 1903 represented a deliberate policy choice, one intended to protect the agency from crippling legal challenges and to ensure flexibility in resolving freight rate grievances.

The Railway Act of 1903 effectively redefined the limits of public and private power. The Act established a special tribunal that would be able to provide relatively constant supervision of railway rate-making practices, and that therefore would be in a far better position to enforce legal requirements with respect to discriminatory and reasonable rates. Moreover, Parliament granted the regulatory agency a very wide discretion to determine how, when, and for what reasons it should interfere with and readjust privately-set freight rates. The Railway Act not only created a new means of regulation, it also enlarged the sphere of public authority with respect to the railway companies' rate-making prerogative.

Once the Board of Railway Commissioners was established, it had a dynamic impact on the interest groups with a stake in its operation. The Canadian Freight Association developed close ties with the board and its staff. Individual railway companies appointed freight officers, statisticians, and lawyers to specialize in appearing at commission hearings. The impact on shipping organizations was even more dramatic. The Canadian Manufacturers' Association, the Dominion Millers' Association, the larger municipal boards of trade and other organizations hired transportation experts, usually former clerks in railway freight offices, to represent their interests before the board on a regular basis. Business leaders in British Columbia, the prairies, and later the Maritimes convinced their provincial governments to pay lawyers and transportation experts to represent their interests. The board proved to be an important impetus for the further organization of business communities throughout Canada, and the creation of policy-oriented business-government networks.[3]

Business leaders, represented through their individual firms, organizations, or governments, applied for commission rulings that would improve their competitive position vis-à-vis other shippers. As often as not, allegations of discrimination or unreasonable rates pitted shippers against other shippers, not against the railways. The interests of aggrieved business communities varied with their particular geographic and market position, so that no single regulatory objective or orientation emerged. Some shippers wanted rates fixed in relation to distance, others in relation to market competition, and still others in relation to costs of operation. The railway commissioners found themselves asked to balance the conflicting demands of many different competing shipping interests.

For their part, railway officials intervened in disputes between shippers over the relative level of rates when the settlement of the issue threatened to produce serious revenue losses. They also sought to protect, as far as possible, their private discretionary authority in the rate-making process. In addition to these defensive goals, railway officials saw a positive use for the new regulatory regime. They attempted to use the greater enforcement of the laws against discrimination to eliminate a number of special rate arrangements into which they had been forced by competition.

The regulatory objectives of shippers and railway officials changed with time. The railway companies, in response to the spiralling costs and acute financial crisis produced by World War I became increasingly active in seeking positive action from the Board of Railway Commissioners. Specifically, they asked the commissioners to help generate revenues for their seriously troubled industry by approving rate increases. Shipping organizations became more defensive as cases focused, not on rate disparities, but on the general level and profitability of the overall rate structure. No common position emerged among shippers. While all agreed that the railways were facing a serious crisis, business organizations disagreed amongst themselves as to whether rate advances were the appropriate means to resolve that crisis.

The regulatory problems posed during the war soon gave way to traditional questions. During the 1920s, the relative level of rates between shippers and regions again became the central issue. Various business communities contested the freight rates enjoyed by their competitors and sought to have the board readjust the structure, under the broad banner of regional "equalization." Mercantile, industrial, and agricultural interests were organized and represented more vigorously by provincial governments, who made freight rate adjustments part of a broader campaign against regional disparities. The railway corporations returned to the defensive, and, more sensitive to costs than prior to the war, took an even more active role in protecting their revenues from major rate readjustments.

Regulation, it has been argued, represents the effort of private groups to manipulate public power in their own interest. Few of the railway commissioners would have disagreed. "From this side of the bench there is a strong family resemblance among all the applicants," Commissioner Rutherford remarked at the conclusion of one of the general rate investigations, "They are all more or less selfish – generally more."[4] The popular and still-widely accepted theory of interest-group "capture" of regulatory agencies, however, does not necessarily follow from such an argument. Neither shippers nor railways could dominate the Board of Railway Commissioners because both groups were effectively organized and influential, and had a substantial interest in the outcome of the board's decisions. Moreover, for most of the period 1904 to 1930, regulation largely involved the resolution of trade disputes between shippers. When freight rates were at issue, railway corporations were not the only industry being regulated.

The conflicts between increasingly organized and sophisticated interest groups, then, provided the regulatory agenda. Faced with disparate and conflicting interests, the Board of Railway Commissioners enjoyed a considerable degree of autonomy in reaching decisions. The board had its own objective – institutional survival. The commissioners had to resolve freight rate disputes without seriously alienating either the railway industry or various groups within the shipping community. Without the co-operation and support of those interests, the board would be neither an effective nor accepted agency. The commissioners therefore engaged in a quest for legitimacy, a quest that involved both substantive and procedural issues.

Parliament delegated the regulation of freight rates to an independent regulatory agency ostensibly to permit the resolution of grievances through the application of scientific expertise to these technical problems. However, the commission eschewed any fixed, scientific system of linking the price and cost of transportation services, as its response to Muller's proposals in the western rate inquiry clearly demonstrated. Instead, the legitimacy of the commissioners rested on their ability to act as good arbitrators. The commissioners actively encouraged and facilitated privately negotiated settlements. Failing this, they presided over relatively informal hearings in which interested parties were encouraged to participate fully. In reaching their decisions, they avoided producing clear losers who might challenge or make the enforcement of their orders difficult. Compromise was as much a part of their decisions as it was of their procedures. These compromises were based on existing business conditions. Quite early in its existence, the board enunciated the regulatory principle that freight rates which shippers had enjoyed for some time were to be considered just and reasonable. The onus of proof would be placed on those who sought change, whether it was railway officials applying to cancel old special arrangements, or shippers challenging the rates enjoyed by competitors. The commissioners left a fair degree of discretion with private railway officials, sanctioning their right to meet, or not to meet, water carrier and American railway competition, as well as the competition of markets. The board hoped to escape serious confrontations with its clients, railways and shippers alike, by protecting the established patterns of trade and investment that had grown up around the rate structure, and by continuing to allow market forces to play a role in rate-making.

The board's "expertise" and authority rested on its ability to concentrate on mediating freight rate disputes. Some cases, however, proved less susceptible to this regulatory strategy. The railway crisis of World War I raised different types of questions, largely unanticipated when the board was created. The mediation approach had been designed to deal with matters of discrimination, not the kinds of general rate increases the railway corporations sought between 1914 and 1920. These cases raised broad questions over the relative impact of increases on shippers, and of the proper distribution of increasing railway costs between shippers and railways.

Faced with such important questions, and in an attempt to maintain its own legitimacy, the railway commission moved cautiously. Railway officials soon chafed at the lengthy hearings and investigations to which their applications were subjected. They sought to circumvent the process, turning to the ultimate power the government enjoyed with respect to freight rates. In 1918, the government used the war emergency as the pretense for becoming directly involved in regulation, granting the railway corporations a 25 per cent advance. To minimize its involvement, the government relied on the expertise of the railway commission to develop the precise details of the increase. This joint approach to an extraordinary regulatory demand was abandoned in 1920, when the railways sought an even more dramatic rate increase. Instead, the railway commission reasserted its exclusive authority over rate questions and granted the railways a 40 per cent increase after a very cursory hearing and investigation. In this second case, the railway commission seriously undermined the legitimacy as a neutral arbitrator it had worked so hard to acquire.

Like applications for rate increases, regional rate grievances involved broader questions of policy than did many of the other freight conflicts with which the board dealt. The extensive western rate inquiry undertaken prior to the war, and the various concessions granted by the railway commission, avoided many of the fundamental policy questions associated with regional economic development. When regional grievances resurfaced following the war, the railway commission had lost much of the legitimacy that would have made its response to such issues acceptable.

The railway commissioners adopted a contradictory approach to the renewed regional grievances. A number of the commissioners began to take a much harder line on the broader questions of regulatory principle raised in the cases. They believed that the resolution of a number of the regional rate grievances might involve them, improperly, in matters of "semi-public" policy. They quite rightly sought to define the limits of their regulatory authority. At the same time, however, they continued to offer various kinds of rate concessions to regional interests, which only led to pressures for further concessions. Furthermore, many of these same commissioners stubbornly insisted on asserting the board's exclusive jurisdiction with respect to rate regulation, denying the right of the government to fix rates in accordance with public policy. They confused legitimate questions of regulatory jurisdiction with their disapproval of rate making by elected politicians.

Railway officials and various politicians actively encouraged the board to assert its exclusive jurisdiction over rate questions. Railway executives, once hostile to the railway commission, now viewed the commissioners as more sympathetic to their economic situation than were the members of Parliament – the alternative regulatory authority. For their part, governments sought to avoid potentially divisive regional policy decisions by referring them to the board.

Regional rate grievances produced a serious crisis within the railway commission. After 1925, the members of the board began to disagree over the legitimate roles of the government and their regulatory agency in the rate-making process. The internal dissension further undermined the credibility of the railway commission. It became increasingly difficult for them to reach authoritative decisions or to be taken seriously by politicians, railway officials, or shipping communities. The railway commission's quest for a measure of legitimacy ended in failure.

Regional shipping interests and their political champions became frustrated with the board's apparent hostility to, and subsequent paralysis over their grievances, particularly in contrast to its accommodating approach to rate increases. Like railway officials before them, shippers sought to circumvent the process, turning to the government to settle their grievances. Appeals from the board to cabinet, the debate over the future of the Crow's Nest Pass agreement, and direct legislative lobbying all provided regional shipping interests with access to the government. Some shipping communities convinced the dominion government to use its ultimate authority over railway corporations to legislate specific rates in the "national" interest. The government, nevertheless, interfered with private rate-making cautiously and reluctantly. The fact that the Canadian Pacific had entered into the Crow's Nest Pass contract voluntarily helped justify the fixing of export grain and flour rates by statute. When the government again directly interfered in the rate-making process in 1927 and ordered the establishment of lower tariffs in the Maritimes, it agreed to compensate the railway companies for any resulting losses in revenue. The Maritime Freight Rates Act, not the statutory grain legislation, introduced the principle that future governments would adopt. Through the principle of compensation, governments sought to introduce a rate policy in the regional and national interest without damaging the earning power of the publicly-owned Canadian National and the last major private railway corporation, the Canadian Pacific. The regulatory struggle of the 1920s again ended with an extension of public authority, although every effort was made to limit this extension and to respect the rights of private capital.

In spite of the direct intrusions of the government into the area of rate regulation in 1925 and again in 1927, the railway commission survived the debacle of the 1920s, but not without a considerable loss of authority and prestige. Some critics complained of the close ties between the commission and the railway industry, while others felt the ties between the commission and elected politicians were too close. Regulation by commission had not failed, it simply had reached its limits. The attempt by politicians and commissioners alike to treat all freight rate conflicts as administrative problems proved futile. A regulatory agency was not the appropriate forum for resolving larger policy questions. That responsibility belonged to Parliament. The 'crisis' facing the railway commission in the 1920s was brought on by the reluctance of railway officials, shippers, politicians and commissioners to recognize the limits of regulation.

By the early 1930s, the pattern of future regulatory initiatives had been established. Between the late nineteenth century and the Great Depression, competition, administrative regulation, contractual agreements, direct legislation, and to a lesser extent, public ownership, had all played a role in reconciling the objectives of railway corporations and the wider community they served. This "regulatory pluralism," the use of a variety of regulatory instruments to resolve conflicts over freight rates, endured.[5] An independent regulatory commission, reorganized in 1938, in 1967, and again in 1987, retained some, albeit increasingly restricted, authority over the rate-making process. Between 1930 and 1970, governments adopted the principle of the Maritime Freight Rates Act – government financial compensation to the railways in exchange for the adoption of "national" policies defined by legislation that were intended to maintain low rates on grain shipped for export through Canadian ports, and on merchandise carried north of Lake Superior. The railway companies also received annual compensation in lieu of a rate increase denied them in 1958.

From the 1960s' onward, the politicians and administrators who have attempted to reformulate transportation and other types of regulation have been conscious of the reform proposals advocated by lawyers, political scientists, and economists. Efforts have been made to prescribe regulatory procedures, to formulate more specific mandates for administrative agencies, to establish mechanisms to make those agencies accountable to governments and Parliament, and to return many key decisions back to private interests operating in the market. The analysis of economists has been particularly influential, appealing to a generation of Canadians increasingly disillusioned with the ability of governments to manage the economy, and less sanguine about giving power to bureaucrats. In the railway sector, there has been a gradual retreat from regulatory pluralism, with the phasing out of most legislated rate arrangements, including the statutory grain rates – the enduring legacy of the Crow's Nest Pass agreement of 1897. Through these and a number of other legislative changes, market mechanisms have been given more free play to shape freight rate decisions.[6]

Particularly since the 1967 National Transportation Act, the history of rate regulation has begun to reverse the developments described in this book. The story recounted here cannot help us to assess recent developments, although it can put them in perspective, and offer a few sobering insights to regulatory reformers. Legal experts anxious to protect individual rights and prevent arbitrary administrative discretion might reflect on the degree to which the procedural flexibility of the early railway commission permitted a considerable degree of participation in regulatory proceedings by non-lawyers and by non-organized interests, and allowed the commissioners to encourage informal negotiations. Those political scientists who are hostile to wide administrative mandates and set the blame on the legislative process might recall Railways Minister Blair's intentions: "The ingenuity of you fellows [counsel for the railways] is so inexhaustible and limitless that we must make the words general." They might examine the way in which vague language allowed the railway commission to arbitrate disputes and seek compromise solutions. They might also consider the problems which "legislative oversight" created that allowed various governments to avoid making tough policy decisions and to foist responsibility on the regulators. And those economists who believe that policy decisions should be returned to the market might pay a little closer attention to the nineteenth-century politics of freight rates, where it is not obvious that bargaining between railway officials and shippers resulted in an optimal distribution of transportation resources, either from an economic or social point of view. Nor does it appear that regulation simply allowed railway officials to engage in cartel-like behaviour.

The history of freight rate regulation does not prove that all these different reform proposals are misguided and doomed to failure, or that they should be abandoned in favour of some ideal model from the past. History cannot refute, although it certainly cannot be shown to confirm, the value or correctness of any of these prescriptions. What the freight rate struggles of the past do seem to demonstrate are the limits of all regulatory regimes – including the market. No single set of reforms, no one type of institutional structure can, or should be expected to, resolve complex economic problems or contain the social conflicts that are a part of a competitive economy. It is precisely for this reason that freight rate controversies led to the development of regulatory pluralism. The conflicts between railways and their customers shifted back and forth between various arenas – the offices of private and public railway managers, the hearing-rooms of the Board of Railway Commissioners, the cabinet chambers in Ottawa and in various provincial capitals, and the halls of various legislatures – leaving in their wake a haphazard set of initiatives and institutions.

Pluralism would seem to be an inevitable part of our regulatory experience, yet it is rarely acknowledged as a potentially useful approach to social problems. Indeed, few reformers sympathize with regulatory pluralism. Supporters of the market dislike all forms of government intervention. Supporters of administrative regulation are suspicious of the market but find direct political interference repugnant. Supporters of legislated standards are suspicious of independent government agencies and of the market. Regulatory pluralism offends our notions of harmony and order, our desire to provide a single scientific solution to socio-economic problems. Haphazard and imperfect though regulatory pluralism may be, it might be worth acknowledging its existence, and finding ways to cope with it, rather than trying to escape it. There may even be some important benefits in the overlapping jurisdictions, institutional duplication, policy confusion and administrative inefficiency that a plurality of governing instruments can engender. Because various interests have a number of points of access to the decision-making process, it becomes more difficult for those that are the best-financed and most highly organized to monopolize control of the process. Similarly, different institutional actors may examine problems from somewhat different perspectives, helping prevent only one mode of analysis or one set of priorities from shaping all decisions.

The history of regulation, then, offers a perspective on the plurality of strategies that have been adopted to allocate scarce resources in our society. The history of regulation is a story of limits. Regulation involves the attempt to draw limits – between the public and private allocation of resources, and between various public decision makers. The theoretical separation of "politics" and "administration" provided the rationale for the creation of the Board of Railway Commissioners. In a democratic capitalist society, this separation provided a thin cloak of legitimacy to regulators who were not directly responsible to the electorate. Twentieth-century attempts to distinguish between the "political" and "administrative" functions of government resembled nineteenth-century efforts to define the public and private sectors of society. The concept of a private sphere of authority permitted corporations and business not directly responsible to the electorate to make critical decisions concerning the distribution of scarce resources within our society, by denying that those decisions were in any way political. Neither the separation between politics and administration nor between public and private authority could be sustained at critical junctures. Freight rate controversies could and did stretch traditionally defined limits, resulting in an overlapping and a redrawing of the boundaries of individual spheres. In the final analysis, however, certain fundamental questions about the allocation of scarce resources were public and political, not private or administrative. Decisions about who would regulate and what they would regulate were returned to the political arena, where they belonged. There, through a process of pressure and compromise, democratically elected legislators reformulated the limits of regulation.

Chronology of Railway Freight Rate Regulation

1851 Railway Clauses Consolidation Act, first general railway act in Canadas, includes provisions requiring cabinet approval of freight tariffs, allowing for parliamentary intervention if profits exceed 15 per cent, and directing railway companies to provide shippers with "equal facilities."

1868 First dominion legislation, General Railway Act for Canada embodies features of 1851 railway law.

1871 In *Scott* v. *Midland Railway*, an Ontario court adopts British interpretation of "equal facilities," making it extremely difficult for shippers to charge railways with unjust discrimination.

1883 D'Alton McCarthy's proposal to create a special "Court of Railway Commissioners" to regulate freight rates and other matters, first introduced as a Private Member's Bill in 1880, overwhelmingly defeated in a parliamentary committee.

1888 Canadian Pacific Railway gives up its monopoly clause, and Northern Pacific leases a competitive line built by the Manitoba government. These developments result in a reduction in the rates between Winnipeg and the Lakehead.

1888 Revision of General Railway Act for Canada. The Railway Committee of the Privy Council, a special cabinet committee, acquires jurisdiction over freight rate matters, as recommended by the Royal Commission on Railways.

1897 The Crow's Nest Pass agreement between the dominion government and the Canadian Pacific provides for reductions in rates on eastbound grain and flour and a number of westbound commodities.

1899 The Canadian Pacific and Grand Trunk railways are charged with offering special rate reductions to Imperial Oil, which had been acquired by Standard Oil. The Railway Committee of the Privy Council grapples with the issue, and in 1900 the government orders a readjustment in the rates.

1901 The government of Manitoba makes an agreement with the Canadian Northern Railway leasing its government line and offering subsidies in exchange for rate reductions and the right to control the railway's freight rates.

1903 A new Railway Act provides for the creation of the Board of Railway Commissioners, and gives the agency the right to supervise and alter all railway rates.

1904 The board is established, its first three commissioners are appointed and it begins hearing complaints.

1906 The railway commission sanctions the use of the mountain scale, the relatively higher tariff applied by the Canadian Pacific on goods moving through British Columbia.

1907 The board's International Rates order results in a number of adjustments, and a general reduction in the merchandise tariffs in Ontario and Quebec. Railway commission outlaws a special distributing tariff enjoyed by the merchants of Winnipeg and approves a new set of reduced distributing rates to be enjoyed by all major prairie western towns.

1908 Membership of the railway commission is expanded from three to six.

1910 In response to complaints of the Regina and Edmonton boards of trade, the commission orders further adjustments in western distributing rates to lessen the advantages enjoyed by Winnipeg merchants. The introduction of the new tariffs is delayed until 1912, however, as

the railways unsuccessfully appeal the decision
to the Supreme Court.

1912   Board agrees to investigate rates in western
Canada; it also makes an inquiry into the
mountain scale, already initiated by the Vancouver Board of Trade, part of the investigation.

1914   Commission's decision in the Western Rates inquiry is rendered: reducing the mountain scale,
merchandise tariffs in Alberta and Saskatchewan, distributing rates and a number of western commodity tariffs.

1915   Railways in eastern Canada apply for a series of
rate advances, averaging 5 per cent. Application follows Interstate Commerce decision in
December 1914.

1916   Government announces intention of appointing
royal commission to investigate railway problem, commission formally appointed in July.

1916   *Eastern Rates Case* decision, commission approves 5 per cent advance on general merchandise tariffs, and a number of other increases.

1917   Release of Report of Royal Commission on
Railways; majority report recommends government ownership of Grand Trunk, Grand
Trunk Pacific, National Transcontinental and
Canadian Northern. Prime minister informs
William Mackenzie of intention to take over
Canadian Northern. Railway commission approves 15 per cent increase in rates, limits advances in mountain scale and in rates
established under Crow's Nest Pass agreement
to 10 per cent.

1918   In March, government supports railway commission's decision to advance rates, but makes
effective only until one year following the war.
In a separate but clearly related order, it provides for taxation of Canadian Pacific earnings
from its railway operations.
In July, government adopts recommendation of
railway commission and grants a further 25 per
cent advance in railway rates. Advance allows
for application of American McAdoo award
concerning wages and hours to Canadian rail-

way workers. Nationalization of Canadian
Northern completed.

1919 Government incorporates Canadian National
Railways Company; independent board to
manage Canadian Northern, National Transcontinental and Canadian government railway
systems.

New Railway Act makes wartime advances permanent and continues to allow rates to exceed
those in the Crow agreement for three more
years.

1920 Government takes possession of Grand Trunk
and Grand Trunk Pacific; nationalization of
railways complete.

Railways apply for 35 per cent advance, increased to 40 per cent when details of American Chicago labour award, which advance
intended to cover, become available. Railway
commission grants 40 per cent advance in eastern rates, 35 per cent advance in western rates,
to be reduced to 35 per cent and 30 per cent in
January 1921. Decision generally upheld by
government on appeal.

1921 Railways reduce a number of rates voluntarily;
railway commission then orders more reductions, so that rates now 30 per cent and
25 per cent higher than those in effect prior
to 1920 decision.

1922 Parliamentary Special Committee on Transportation Costs studies restoration of Crow agreement rates. Grain and flour rates based on
Crow restored, the tariffs on other commodities
outlined in agreement suspended for a maximum of two years.

Railway commission responds to parliamentary
committee's recommendation concerning the
need for rate reductions, and to the demands
from a number of regional interests for rate
"equalization." The commission orders reductions in the level of the mountain tariff, rates
between Maritimes and the prairie west, and
coal and a number of other important commodity rates throughout the country.

1923 Formal amalgamation of Canadian government
and Grand Trunk Railway systems with Canadian National Railways.
Cabinet generally upholds railway commission's
1922 decision, but orders it to consider the
question of export rates on grain via Vancouver. As a result, the board orders a 10 per cent
reduction in those rates.

1924 All Crow-based rates restored; result is chaotic
since railways apply only to those points served
at the time of the original 1897 agreement.
Railway commission effectively cancels Crow-
based rates on various commodities, status of
grain rates remains uncertain. Government
overrules commission; takes no further action
but awaits Supreme Court decision.

1925 Supreme Court rules that railway commission
cannot alter Crow-based rates and that narrow
application of the agreement adopted by railways is legal. Government adopts PC 886: cancels all Crow-based rates, except those on grain
and flour which are confirmed by a subsequent
amendment to the Railway Act. PC 886 orders
and provides terms of reference for a general
inquiry by railway commission into other regional rate issues. Chief Commissioner Mc-
Keown and Commissioner Oliver approve
fixing of grain rates to Vancouver on basis of
Crow agreement, in spite of the opposition of
the three other members of the railway commission.

1926 Royal Commission on Maritime Claims recommends statutory reduction of freight rates in
Maritimes.

1927 Maritime Freight Rates Act adopted, reducing
by 20 per cent local Maritime tariffs and rates
on freight originating in the Maritimes and
bound for other parts of Canada. Railways to
be compensated for any losses resulting from
the reductions.
Railway commission renders decision in General Rates Investigation: rejects further reductions in mountain tariff or in application of

transcontinental rates to interior points; orders low rate on grain over Canadian National from west to Quebec City and requires railways to adopt a somewhat more liberal interpretation of the 1925 grain legislation.

1933 Government adopts Canadian Pacific-Canadian National Railways Act to encourage co-operation and co-ordination of railway system. Government dismisses appeal from decision of railway commission in General Rates Investigation.

Statistics on Railway Freight Operations

For most readers, the graphs in the text probably provide as much information on railway operations as they want. This appendix is offered to those who are more interested in the subject and wish a little more detail than those graphs provide. The following five tables provided the statistics on which those graphs have been based. The sources of the data are listed, although it is worth mentioning that for the Grand Trunk I have relied as much as possible on *Poor's Railroad Manual of the United States* and a statistical table contained in an unpublished history of the railway. The Canadian Pacific material is more readily available; I have relied on the statistics Harold Innis republished from the annual reports in his *History of the Canadian Pacific Railway*. Anyone who may have consulted my thesis, or my article in *Historical Papers*, may notice some discrepancies between the data presented there and here. In the other material I was not always successful in providing the different types of statistics covering the exact fiscal year; I have corrected those errors here.

Table B.1
Grand Trunk Freight Operations, 1860 – 1900
(Index, 1860 = 100)

Year	Average Trainload*		Tons of Freight Carried		Miles Travelled by Freight Trains		Expenses per Ton-mile**	
	Tons	Index	Tons	Index	Miles	Index	Cents	Index
1860	54	100	685,624	100	1,804,347	100	1.68	100
1872	103	190	1,535,296	224	4,197,050	233	1.10	66
1873			1,608,584	235			1.15	69
1874			1,920,722	280			0.91	54
1875	118	217	1,951,151	285	5,272,557	292	0.79	47
1876	129	238	2,172,030	317	5,631,179	312	0.64	38
1877	137	253	2,284,770	333	5,643,509	313	0.61	36
1878	132	243	2,302,432	336	5,944,365	329	0.56	33
1879	161	296	2,532,396	369	5,492,792	304	0.49	30
1880	172	317	3,057,138	446	5,912,364	328	0.48	29
1881	176	324	3,516,062	513	6,036,762	335	0.47	28
1882	255	470	5,986,584	873	5,495,742	305	0.51	31
1883	187	345	5,510,794	804	7,263,341	403	0.57	34
1884	190	350	6,114,548	892	7,554,914	419	0.53	32
1885	189	348	6,157,151	898	7,555,536	419	0.50	30
1886	198	364	6,609,969	964	7,899,545	438	0.49	29
1887	199	366	6,990,701	1020	8,147,774	452	0.50	30
1888	191	353	7,330,559	1069	8,278,975	459	0.52	31
1889	182	335	7,955,965	1160	9,535,293	528	0.52	31
1890	193	356	8,399,524	1225	9,331,703	517	0.51	30
1891	200	368	8,274,009	1207	8,790,688	487	0.51	31
1892	218	401	9,023,278	1316	8,988,806	498	0.47	28
1893	202	371	8,667,933	1264	9,291,593	515	0.47	28
1894	195	359	8,115,095	1184	8,946,684	496	0.46	28
1895	224	412	8,394,104	1224	7,851,463	435	0.46	27
1896	226	416	8,787,293	1282	8,520,970	472	0.45	27
1897	209	385	9,186,206	1340	9,621,627	533	0.41	25
1898	206	379	9,193,654	1341	9,885,917	548	0.42	25
1899	224	412	10,300,793	1502	10,425,247	578	0.39	23
1900	225	414	10,393,986	1516	10,166,826	563	0.42	25

Sources: CNR, "History of the Grand Trunk Railway of Canada," vol. 10394, Appendix, "Statistics"; Royal Commission Evidence, testimony of Lewis J. Seargeant, Montreal, 16 December 1887; province of Canada, Sessional Papers, 1862, no. 13, Grand Trunk Railway Statistics; Poor's Railroad Manual of the United States, 1870–1901.
  *Average trainload = ton-miles / miles travelled by freight trains
**Expenses per ton-mile is an estimate, since the railways did not separate expenses associated with their freight and passenger service. I have adopted a simple method used by railway officials: calculating the proportion of freight earnings to overall earnings in the year: e.g., if freight earnings accounted for 75 per cent of total earnings, freight expenses have been calculated on the basis of 75 per cent of total expenses.

Table B.2
Grand Trunk Freight Operations, 1901–21
(Index, 1901 = 100 miles)

Year	Average Trainload*		Tons of Freight Carried		Miles Travelled by Freight Trains		Expenses per Ton-mile*	
	Tons	Index	Tons	Index	Miles	Index	Cents	Index
1901	248	100	11,080,037	100	9,729,297	100	0.42	100
1902	268	108	11,823,868	107	9,673,726	99	0.43	102
1903	257	103	13,484,056	122	11,033,178	113	0.47	112
1904	252	101	12,971,370	117	9,761,940	100	0.50	120
1905	260	105	14,143,210	128	10,188,296	105	0.49	117
1906	288	116	15,916,859	144	10,552,758	108	0.47	112
1907	296	119	17,391,921	157	11,274,316	116	0.48	115
1908	273	110	15,309,716	138	10,032,310	103	0.49	117
1909	299	120	16,772,569	151	10,037,408	103	0.48	116
1910	309	125	17,722,496	160	10,116,510	104	0.50	120
1911	328	132	19,311,925	174	10,465,910	108	0.50	120
1912	326	131	21,347,565	193	11,748,519	121	0.49	116
1913	338	136	23,218,982	210	12,110,763	124	0.50	119
1914	339	137	23,218,982	210	11,465,987	118	0.53	126
1915	351	141	20,696,509	187	10,685,171	110	0.53	127
1916	361	146	22,710,527	205	12,821,281	132	0.48	114
1917	424	171	25,272,449	228	11,098,679	114	0.62	148
1918	454	183	25,272,449	228	10,363,385	107	0.81	194
1919	460	185	23,292,706	210	9,959,214	102	0.93	221
1920	489	197	26,322,423	238	10,290,183	106	1.08	258
1921	443	178	21,687,749	196	9,156,633	94	1.24	296

Sources: CNR, "History of the Grand Trunk Railway of Canada", vol. 10394, Appendix, "Statistics"; *Poor's Railroad Manual of the United States*, 1902–23.
* See Table B.1.

Table B.3
Canadian Pacific Freight Operations, 1886–1921
(Index, 1901 = 100)

	Average Trainload*		Tons of Freight Carried		Miles Travelled by Freight Trains		Expenses per Ton-mile*	
Year	Tons	Index	Tons	Index	Miles	Index	Cents	Index
1886	220	96	2,046,195	29	2,525,572	24	0.70	152
1887	212	93	2,144,327	30	3,238,103	31	0.69	150
1888	138	60	2,496,557	35	5,702,948	55	0.73	158
1889	162	71	2,638,960	37	5,964,585	57	0.63	137
1890	160	70	3,378,564	47	7,547,058	72	0.51	110
1891	162	71	3,846,710	54	8,605,829	83	0.55	119
1892	182	80	4,230,670	59	8,691,132	83	0.51	111
1893	173	76	4,226,959	59	8,385,880	81	0.55	119
1894	186	81	3,891,884	54	7,082,645	68	0.57	124
1895	195	85	4,274,667	60	7,625,462	73	0.48	105
1896	200	87	4,420,550	62	8,870,134	85	0.45	98
1897	199	87	5,174,484	72	9,826,734	94	0.45	97
1898	204	89	5,582,038	78	10,496,129	101	0.45	99
1899	231	101	6,620,903	93	10,982,873	105	0.43	93
1900	–	–	–	–	–	–	–	–
1901	229	100	7,155,813	100	10,415,831	100	0.46	100
1902	275	120	8,769,934	123	11,792,221	113	0.47	101
1903	276	120	10,180,847	142	13,353,188	128	0.50	107
1904	276	121	11,135,896	156	13,810,180	133	0.53	116
1905	288	126	11,892,204	166	14,429,739	139	0.53	115
1906	311	136	13,933,798	195	17,186,263	165	0.46	101
1907	327	143	15,733,306	220	18,187,263	175	0.50	109
1908	330	144	15,040,325	210	17,788,649	171	0.52	113
1909	339	148	16,549,616	231	18,816,900	181	0.53	115
1910	378	165	20,551,368	287	20,574,576	198	0.50	108
1911	371	162	22,536,214	315	21,701,893	208	0.53	114
1912	405	177	25,940,238	363	25,638,692	246	0.50	108
1913	415	182	29,471,814	412	27,611,103	265	0.52	113
1914	448	196	27,801,217	389	24,164,242	232	0.50	110
1915	470	205	21,490,596	300	16,896,368	162	0.50	109
1916	554	242	29,276,872	409	25,355,997	243	0.40	86
1917	583	255	31,198,685	436	25,182,863	242	0.49	106
1918	577	252	29,856,694	417	22,326,115	214	0.67	145
1919	556	243	25,102,821	351	19,994,867	192	0.81	176
1920	538	235	30,160,134	421	24,335,581	234	0.94	204
1921	536	234	22,710,606	317	18,828,421	181	1.05	228

Source: Harold Innis, Canadian Pacific Railway.
* See Table B.1.

Table B.4
Grand Trunk Railway/Canadian Pacific Railway, General Rate Level Estimate,
Freight Earnings per Ton-mile, 1860–1900
(Index, 1900 = 100)

	Grand Trunk Railway				Canadian Pacific Railway			
	Earnings Per Ton-mile		Real Earnings Per Ton-mile*		Earnings Per Ton-mile		Real Earnings Per Ton-mile	
	Cents	Index	Cents	Index	Cents	Index	Cents	Index
1860	1.99	316	n.a.	n.a.				
1872	1.36	216	1.03	164				
1873	1.42	225	1.09	173				
1874	1.15	183	0.88	140				
1875	0.99	157	0.79	125				
1876	0.81	129	0.69	110				
1877	0.80	127	0.70	111				
1878	0.74	117	0.71	113				
1879	0.67	106	0.63	100				
1880	0.71	113	0.62	98				
1881	0.67	106	0.58	92				
1882	0.73	116	0.61	97				
1883	0.80	127	0.70	111				
1884	0.73	116	0.66	105				
1885	0.66	105	0.65	103				
1886	0.71	113	0.73	116	1.10	139	1.13	143
1887	0.71	113	0.69	110	1.01	128	0.99	125
1888	0.73	116	0.69	110	1.02	129	0.96	122
1889	0.74	117	0.70	111	0.92	117	0.88	111
1890	0.71	113	0.68	108	0.84	106	0.81	103
1891	0.70	111	0.67	106	0.91	115	0.87	110
1892	0.65	103	0.68	108	0.84	106	0.87	110
1893	0.64	102	0.65	103	0.87	110	0.88	111
1894	0.65	103	0.70	111	0.87	110	0.95	120
1895	0.64	102	0.73	116	0.80	101	0.91	115
1896	0.63	100	0.76	121	0.75	95	0.90	114
1897	0.64	102	0.75	119	0.78	99	0.91	115
1898	0.64	102	0.69	110	0.76	96	0.83	105
1899	0.60	95	0.66	105	0.74	94	0.81	103
1900	0.63	100	0.63	100	–	–	–	–

Sources: See Table B.1; M.C. Urquhart and K.A.H. Buckley, eds., Historical Statistics of Canada, Series J1, s149.
* Michell's general wholesale price index is utilized.

Table B.5
Grand Trunk Railway / Canadian Pacific Railway, General Rate Level Estimate,
Freight Earnings per Ton-mile, 1901–21

	Grand Trunk Railway				Canadian Pacific Railway			
	Earnings Per Ton-mile		Real Earnings Per Ton-mile*		Earnings Per Ton-mile		Real Earnings Per Ton-mile	
	Cents	Index	Cents	Index	Cents	Index	Cents	Index
1901	0.62	100	0.63	100	0.80	100	0.80	100
1902	0.63	101	0.62	99	0.75	94	0.74	92
1903	0.67	107	0.65	104	0.77	96	0.75	95
1904	0.71	113	0.70	112	0.77	96	0.76	95
1905	0.70	112	0.66	105	0.76	95	0.72	90
1906	0.67	107	0.60	96	0.74	93	0.66	83
1907	0.67	108	0.57	92	0.77	96	0.66	82
1908	0.69	111	0.60	95	0.75	94	0.65	81
1909	0.67	107	0.58	93	0.76	95	0.66	82
1910	0.69	111	0.58	93	0.77	96	0.65	82
1911	0.69	111	0.57	91	0.81	101	0.67	84
1912	0.69	110	0.52	84	0.77	96	0.59	74
1913	0.69	110	0.53	85	0.78	98	0.60	76
1914	0.68	109	0.52	83	0.75	94	0.57	72
1915	0.70	112	0.49	78	0.76	95	0.54	67
1916	0.67	107	0.38	61	0.64	80	0.36	45
1917	0.76	122	0.32	51	0.71	89	0.30	37
1918	0.96	155	0.37	59	0.86	108	0.34	43
1919	1.05	170	0.39	62	1.00	125	0.37	46
1920	1.16	187	0.40	64	1.11	139	0.39	49
1921	1.34	216	0.68	108	1.28	160	0.65	81

Sources: See Tables B.2 and B.3; Urquhart and Buckley, eds., *Historical Statistics*, Series J1.
* Michell's general wholesale price index is utilized.

Table B.6
Grand Trunk Railway Earnings, Expenses, and Fixed Charges, 1906–21

	Earnings	Expenses	Fixed Charges
1906	32,151,770	22,370,752	5,725,497
1907	34,769,929	24,782,684	5,887,107
1908	30,669,896	21,637,787	6,005,303
1909	31,630,273	22,935,026	5,394,935
1910	34,171,740	24,887,071	5,716,793
1911	37,458,523	27,261,883	6,157,857
1912	41,109,154	29,179,398	7,231,308
1913	44,454,829	32,142,649	7,556,851
1914	41,837,603	32,494,129	7,274,578
1915	40,357,748	30,689,989	7,182,431
1916	47,789,403	34,101,509	7,836,794
1917	52,197,349	42,619,759	9,449,696
1918	61,588,759	52,379,783	9,200,216
1919	68,744,358	60,374,431	8,364,371
1920	81,442,647	76,213,815	9,751,347
1921	76,858,032	71,179,292	18,871,395

Sources: See Table B.2.

Table B.7
Canadian Pacific Railway, Earnings, Expenses, and Fixed Charges, 1906–21

	Earnings	Expenses	Fixed Charges
1906	61,669,758	38,696,446	8,350,545
1907	72,217,528	46,914,219	8,511,756
1908	71,384,173	49,591,808	8,770,077
1909	76,313,321	53,357,748	9,427,033
1910	94,989,490	61,149,534	9,916,940
1911	1,04,167,808	67,467,978	10,011,071
1912	1,23,319,541	80,021,298	10,524,938
1913	1,39,365,700	93,149,826	10,876,352
1914	1,29,814,823	87,388,896	10,227,311
1915	99,865,210	65,290,502	10,446,510
1916	1,29,481,886	80,255,966	10,306,196
1917	1,52,389,335	1,05,843,316	10,229,143
1918	1,57,532,698	1,23,035,310	10,177,513
1919	1,76,929,060	1,43,996,524	10,161,510
1920	2,16,641,349	1,83,488,304	10,177,409
1921	1,93,021,854	1,58,820,114	11,519,072

Sources: See Table B.3.

Table B.8
Canadian Northern Railway Earnings, Expenses, and Fixed Charges, 1910–19

	Earnings	Expenses	Fixed Charges
1910	13,833,062	9,194,510	3,342,048
1911	18,005,032	12,550,395	4,295,523
1912	23,069,581	16,918,957	5,305,648
1913	27,157,551	20,119,172	6,179,138
1914	26,913,339	19,495,306	7,146,057
1915	25,912,106	19,288,814	8,263,575
1916	35,476,275	26,102,744	9,621,657
1917	43,495,077	31,349,408	16,550,901
1918	49,062,712	44,062,950	17,898,247
1919	55,353,930	60,034,024	19,969,710

Sources: *Poor's Railroad Manual of the United States*, 1911–21; Regehr, *Canadian Northern Railway*, Appendix I.

Notes

ABBREVIATIONS

Annual Report	Dominion of Canada, Board of Railway Commissioners, Annual Reports
BRC Transcripts	NA, Records of the Canadian Transport Commission, RG 46, Board of Railway Commissioners, Transcripts of Hearings
CNR	NA, Canadian National Railways Records, RG 30
CPR	NA, Canadian Pacific Railway Records, MG 28 II 20
C.R.C.	*Canadian Railway Cases*
Debates	Dominion of Canada, Parliament, House of Commons, *Debates*
J.O.R.R.	Board of Railway Commissioners, *Judgments, Orders, Regulations and Rulings*
NA	National Archives
Royal Commission Evidence	NA, Privy Council Office, RG 2, Series 3, Dormants, Volume 46

CHAPTER ONE

1 Toronto *Globe*, 13, 14 November 1856; Montreal *Gazette*, 12, 13 November 1856.
2 Canada, Parliament, *Sessional Papers*, 1888, no. 8A, 1; Toronto *Globe*, 22 October 1886.
3 Emerson cited in Kasson, *Civilizing the Machine*, 122,
4 For a similar explanation of government promotion in the United States, see Goodrich, *Government Promotion of American Canals and Railroads*, 8–10. As Goodrich has noted elsewhere, what makes the United

States different from other countries, including Canada, is the degree to which the state ceased to be a key source of financing after its initial investment: "State In, State Out: A Pattern of Development Policy," 365–72.

5 E.C. Kirkland emphasizes this fundamental contradiction throughout volume I of his majesterial study of railways in New England: *Men, Cities and Transportation*.

6 Doern, ed. *The Regulatory Process in Canada*; Dwivedi, *The Administrative State in Canada*; Law Reform Commission, *Independent Administrative Agencies*; Evans et al. *Administrative Law*; Economic Council of Canada, *Reforming Regulation*. For surveys of the American literature, see Thomas McCraw, "Regulation in America: A Review Article," 159–83; Mitnick, *The Political Economy of Regulation*; Horwitz, *The Irony of Regulatory Reform*, 22–89.

7 Kolko, *Railroads and Regulation*; Stigler, "The theory of economic regulation," 3–21; Fellmeth, *The Interstate Commerce Commission*.

CHAPTER TWO

1 Constitution Act, 1867 (30 & 31 Vict.), c. 3, s. 145; McLean, "The Railway Policy of Canada, 1849–67, Parts I and II," 191–217, 351–83.

2 Currie, *Grand Trunk Railway*, 220–2.

3 Ibid., 199–204.

4 Lamb, *Canadian Pacific Railway*, 94–103, 165–75.

5 Currie, *Grand Trunk Railway*, 294–8, 314–24, 345–9; statistics from Canada, Parliament, *Sessional Papers*, 1891, no. 20b, Railway Statistics.

6 Lamb, *Canadian Pacific Railway*, 195–211, 233–8; Cruise and Griffiths, *Lords of the Line*, 278–87; Regehr, *Canadian Northern Railway*, 128–9, 187–219.

7 Currie, *Grand Trunk Railway*, 118–22, 349–52; CPR, Shaugnessy Letterbooks, no. 76, 59–65, Shaugnessy to Lord Strathcona, 16 November 1901; *Monetary Times*, 25 September 1885; Lamb, *Canadian Pacific Railway*, 179; Martin, *Enterprise Denied*, 55–71.

8 The burden of the Grand Trunk's fixed charges can be calculated from *Poor's Railroad Manual of the United States*, [later *Poor's Manual of Railroads*] *1875–1905*, and those of the Canadian Pacific from Innis, *Canadian Pacific Railway*, 247, 279. Matthew Simon notes the preference of British investors for safe Canadian securities in his "New British investments in Canada, 1865–1914," 238–54.

9 Jackman, *Economic Principles of Transportation*; Currie, *Economics of Canadian Transportation*; Locklin, "The Literature on Railway Rate Theory," 167–230; J.M. Clark, *Standards of Reasonableness*; Ripley, *Railroads: Rates and Regulations*.

10 Chandler, *The Visible Hand*, 109–20; BRC Transcripts: vol. 13, file
    vol. 31, 3088 (Olds), 29 May 1906; vol. 12, file vol. 29, 1904 (Loud),
    20 April 1906.

11 Currie, *Grand Trunk Railway*, 336–41; Royal Commission Evidence,
    Lewis J. Seargeant, Montreal, 16 December 1887; Ulen, "Railroad
    Cartels Before 1887," 125–44; CNR, Canadian Freight Association/
    Association of General Freight Agents of Canada, Minutes,
    vol. 10817; 1074, 25 February 1898; 1123, 18 February 1898; BRC
    Transcripts, vol. 8, file vol. 10, 2851–71 (discussion of grain rate
    structure), 30 August 1905.

12 CPR, Van Horne Letterbooks: no. 28, 588–93, Van Horne to Charles
    Owens, 20 December 1888; no. 9, 374–7. Van Horne to Joseph Hick-
    son, 22 December 1884; no. 10, 730–2, Van Horne to Hickson,
    21 March 1885; no. 11, 293–6, Van Horne to Hickson, 25 April
    1885; no. 14, 522–3, Van Horne to G.M. Bosworth, 5 December
    1885. For further details on this and other issues discussed below, see
    Cruikshank, "The Transportation Revolution and its Consequences."

13 Royal Commission Evidence, Lewis J. Seargeant, Montreal, 16 Decem-
    ber 1887.

14 Inwood, "Effective Transportation and Tariff Protection"; North,
    "Ocean Freight Rates and Economic Development"; cf. BRC Tran-
    scripts, vol. 77, file vol. 170, 1051–68.

15 Royal Commission Evidence: William Ogilvie, Montreal, 21 January
    1887; John Earls, Montreal, 15 December 1887; George Olds,
    9 December 1887.

16 NA, Records of Department of Railways and Canals, RG 43, vol. 867,
    file 87173, Pottinger to A.C. Blair, 15 February 1900; NA, Records of
    Canadian Transport Commission, RG 46, vol. 107, file vol. 229, 3227–
    49, 10 May 1915.

17 Cruikshank, "The Transportation Revolution and its Consequences,"
    124–6; Kerr, "Wholesale Trade on the Canadian Plains in the Late
    Nineteenth Century." On Winnipeg merchants, see Bellar, *Winnipeg
    First Century*, 73.

18 Van Horne Letterbooks: no. 3, 844–6, 3 December 1883; no. 4, 180–
    2, Van Horne to John Egan, 6 January 1884; 289–92, Van Horne to
    Stephen, 14 January 1884; Shaugnessy Letterbooks: no. 3, 626–8,
    Shaugnessy to Egan, 27 December 1884; no. 5, 558–9, Shaugnessy to
    Egan, 8 September 1885.

19 Van Horne Letterbooks: no. 2, 633–4, Van Horne to William Harder,
    11 October 1883; no. 3, 757, Van Horne to Harder, 1 December
    1883; no. 4: 187–8, Van Horne to Harder, 7 January 1884; 407–8,
    Van Horne to Harder, 20 January 1884.

20 Ripley, *Rates and Regulations*, 186–90; J.M. Clark, *Standards of Reason-
    ableness*, 74–87.

21 Van Horne Letterbooks, no. 53, 214–7, Van Horne to John J. Young, 23 April 1897.

22 Chandler, *The Visible Hand*, 207–8. For a fine discussion which emphasizes the competitiveness of the nineteenth-century economy, see Forster, "Finding the Right Size: Markets and Competition in Mid- and Late-Nineteenth Century Ontario," 150–73.

23 McCalla, *The Upper Canadian Trade*, 109–13, 179; McCalla, "The Decline of Hamilton as a Wholesale Centre," 247–54; *Sessional Papers*, 1876, 1886, 1901, Trade and Navigation Returns.

24 Royal Commission Evidence, John Tilden, Hamilton, 19 April 1887.

25 Ibid.: Quebec City, 9–10 December 1886; Ottawa, 4, 6–7 December 1886; Toronto, 21, 23, 28–9 October 1886, 14 April 1887.

26 Ibid.: Montreal, 17, 21, 25 January 1887; Quebec City, 9–10 December 1886.

27 Statistics on Montreal grain trade drawn from Montreal *Gazette*, 1 January 1880, 5 January 1882, 6 January 1885, 7 January 1887, 5 January 1888, 4 January 1890.

28 Royal Commission Evidence, Alexander Tough, George McBean, Montreal, 15 January 1887.

29 NA, RG 43, vol. 200, file 238, Evidence, Commission on Railway Rate Grievances; R. Kerr, W.C. Duffy, Windsor, 19 July 1901; John Bowman, London, 22 July 1901; see also F.W. Macpherson, Windsor, 19 July 1901; "Discrimination in Railway Freights," *Canadian Manufacturer*, 15 March 1895; "They Want Fair Play," 21 June 1895; NA, Canadian Manufacturers Association Papers, MG 28 I 230, Railway and Transportation Committee, vol. 67: Minutes, Meeting with Simon James McLean, Rate Grievance Commissioner, 12 July 1901; Report of Committee to Annual Meeting, 5,6 November 1901; Windsor *Evening Record*, 15, 19 July 1901.

30 "The High Freight Rates," Winnipeg *Daily Tribune*, 10 December 1894 (evidence heard at Brandon by investigation); "The Commission," *Brandon Daily Mail*, 13 December 1894; "The Rates Commission," *Calgary Daily Herald*, 18, 19 February 1895; RG 43, vol. 200, file 238, Evidence, Commission on Railway Rate Grievances: W.J. Cummings (McCormick Harvesting Co.), J.M. Young (Regina), 15 August 1901; Mr Munroe (British America Paint Co., Victoria), 28 August 1901, F. Boscombe, W.H. Malkins (Vancouver), 30 August 1901.

31 For the rate investigation of 1894, in which Winnipeg and the province of Manitoba outlined their case, see "Freight Rates Commission," Winnipeg *Daily Tribune*, 13, 14 December 1894, 21 January 1895. The brief was resubmitted to the 1901 investigation, "Freight Rate Enquiry," Winnipeg *Daily Tribune*, 12 September 1901.

32 The kind of support the general question of western rates received is

reflected in the voluminous set of petitions, about 125 in all with 20–2 names on each, signed by local merchants and farmers throughout the west. These petitions helped prompt the 1894 investigation in the first place: NA, Privy Council Records, RG 2, Series 3, Dormants, vol. 105, file 1894, no. 1500.

CHAPTER THREE

1 Willison, *The Railway Question*, 18, 27–31. On Willison's western tour and the letters for the *Globe*, see Clippingdale, "J.S. Willison, Political Journalist," 355–8, 374.
2 J.S.W. Lyon to Willison, 15 May 1897, cited in Clippingdale, "J.S. Willison, Political Journalist," 375.
3 Filby, *Credit Valley Railway*, 21–9 (The "King of the Bonus Hunters" phrase comes from Toronto *World*, 20 November 1883, cited in Filby, 93); NA, John A. Macdonald Papers, MG 26 A 1: 57598–607, James White (Oxford County Clerk, Woodstock) to Macdonald, 7 February 1882; 139254–69, Petition, George Laidlaw to Governor General, n.d. [1879].
4 Laidlaw, *The Credit Valley Railway*, particularly 6–9, 17.
5 "The CVR," Toronto *Globe*, 28 November 1872; "BOT: CVR, The Cordwood Question," ibid., 11 December 1972; An Act to Incorporate the Credit Valley Railway Company, S.O. 1871, c. 38, s. 41; An Act to Amend Several Acts Relating to the Credit Valley Railway Company, S.O. 1873, c. 80, s. 4.
6 Toronto, City Council, Minutes, 1872: minute 811, 18 November 1872; Appendix 177, 16 December 1872; "Poll Taken on Credit Valley Railroad," Appendix 185; By Law no. 572, 30 December 1872; Minutes, 1876: minute 367–85, 6 March 1876, minute 677, 18 April 1876, minute 734, 26 April 1876; Minutes, 1877: minute 120–4, 143, 161, 15 January 1877; Appendix 32, Report no. 8 of Standing Committee on Finance and Assessment, 26 February 1877; minute 294–302, 28 February 1877; minute 341–4, 7 March 1877; Appendix 68, Return of Voting, 9 April 1877. See "The CVR," Toronto *Globe*, 30 January 1877; "Finance Committee," ibid., 27 February 1877.
7 Macdonald Papers, 139235–39, Blake, Kerr, Boyd, and Cassels to George Laidlaw, 21 January 1879; *Grand Trunk Railway Co.* v. *Credit Valley Railway Co.* (1879), 26 *Grant's Chancery Reports*, 572–89; ibid., 232–52.
8 Macdonald Papers: 178872–73, George J. Jaffery, George Galt to Macdonald, 10 March 1882; 57598–607, James White (Oxford County Clerk, Woodstock) to Macdonald, 7 February 1882; 57612–16, Duncan McIntyre (VP, CPR) to Macdonald, 20 April 1883;

Toronto, City Council, Minutes, 1882: minute 214, 14 February 1882;
Appendix 14, no. 87, Committee on Legislation, 20 February 1882;
An Act Respecting the Credit Valley Railway Company, S.O. 1883,
c. 50; An Act Respecting the Canadian Pacific Railway Company, S.C.
1883, c. 55; An Act to Amend an Act Respecting the Credit Valley
Railway Company, S.C. 1883, c. 57; An Act to Amend an Act to Incorporate the Ontario and Quebec Railway Company, S.C. 1883,
c. 58.

9 Cooper, *Rails to the Lakes*, 16–21; Hunter, *History of Simcoe County*,
187–93; Hamilton *Daily Spectator*, 19, 22 May, 2, 3 June 1873.

10 An Act Respecting the Northern Railway of Canada, S.C. 1878, c. 26.

11 Cooper, *Rails to the Lakes*, 24–8; *Campbell* v. *Northern Railway* (1879),
26, *Grant's Chancery Reports*, 522–43.

12 Ibid., 542–3.

13 Ibid., 526–34, 541.

14 Cited at ibid., 535–6.

15 E.g., *City of St Thomas* v. *Credit Valley Railway* (1884), 7 *Ontario Reports*
332, affirmed (1885), 12 *Ontario Appeal Reports* 273, in which the city
had some success in an action against the railway for failing to run
trains from the eastern to the western part of the city, as the railway
promoters had agreed.

16 Hunter, *History of Simcoe County*, 194–5.

17 Macdonald Papers, 139270–7, "Memorandum in Reference to Railway Commission," 28 March 1879; Toronto, City Council, Minutes,
1879: minute 29, 20 January 1879; Appendix 29, Executive Committee Report, 20 March 1879; Minutes, 1880: minute 231, 23 February
1880; minute 322, 8 March 1880.

18 Macdonald Papers: 123373–6, George Stephen to Macdonald,
23 April 1887; 123566–81, Stephen to Macdonald, 12 July 1887;
CPR, Van Horne Letterbooks, no. 21, 921–3, Van Horne to Stephen,
17 June 1887. On the politics of the disallowance question, see Jackson, "The Disallowance of Manitoba Railway Legislation in the
1880s"; Regehr, *Canadian Northern Railway*, 1–20; Hall, *Clifford Sifton*,
vol. 1, 32–3.

19 Van Horne Letterbooks, no. 21: 364, Van Horne to W. Whyte (Gen-
eral Superintendent Winnipeg), 3 May 1887; 489–93, Van Horne to
Acton Burrows (Winnipeg), 13 May 1887; 556–7, Van Horne to John
Norquay, 16 May 1887; "Letter to Editor, from Stephen," Winnipeg
Morning Call, 21 May 1887, cited in Gilbert, *Awakening Continent*, 211;
Macdonald Papers: 123623–30, Stephen to Macdonald, 2 September
1887; 221936–7, T. Mayne Daly to Macdonald, 8 April 1887.

20 Ibid., 123461–43, Stephen to Macdonald, 14 September 1887; Gilbert, *Awakening Continent*, 213–17.

21 Van Horne Letterbooks no. 23, 84, Van Horne to Whyte, 13 September 1887; Macdonald Papers, 120113; Press Clipping, Winnipeg *Morning Call*, 2 November 1888. For a good account of the controversy surrounding the Northern Pacific negotiations, see Hall, *Clifford Sifton*, vol. 1, 35–38.

22 Regehr, *Canadian Northern Railway*, 15–16.

23 Hall, *Clifford Sifton*, vol. 2, 15–20; Regehr, *Canadian Northern Railway*, 85–100.

24 *Railway and Marine World*, February 1901, 43–5.

25 Ibid., 41–3; An Act Confirming a Certain Agreement Respecting Certain Railways and Passenger Rates, S.M. 1901, c. 39.

26 Argo, "Historical Review of Canadian Railway Freight Rate Structure, 1876–1938," 115.

27 Macdonald Papers; 132306–7, 132310–12, Van Horne to Macdonald, 9, 15 May 1891; Van Horne Letterbooks: no. 50, 703–5, Van Horne to Hon. J. H. Turner, 7 February 1896; no. 52, Van Horne to Hon. J. D. Edgar, 116–9, 10 February 1896; NA, Wilfrid Laurier Papers, MG 26 G1, 6990, Thomas Shaugnessy to Laurier, 12 September 1896.

28 Van Horne Letterbooks, no. 51, 970, Van Horne to Thomas C. Irving, 10 September 1896; no. 52: 5, Van Horne to Wilmot D. Matthews, 16 September 1896; 168, Van Horne to Fred Cook, 7 October 1896; Hall, *Clifford Sifton*, vol. 1, 150–1; NA, Records of Department of Railways and Canals, RG 43, A1 vol. 4, file 796: no. 76497, encl. Wesley Orr (Calgary) to Frank Oliver, 17 August 1896; no. 77013, C.B. Bowman (Secretary Lethbridge Board of Trade) to Minister of Railways, 12 November 1896; no. 77299, W. Findlay (Clerk Wolseley Council) to Minister of Railways, 28 November 1896; no. 77292, George H. Healey (Secretary Virden Board of Trade), 2 December 1896; no. 77273, James Balfour (Secretary Regina Board of Trade) to R.W. Scott (Secretary of State), 19 December 1896; Laurier Papers: 9248, W. Trant (Secretary Regina Board of Trade) to Laurier, 18 November 1896; 11945, Daniel O'Hara to Laurier, 2 October 1897; 12484–86, T.H. Macpherson to Laurier, 25 February 1897; 12487–90, Richard Armstrong to Laurier, 25 February 1897; 12516–17, D.J. O'Donoghue (Secretary Toronto Trades and Labour Congress) to Laurier, 26 February 1897; 12702, George W. Dower (Secretary Trades & Labour Congress of Canada) to Laurier, 1 March 1897; 12725–6, M.K. Cowan to Laurier, 2 March 1897; 12733, John Proctor to Laurier, 3 March 1897; 12737–8, A.B. McCallum to Laurier, 3 March 1897; 12756, Robert J. Fleming (Mayor of Toronto) to Laurier, 3 March 1897; 12787, James Sutherland (Ontario Liberal Association) to Laurier, 5 March 1897; 14421–2, H.F.

Gardiner to Laurier, 4 March 1897; 13356–55, J.L. Bennet (Secretary Kamloops District Liberal Association) to Laurier, 23 March 1897; 13487, Frank Oliver to Laurier, 29 March 1897.

29 Van Horne Letterbooks, no. 52: 643–7, Van Horne to Hon. Col James Baker, 21 January 1897; 837–8, Van Horne to Donald Smith, 16 February 1897; Laurier Papers: 12476, A.T. Wood (Wholesale Hardware Merchants of Hamilton) to Laurier, 24 February 1897; 12542, Laurier to A.T. Wood, 26 February 1897; 12556–7, Laurier to Richard Armstrong, 27 February 1897; 12379–80, Laurier to A.B. McCallum [n.d.].

30 Van Horne Letterbooks, no. 52: 116–19, Van Horne to Hon. J.D. Edgar, 2 October 1896; 287–9, Van Horne to Hon. J.D. Edgar, 6 November 1896; Willison, *The Railway Problem*, 36–7; NA, Clifford Sifton Papers, MG 27 II D 15, vol. 37, file J.S. Willison, 1897, 24219, Willison to Sifton, 15 March 1897.

31 CPR, Shaugnessy Letterbooks, no. 49, 202–4, Shaugnessy to E.B. Osler, 22 October 1896; Van Horne Letterbooks, no. 52: 532–8, Van Horne to Hon. John Turner, 28 November 1896; 458, Van Horne to Sir Donald Smith, 8 December 1896.

32 An Act to authorize a Subsidy for a Railway through the Crow's Nest Pass, S.C. 1897, c. 5; Hall, *Clifford Sifton*, vol. 1, 152–5; Sifton Papers: vol. 32, file T.G. Shaugn, 1897, 21433, Shaugnessy to Sifton, 15 June 1897; vol. 11, file J.H. Ashdown, 1897, 6731–2, Ashdown to Sifton, 24 June 1897.

33 Van Horne Letterbooks, no. 53, 422–3, Van Horne to Sir Donald Smith, 3 June 1897; cf. Sifton Papers: vol. 11, file J.H. Ashdown, 1897: 6708–18, J.H. Ashdown to Sifton, 2 March 1897; 6721–2, Ashdown to Sifton, 13 March 1897.

34 Van Horne Letterbooks, no. 53, 422–3, Van Horne to Sir Donald Smith, 3 June 1897.

35 Laurier Papers, 14024–32, Sifton to Laurier, 19 April 1897.

36 Roy, "Progress, Prosperity and Politics," 3–28; BRC Transcripts, vol. 88, file vol. 192, 10323 (M.K. Cowan), 12 December 1913; Laurier Papers, 100643, Laurier to J.W. Dafoe, 8 May 1908. *In re Western Tolls* (1914), 17 *C.R.C.* 123 at 180–6 offers an excellent analysis of duplication in the prairies.

37 For the Canadian Northern and British Columbia, see An Act to Ratify an Agreement ... between His Majesty the King and the Canadian Northern Railway Company, S.B.C. 1910, c. 3, and Regehr, *Canadian Northern Railway*, 291–9; for Grand Trunk Pacific provisions, see *In re General Freight Rates Investigation* (1927), 33 *C.R.C.* 127 at 204–8; for Canadian Northern subsidies, see An act respecting certain aid for the extension of the Canadian Northern Railway, S.C. 1903, c. 7, s. 6, and discussion in *Re Crow's Nest Pass Rates* (1925), 30 *C.R.C.* 44–5.

CHAPTER FOUR

1 Mills, "Railway Reform – The CPR," 437–9.
2 Cruikshank, "The People's Railway," 87–90.
3 E.g. NA, Robert Borden Papers, MG 26 H: 8919–22, J. Picard (Quebec City Board of Trade) to Bordon, 6 June 1914; 98171–2, Quebec City Board of Trade to Borden, 1 May 1914.
4 Cruikshank, "The People's Railway," 78–100.
5 Railway Clauses Consolidation Act, 1851 (14 & 15 Vict.), c. 51, s. 22(7); NA, Records of NA, Canadian Transport Commission, RG 46: vol. 718, file 8764, Reporters' Notes, Argument of B.B. Osler of the Grand Trunk Railway, 22 March 1900; vol. 1490, file 7493, document 73186, A.G. Blair Jr. (Law Clerk of Board of Railway Commissioners) to Cartwright (Secretary of Board), 21 October 1908. The dominion government almost sent a reference to the Supreme Court on the matter shortly after the creation of the Board of Railway Commissioners in 1930, but the Canadian Pacific apparently voluntarily agreed not to challenge the board's authority: *Railway and Shipping World*, October 1904, 371; BRC Transcripts, vol. 187, file vol. 190, 9398–400, 12 April 1913.
6 Railway Clauses Consolidation Act, 1851, s. 16(4), (5); NA, Records of Department of Railways and Canals, RG 43, vol. 253, file 2092, pt no. 1, 47892, Minister of Justice to A.P. Bradley, 7 March 1888; CPR, Shaugnessy Letterbooks, no. 40, 792–3, memorandum to President, 29 August 1894.
7 Railway Clauses Consolidation Act, 1851, s. 16(1).
8 These statistics are drawn from an analysis of the records of the Middlesex County Court and of the Courts of Assize and Nisi Prius for Middlesex, Wentworth, and York counties. For precise details, see Cruikshank, "Law versus Common Sense," footnote 6; Abbott, *Treatise on the Railway Law of Canada*, 273–7; MacMurchy and Denison, *Canadian Railway Act 1903*, 381, 490–511.
9 *Scott* v. *Midland Railway* (1873), 33 *Upper Canada Queen's Bench Reports*, 580–92.
10 Ibid., 595–6. In an earlier decision, Ontario's Chancery Court had ruled against such a distinction being made (*Attorney General* v. *Ontario, Simcoe, & Huron Railways* (1858), 6 *Grant's Chancery Reports*, 446–51). However, in *Scott*, the court argued that the language of the railway charter involved in the 1858 case was more explicit than the language applicable to the Midland Railway.
11 Ibid., 592–603.
12 On business attitudes towards lawyers and courts, see Michael Bliss, *A Living Profit*, 117; Cruikshank, "Law versus Common Sense"; "A Railway Commission," Toronto *Globe*, 29 January 1879; "The Railway

Commission," ibid., 27 September 1879; "Railway Abuses and their
Cure," ibid., 3 March 1880. A number of business leaders also advocated the creation of tribunals of commerce for resolving other kinds
of disputes: "Tribunals of Commerce," Toronto *Globe*, 15 November
1871, 21 January 1875. For a fascinating discussion of tribunals of
commerce and other alternatives to the court system in nineteenth-
century England, see Harry Arthurs, '*Without the Law.*'

13 *Debates*: 23 February 1880, 153–4; 10 January 1881, 926–31.

14 Canada, Parliament, House of Commons, *Journals*, Appendix no. 1,
43–6, "Third Report, Select Standing Committee on Railways and Canals"; NA, John A. Macdonald Papers, MG 26 A 1, 61187–96, Bill
No. 12, An Act for Constituting a Court of Railway Commissioners
for Canada, and to amend the Consolidated Railway Act, 1879, 6 February 1885; *Debates*: 2 March 1882, 173–6; 8 March 1883, 140–2;
11 April 1883, 558–63.

15 E.g., Aemilus Irving's earlier proposal to give the Exchequer Court
of Canada responsibility for enforcing railway legislation: *Debates*,
16 April 1877, 1521–29; Macdonald Papers, 139270–7, "Memorandum in Reference to Railway Commission," 28 March 1879.

16 Miller, "'As A Politician He Is A Great Enigma'," 399–422; Waite, *The
Man from Halifax*, 237–8.

17 *Debates* (Charles Tupper), 10 February 1881, 931–2; 2 March 1882,
174–6; 8 March 1883, 142–4. Petitions in support of the proposal
(found in RG 2) were received from: Toronto Board of Trade,
PC 192, 5 February 1880; city of Toronto, PC 467, 12 March 1880;
Port Hope, PC 672, 9 April 1880; County Council of Lambton,
PC 409, 20 February 1883; County Council of Huron, PC 410, 20 February 1883; Ottawa Board of Trade, PC 663, 7 April 1886. Petitions
could, of course be presented in other ways. A. McNeill estimated in
1886 that some sixteen counties and thirty-two towns had adopted petitions in favour of the proposal: *Debates*, 8 April 1886, 585–7.

18 NA, Joseph Hickson Papers, MG 29 A 29, vol. 1, 77–9, Hickson to Macdonald, 16 February 1883; Macdonald Papers, 95397–8, Hickson to
Macdonald, 25 February 1883. Formal petitions opposing the proposal (found in RG 2) were received from the following railway companies: Grand Trunk, PC 445, 11 March 1880, PC 81, 13 January
1881; Toronto, Grey, and Bruce, PC 449, 11 March 1880; Port Dover
and Lake Huron, Sratford and Huron, PC 460, 11 March 1880;
Toronto and Nipissing, PC 466, 12 March 1880; Midland, PC 466,
12 March 1880, PC 111, 17 January 1881; Quebec Central, PC 470,
13 March 1880, PC 143, 22 January 1881; Northern, PC 475.5,
13 March 1880, PC 146, 24 January 1881; Great Western, PC 485,
15 March 1880; PC 439, 6 March 1882; Canada Southern, PC 520,

17 March 1880; South Eastern Pacific, PC 536, 20 March 1880; Albert, PC 568, 24 March 1880; Montreal and Champlain Junction, PC 82, 13 January 1881; Simcoe Junction, PC 116, 18 January 1881; Massawippi Valley, PC 126, 20 January 1881; International, PC 186, 28 January 1881; St Lawrence and Ottawa, PC 192, 29 January 1881; Whitby, Port Perry, and Lindsay, PC 263, 11 February 1881.

19 *Debates*, 8 March 1883, 148–50; "Editorial Notes," *Canadian Manufacturer*, 6 April 1883; "Railway Commission," Toronto *Globe*, 30 March 1883; "Railway Commission Bill," ibid., 2 April 1883.

20 *Journals*, Appendix no. 1, 1–19, "Third Report, Select Standing Committee on Railways and Canals."

21 "Railway Commissions," Toronto *Globe*, 4 April 1883; "Editorial Notes," *Canadian Manufacturer*, 6 April 1883. The group of twelve who supported the measure were: T. Bain (Reform, Wentworth North), G.E. Casey (Reform, West Elgin), J.H. Fairbank (Reform, East Lambton), D'Alton McCarthy (Conservative, North Simcoe), Peter Mitchell (Independent, Northumberland), William Mulock (Reform, North York), G.T. Orton (Conservative, Centre Wellington), J. Small (Conservative, East Toronto), T.S. Sproule (Conservative, East Grey), N.C. Wallace (Conservative, West York), R.M. Wells (Reform, East Bruce), Peter White (Conservative, Renfrew).

22 *Debates*, 18 May 1883, 1308; "Railway Legislation," *Monetary Times*, 25 May 1883, 1315.

23 First announced by Hon. John Thompson: *Debates*, 8 April 1886, 596–9. On the appointment of the other royal commission, see Greg Kealey, ed. "Introduction," ix–xiv. P.B. Waite rightly places the debate over railway regulation in the context of contemporary debates over factory and combines legislation: *Canada, 1874–1896*, 179–83.

24 NA, Alexander Galt Papers, MG 27 I D8, Galt to his wife, 24 October 1886; NA, Department of Railways and Canals Records, RG 43, Correspondence Register, vol. 173, no. 41371 refers to appointments, 6 July and 14 August 1886; Baker, "Isaac Burpee," 134, refers to his brother; "George Moberly," *Canadian Biographical Dictionary*; "Sir Collingwood Schreiber," in Wallace, *Macmillan Dictionary of Canadian Biography*. A second Maritime appointment, T.E. Kenny, was preoccupied with getting elected to Parliament and formally resigned from the commission when he succeeded: RG 43, vol. 173, no. 42466, 9 February 1887; "T.E. Kenny," *Morgan's Canadian Men and Women of the Times*.

25 Figures based on my analysis of the evidence heard before the royal commission: NA, Privy Council Records, RG 2, Series 3, Dormants, vol. 46. Comments on the unsatisfactory nature of testimony can be found in "Railway Commission Enquiry," *Monetary Times*, 29 Octo-

ber 1886, 496; "Railway Commission," ibid., 17 December 1886, 693; "The Proposed Railway Commission," Toronto *Globe*, 29 October 1886. Royal Commission Evidence, testimony of: Barlow Cumberland, Hugh Blain, Toronto, 23 October 1886; Daniel Defoe, Toronto, 25 October 1886; William Galbraith, Toronto, 28 October 1886; Alexander Orsali, Montreal, 20 January 1887. Thomas Andrew coined the phrase "come-at-able," Quebec, 10 December 1886.

26 For the "circumlocution office" comment, see ibid., testimony of Thomas Hobbs, London, 25 May 1887; for concern with special rates see testimony: Toronto, 25–27 October 1886; Halifax, 16 November 1886; Ottawa, 4 December 1886; Montreal, 13, 17 January 1887; Kingston, 11 April 1887; Hamilton, 18 April 1887; London, 23 May 1887; Shaugnessy Letterbooks, no. 11, 135–6, Shaugnessy to Col John Walker, and to Hon. E.R. Burpee, 18 May 1887.

27 The advantage the Interstate Commerce Act would afford the Grand Trunk were noted in the trade journal, *Railway Age Gazette*, cited in "Miscellaneous," Montreal *Gazette*, 23 March 1887; American concerns about the impact of the act on Canadian competition can be found in United States, Senate, 51st Congress, 1st Session, Report no. 847. *Report on the Transportation Interests of the United States and Canada* (1889).

28 Royal Commission Evidence, William Van Horne, Joseph Hickson, Montreal, 20 December 1887.

29 Ibid., 17–19.

30 An Act Respecting Railways, S.C. 1888, c. 29, ss. 225, 232–3, 226–7. A further amendment, not recommended by the royal commission, established that railway companies could not collect any money in return for their services until their tolls were formally sanctioned by cabinet. With this last amendment, legislators finally responded to the ruling in *Scott*, which had permitted railways to avoid one of their basic public responsibilities.

31 Ibid., ss. 8–25. The failure to adopt the recommendation concerning provincial officers was noted with concern in "The Railway Act," *Monetary Times*, 20 April 1888, 1308.

32 Macdonald Papers, 95547–51, Hickson to Macdonald, 5 May 1888 (and copy of undated reply of minister of railways).

33 *Debates*, 2 May 1892, 1948–9; general conclusions based on my analysis of the correspondence files and minutes of the proceedings of the Railway Committee of the Privy Council, RG 46, vols. 778–82, 679–722, 809.

34 Ibid.: vol. 702, file 5256a *R.E.A.* Leech (Secretary, Manitoba Central Farmers' Institute) to Minister of Justice, 12 July 1893; Leech to Secretary, Railway Committee of the Privy Council, 6 Novembver 1893;

George M. Clark (Canadian Pacific), to Schreiber, 20, 23 November 1893; Leech to Schreiber, 7 December 1893; J. Elder (Manitoba Central Farmers' Institute) to Schreiber, 2, 8 December 1893; Leech to Schreiber, 31 January, 23 February 1894; vol. 703, file 5510, Memorial of Manitoba Central Farmers' Institute, 27 July 1894; vol. 780, 203–4, 221, 232; Manitoba Central Farmers Institute v. Railroad Companies in Manitoba, 16 December 1893, 9, 23 February 1894.

35 Ibid., vol. 703: file 5454, C.A. Boulton to Secretary, Railway Committee of the Privy Council, 20 June 1894; file 5469, C.A. Boulton to Minister of Railways and Canals, 20 July 1894. On the organizational strength of the Patrons in Western Canada in 1894, see Wood, *A History of Farmers' Movements in Canada*, 127–9.

36 RG 46: vol. 780, 268, Regina County Association of the Patrons of Industry of the North West Territories v. C.P.R., 31 July 1894; vol. 703, file 5514, Reporters Notes, Railway Committee of the Privy Council, 31 July 1894; "Despotism of a Railway," *Canada Farmers' Sun*, 8 August 1894.

37 CPR, Van Horne Letterbooks, no. 46: 220–2, Van Horne to Senator D. MacInnes, 7 April 1894; 918, Van Horne to Nicholas F. Davin, 3 July 1894; Shaugnessy Letterbooks: no. 40, 224–5, Shaugnessy to Haggart, 3 July 1894; no. 41, 84, 86, Shaugnessy to Haggart, 3 October 1894; 451–2, Shaugnessy to William Whyte, 17 November 1894.

38 Canada, Parliament, *Sessional Papers*, 1895, no. 30, Report of the Railway Rates Commission; "A Report," *Edmonton Bulletin*, 26 September 1895; Willison, *Railway Question in Canada*, 22.

39 E.g., RG 46; vol. 709, file 6868, George Henry New to Schreiber, 26 March 1897; New to Schreiber, 16 February 1897; W.J. Fielding to A.G. Blair, 2 March 1897; vol. 715, file 8211, George Casey MP to A.G. Blair, 4 June 1899; vol. 717, 8627, J. Campbell to Collingwood Schreiber, 29 January 1900; vol. 781, 281, John Campbell v. Grand Trunk Railway, Canadian Pacific Railway, and others, 30 January 1900.

40 Willison, *Railway Question in Canada*, 7.

41 Shaugnessy Letterbooks: no. 61, 483–4, Shaugnessy to Charles M. Hays, 9 August 1898; no. 70, 418, Shaugnessy to Charles M. Hays, 1 March 1900; RG 46, vol. 718, file 8764, Reporters' Notes, 20, 21 March 1900. For an analysis and description of Standard's takeover of the Canadian refining industry, I am indebted to Hugh Grant for lending me early versions of Chapters 3 and 4 from his PhD thesis in progress on foreign ownership and the Canadian oil industry.

42 On oil rates, see CNR, vol. 8456, Grand Trunk Railway, *History of Freight Rates in the Provinces of Ontario and Quebec* (Montreal, 10 Janu-

ary 1912); cf. RG 46, vol. 718, file 8764, testimony of John Loud and George M. Bosworth, 21 March 1900.

43 RG 46, vol. 718, file 7987, Reporters Notes, testimony of A.D. Gall, 22 February 1899; United States, Industrial Commission, *Hearings*, Standard Oil Combinations (Washington, 1899), 378, cited in Grant's thesis. For the protests concerning the oil freight tariff, see RG 46: vol. 713, file 7901, Germania Refining Company to Collingwood Schreiber, 16 December 1898, 25 February 1898; Fredericton Board of Trade to Minister of Railways and Canals, 9 February 1899; Canadian Packing Company, London to A.G. Blair, 18 February 1899; Hamilton Board of Trade to Railway Committee of the Privy Council, 15 February 1899; vol. 714, file 8002: Kingston Board of Trade to Railway Committee of Privy Council, 11 March 1899; Montreal Board of Trade to Blair, 19 May 1899; vol. 719, file 8848, John Osborne, Vice-President Massey-Harris Company to Blair, 5 April 1900.

44 NA, John S. Willison Papers, MG 30, D 29, vol. 37, folder 286, 27393, Sifton to Willison, 15 February 1899; RG 46, vol. 713, file 7901: Sun Oil Refining Company to Blair, 26 January 1899; Staunton and O'Heir to Blair, 31 January 1899.

45 Ibid.: vol. 714, file 7987, Reporters Notes, 22 February 1899; vol. 780, 220–3, Minutes, Sun Oil Refining Company v. Grand Trunk and Canadian Pacific Railways.

46 Ibid., vol. 714, file 8002, Staunton to Blair, 7 March 1899; Hon. William Mulock to Blair, 8 April 1899; Order, Railway Committee of the Privy Council, 11 April 1899; Gall-Schneider to Blair, 12, 19 May 1899; E.R. Clarkson (Sun Oil Company) to Blair, 22, 27 May 1899, 19 June 1899; Shaugnessy Letterbooks, no. 67, 611, Shaugnessy to Collingwood Schreiber, 2 June 1899; *Debates*, 2 August 1899, 9175; RG 46: vol. 719, file 8882, L. Brodeur to Blair [n.d.] (request for government to pay related expenses, amounting to over $700) vol. 718, file 8676, Reporters Notes, 1 January 1900; vol. 717, file 8602, George M. Clark to Schreiber, 26 January 1900, Amended Complaint of Sun Oil and Gall-Schneider, 5 February 1900.

47 Ibid., vol. 718, file 8764, Reporters Notes, 20–2 March 1900.

48 Ibid., vol. 718, file 8764, Reporters Notes, 22 March 1900, x–36.

49 Ibid.: vol. 718, file 8764, Reporters Notes, 21 March 1900, 87; cf. vol. 714, file 7987, Reporters Notes, 22 February 1899, 75.

50 Ibid., Reporters Notes, 22 March 1900, x–47.

51 Ibid., vol. 719, file 8806, Order, Railway Committee of the Privy Council, 24 April 1900, Approved by cabinet 1 May 1900.

52 *Debates*: John MacMillan (Liberal, South Huron), 3 May 1899, 2498–509; N. Clark Wallace (Conservative, West York), 3 May 1899, 2509–12; T.S. Sproule (Conservative, East Grey), 21 February 1900, 768–71.

CHAPTER FIVE

1 NA, William Lyon Mackenzie King Papers, MG 26 J1, 2517, S.J. Mc-Lean to King, 28 December 1901. King and McLean travelled to the University of Chicago on the same train (NA, William Lyon Mackenzie King Diaries, MG 26 J13, 30 September 1896) and kept in touch, both at the university (13 January, 19 June 1897) and afterwards (King Papers: 605–7, McLean to King, 18 October, 12 December 1897; 1852–4, McLean to King, 11 July, 20 October, 16 December 1900).

2 For Blair's statement see "Intercolonial Traffic," Toronto *Globe*, 15 January 1901; for examples of the Toronto *Globe*'s campaign on behalf of the commission, see the following editorials: "Excessive Freight Rates," 4 January 1901; "The Transportation Problem," 10 January 1901; "Transportation Problems," 14 January 1901; "Railway Discrimination," 21, 31 January 1901; "Railway Problems," 4 February 1901; on the House of Commons resolution, see *Debates*, 816–81, 4 March 1901.

3 King Diaries, 28 January 1902; McLean's personal ambitions concerning the railway commission are clear: see NA, John S. Willison Papers, MG 30 D 29, vol. 3, folder 28, 2053–4, A.G. Blair to Willison, 3 November 1898; King Papers, 3039, 5 August 1903.

4 NA, Public Service Commission, RG 32, Historical Personnel Files, vol. 181, Simon James McLean; "Simon James McLean," *Who's Who in America*, vol. 2 (1901–03), 736; University of Toronto Archives, Department of Graduate Records, A73–0026/228, file Simon J. McLean; McLean, *Tariff History of Canada*; Drummond, *Political Economy at the University of Toronto*, 19. On King, see Craven, '*An Impartial Umpire*,' 31–73; Dawson, *William Lyon Mackenzie King*, vol. 1, 3–93. On Wickett, see Weaver, "Order and Efficiency," 220–34.

5 University of Toronto Rare Book Room, James Mavor Papers, MSS 119, Box 12, McLean to Mavor, 23 December 1896, 22 October 1899; McLean, "Railway Policy of Canada"; "An Early Chapter in Canadian Railway Policy," 323–52, "The Railway Policy of Canada, 1849–67, Parts I and II," 191–217, 351–83, "Canadian Railways and the Bonding Question," 500–42, "Federal Regulation of Railways in the United States," 151–71, "State Regulation of Railways in the United States," 349–69, "Railway Rate Regulation in Canada," 419–29; University of Toronto Archives, Department of Graduate Records, A73–0026/228, file Simon J. McLean; NA, Wilfrid Laurier Papers, MG 26 G 1, 27662–3: J.S. Willison to Laurier, 31 October 1898; Laurier to Willison, 1 November 1898.

6 Willison Papers, vol. 3, folder 28, 2052–4, A.G. Blair to Willison, 19 October, 3 November 1898. The Railways Department already had begun gathering information for a study: NA, Records of Department

of Railways and Canals, RG 43, A1, vol. 950, pt 3, file 81981, response of American Railroad Commissions to Collingwood Schreiber, 1897.

7 Canada, Parliament, *Sessional Papers*, 1902, no. 20a, Reports Upon Railway Commissions, Railway Rate Grievances and Regulative Legislation, 4–5, 35–6.

9 Haskell, *Emergence of Professional Social Science*; Skowronek, *Building a New Administrative State*, 42–5, Goodnow, *Politics and Administration*; Gerald E. Caiden, "In search of an Apolitical Science of American Public Administration"; Robert D. Miewald, "The Origins of [Woodrow] Wilson's Thought," in Rabin and Bowman, eds. *Politics and Administration*, 51–76, 17–30. The possible link between McLean and Goodnow was first noted by *R.C.B.* Risk, "Lawyers, Courts and the Rise of the Regulatory State."

10 Owram, *The Government Generation*, 41–79 (quotation is from O.D. Skelton, cited at 47–8); for interpretations of progressive reform in America, see Hays, *Conservation and the Gospel of Efficiency*; Hays, *American Political History as Social Analysis*, Part III; Hammack, *Power and Society*.

11 *Sessional Papers*, 1902, no. 20a, Reports Upon Railway Commissions 22–4.

12 On the Interstate Commerce Commission and the Supreme Court, see Skowronek, *Building a New Administrative State*, 150–60.

13 *Sessional Papers*, 1902, no. 20a, Reports Upon Railway Commissions, 38–40.

14 For Blair and the Intercolonial, see *Debates*, 2792–897, 9 May 1899, and the subsequent debate throughout the 1899 session. For his concern over the Senate and the railway commission proposal, see Willison Papers, vol. 3, folder 28, 2053–4, Blair to Willison, 3 November 1898. Laurier denied the division in Laurier Papers, 34074, Laurier to D.C. Barker, 2 June 1899, but for a discussion of the ideological divisions within the Laurier cabinet, see Owram, *The Government Generation*, 34–41, and Hall, *Clifford Sifton*, vol. 2, 19, 101–6.

15 King Papers, vol. 3, 250–6; McLean to King, 15 February 1901; King to McLean, 19 February 1901; Laurier Papers, 53829, Laurier to E.H. Horsey, 4 March 1901; *Sessional Papers*, 1902, no. 20a, Reports Upon Railway Commissions, 41–2; "Professor McLean was Previous," Toronto *World*, 16 July 1901. To get some idea of political party fortunes in Ontario around 1900, see Stevens, "Laurier and the Liberal Party in Ontario" and Humphries, *'Honest Enough to Be Bold,'* 53–61. For the west and the 1900 election, see Hall, *Clifford Sifton*, vol. 1, 293–301.

16 RG 43, vol. 200, file 238, Evidence, Railway Rates Commission (Oliver Twist quote from evidence of W.R. McInnes, 12 September 1901).

17 *Sessional Papers*, 1902, no. 20a, Reports Upon Railway Commissions, 42–74.
18 Ibid., 77–8.
19 *Debates*, 1902, 9 April 1902, 2431–42.
20 CNR, Grand Trunk Railway – General Manager's Letterbooks, vol. 1783: 406, Geo. M. Reeve to Shaugnessy, 16 July 1901; 465, Reeve to J.W. Loud, 18 July 1901; Montreal *Star*, 26 March 1902.
21 "CPR Rates for Freight," Toronto *Globe*, 9 January 1901; McLean, "Canadian Railways and the Bonding Question," 500–42; CPR, Shaugnessy Letterbooks: no. 74, 522, Shaugnessy to McLean, 24 June 1901; no. 77, 411–12, Shaugnessy to Collingwood Schreiber, 4 April 1902.
22 Statistics from CNR, vol. 10394, History of the Grand Trunk Railway Company of Canada, Appendix Statistics; Innis, *Canadian Pacific Railway*, 143–51, 58–70, 244–8.
23 Kolko, *Railroads and Regulation*, 7–15; Canadian Freight Association, "History of Canadian Freight Association" (pamphlet kindly provided to me by J.R. McMaster, Assistant Chairman of the Association); CNR, Canadian Freight Association Minutebooks, vol. 10820, note re J. Earls, 4 September 1896, and for examples of various activities, see minutes: 413.5, 1 November 1896 (outlining general principle to be followed in establishing commodity rates from Ontario to Montreal and points east); 510, 14 December 1896 (committee to study modernization Maritime rates); 640, 10 March 1897 (presentation by canning industry); 767, 24 June 1897 (report of violations by railways of classification rules); 1205, 28 April 1898 (presentation by fruit growers); 2123, vol. 10830, 21 February 1900; 2144, 21 February 1900 (committees studying advances in cotton and paper special rates); vol. 10818, 827, 9 December 1902 (advancing iron commodity rate 10 per cent).
24 Hall, *Clifford Sifton*, vol. 2, 97–109.
25 RG 43, vol. 697, *The Railway Act 1903*, Report of the Legal Committee to the General Committee of Executive Officers of Railway Companies [hereafter Report of Legal Committee], 2.
26 *Debates*, 20 March 1903, 244–61; RG 43, vol. 697, *The Railway Act 1903*, Charles Fitzpatrick's annotated copy of Railway Act.
27 NA, Canadian Manufacturers' Association Papers, MG 28 I 230, vol. 67, Minutes Railway and Transportation Committee, 24 November 1902, 12 January 1903; Laurier Papers, 69812–3; W. Purcell to Laurier, 2 February 1903; W.L. Smith (Secretary to Laurier) to Purcell, 5 February 1903; RG 43, vol. 697, Memorandum of Suggested Amendments, Toronto Board of Trade, 12 May 1903; NA, Records of the Canadian Transport Commission, RG 46, vol. 1589, file PAC1, Confer-

ence re Railway Bill 1903, between Ministers of Railway and Justice
and Representatives of Railway Companies and Shipping Interests
[hereafter Conference], 1–21, 14 May 1903.

28 See e.g., *Debates*: 27 May 1903, 3538–78; 29 May 1903, 2713–51;
26 June 1903, 5568–72; 9 July 1903, 6284–99.

29 Conference, 21–30.

30 Ibid., 318–28.

31 Ibid., 40, 331–6, 393.

32 Ibid., 389–97.

33 Ibid., 397; The Railway Act, 1903, S.C. 1903, c. 58, ss. 257, 260–2,
274.

34 Conference, 305; The Railway Act, 1903, ss. 253(2), (3), 254.

35 Report of Legal Committee, 5; Conference, 61–69, 453–60; cf. RG 43,
vol. 697, Charles Fitzpatrick's annotated copy of Railway Act, s. 42
and related notes.

36 Canada, Senate, *Debates*: 3 September 1903, 1002–7; 20 October
1903, 1678–9; 22 October 1903, 1751–65; 24 October 1903, 1814–
16; *Debates*, 13 October 1903, 13840; Laurier Papers: 78212, Shaugnessy to Laurier, 23 October 1903; 78208–10, Chas. M. Hays to Laurier, 23 October 1903; RG 43, vol. 220, no. 900, R.J. Young to
Fielding, 21 October 1903; *Debates*: 20 October 1903, 14519–20;
22 October 1903, 14760–63; 24 October 1903, 14844–5; The Railway
Act, 1903, ss. 43–4. Almost all of the other Senate amendments concerned constitutional questions, in particular the efforts of the federal
government to extend the jurisdiction of the *Railway Act*.

37 For Britain, see Alderman, *The Railway Interest*, particularly 146–58,
and Cain, "Traders versus Railways," 65–84; for the United States,
see Martin, *Enterprise Denied*. Although the American situation remains somewhat more controversial, one does not need to accept
Martin's overall thesis that regulation crippled the railway industry to
appreciate the accuracy of his portrayal of the extension of state control involved in the 1906 legislation. For an even more convincing re-
futation of the claim of historian Gabriel Kolko that shippers took no
interest in the 1906 legislation, see Vietor, "Businessmen and the Political Economy," 47–66.

38 Laurier Papers, 78723–4, Shaugnessy to Laurier, 10 November 1903;
Conference, 524.

39 Laurier Papers: 138380–2, Hon. W.C. Edwards to Laurier, 26 March
1908; 14463–6, Laurier to Cartwright, 9 September 1908; Cartwright
to Laurier, 11 September 1908; NA, George P. Graham Papers, MG 27
II D8, vol. 47, file 418, 25922–49, McLean to G. Graham, 11 January
1908; cf. biographical sources in footnote 4 of this chapter.

CHAPTER SIX

1 BRC Transcripts, vol. 1, file vol. 1, 3 (A.G. Blair), 9 February 1904.
2 *Stamford Junction Case* (1904), 3 *C.R.C.* 256.
3 *Annual Report*, 1904–06, 1907–08, 1908–09, 1911–12, 1913–14 (Ottawa, 1907, 1909, 1910, 1913, 1915); *Railway and Shipping World* (November 1911), 1013.
4 "Report of the Chief Traffic Officer," *Annual Report*, 1913–14 (Ottawa, 1915).
5 NA, Wilfrid Laurier Papers, MG 26 G1, 78504–12, Blair to Laurier, 24 November 1903.
6 Ibid., 88098, Blair to Laurier [resignation], 18 October 1904. When Blair resigned, it was not to join the Canadian Pacific legal office but to become part of a rather complex and somewhat sordid scheme to return to politics, as a Conservative. The story of the *La Presse* affair, in which Blair, Robert Borden, officials from the Canadian Northern and Canadian Pacific railways, and a number of other key figures plotted to try to defeat the Laurier government over its railway policy, is outlined by Brown, *Borden*, 78–85.
7 "A.C. Killam," *Railway and Shipping World* (January 1905) 21; "Board of Railway Commissioners," ibid. (April 1908), 275; "Death of Chief Commissioner Mabee," ibid. (June 1912), 286; Laurier Papers, 144463–66: Laurier to Cartwright [re Scott and other appointments], 9 September 1908; Cartwright to Laurier, 11 September 1908; *Annual Report*, 1907–08, 1908–09 (1909, 1910).
8 BRC Transcripts: vol. 12, file vol. 29, 1879–80 (Loud's career), 20 April 1906; vol. 13, file vol. 32, 3615 (Bosworth's career), 6 June 1906; vol. 24, file vol. 59, 1510 (MacInnes' career), 5 February 1908; vol. 23, file vol. 58, 1072, (Peters' career), 30 June 1908; 1510 (Shaw's career), 2 August 1908.
9 Ibid.: vol. 5, file vol. 11, 5588 (on A. White, Toronto Board of Trade expert), 11 October 1904; vol. 23, file vol. 58, 1034 (on G.E. Carpenter, Winnipeg Board of Trade expert), 30 January 1908; vol. 60, file vol. 135, 6175 (on W. Power, Vancouver Board of Trade expert), 9 February 1911; "The New Transportation Expert" [on W.H.D. Miller, Canadian Manufacturers' Association, who later represented some other shippers], *Industrial Canada* (December 1903); "Transportation Department" [on J.R. Marlow, Canadian Manufacturers' Association], ibid. (January 1905); "J.R. Marlow," *Railway and Shipping World* (January 1905), 17.
10 "Death of James Hardwell," *Railway and Shipping World* (July 1921), 355.

11 Bernstein, *Regulating Business by Independent Commissions*; Kolko, *Railroads and Regulation*; Armstrong and Nelles, *Monopoly's Moment*, particularly pts 3 and 4.

12 BRC Transcripts: vol. 2, file vol. 5, 1975, (G.M. Bosworth), 20 June 1904; vol. 13, file vol. 32, 3473 (C.E. Dewey), 31 May 1906. Cf. vol. 2, file vol. 3, 1157, (John Loud), 5 June 1904; vol. 13, file vol. 32, 3431–3, (W.R. MacInnes), 31 May 1906.

13 *Sydenham Glass Company Case* (1904), 3 *C.R.C.* 409; BRC Transcripts: vol. 2, file vol. 5, 1963–78 (Sydenham Glass Company re Rates Detroit vs. Wallaceburg to Toronto), 20 June 1904; vol. 3, file vol. 8, 3070–3 (Judgment), 30 July 1904; vol. 13, file vol. 31, 3030–4, file vol. 32, 3377–511 (Staunton Limited asking Board of Railway Commissioners to restore rates in effect prior to 15 November 1905), 10, 31 May 1906; "Re-complaint of Staunton's Ltd., Toronto," *Annual Report*, 1908–09 (Ottawa, 1910), 171. The board ruled that the advance resulting from the cancellation of a special rate was reasonable in another 1904 case: BRC Transcripts: vol. 1, file vol. 2, 978–1023; vol. 2, file vol. 3, 1111–63 (Case 22, United Factories and Grand Trunk Railway in matter of advance rate), 28 April, 5 June 1904; *United Factories v. Grand Trunk Railway Co.* (1904), 3 *C.R.C.* 424.

14 Ibid.: vol. 12, file vol. 29, 1874 (Blair), 1887–1928, 20 April 1906; vol. 13, file vol. 31, 2964 (Miller), 3001–2, 10 May 1906.

15 Ibid., vol. 12, file vol. 29, 1838–9 (Killam on procedure), 20 April 1906.

16 Canadian Freight Association, *Decisions of the Board of Railway Commissioners*, no. 42, Davies Limited – Rates on Packing House Produces for Export, 29 June 1906.

17 *In re Joint Freight and Passenger Tariffs* (1909), 10 *C.R.C.* 343, at 347.

18 For a thorough discussion of the board's pre-war regulatory principles, see MacGibbon, *Railway Rates and the Canadian Railway Commission*.

19 For this discussion of the oil industry, I have relied on an early draft of Hugh Grant's PhD dissertation on the oil industry, chapter 4, "The Effective Monopoly of Imperial Oil, 1900–1920."

20 BRC Transcripts, vol. 41, file vol. 95, 13097–112 (Application from British American Oil Company for order directing Grand Trunk Railway and Canadian Pacific Railway to adjust rates from Toronto on petroleum and products), 2 December 1909; Saywell, "The Early History of Canadian Oil Companies," 67–72.

21 The firm also sought improved inbound rates and successfully acquired them due to a technical mistake made by railway officials: *British American Oil Co. v. Grand Trunk Railway* (1909), 9 *C.R.C.* 178;

Grand Trunk Railway v. *British American Oil Co.* (1910), 43 *Supreme Court Reports* 311.

22 BRC Transcripts: vol. 41, file vol. 95: 13102–6 (Remarks of Pullen); 13142.1–42.87 (Conference arising from British American Oil Case), 3 December 1909; vol. 42, file vol. 98, 15267 (Exchange between C.D. Chamberlin and Mabee), 21 December 1909.

23 Ibid., 15265–306 (British American Oil Company application, remark by Parsons of British American, 15299), 21 December 1909.

24 Canadian Freight Association, *Decisions of Board of Railway Commissioners*, Judgment – application of the British American Oil Company, file 12203, 30 March 1910.

25 BRC Transcripts, vol. 79, file vol. 174, 2655–73 (Application of Dominion Sugar Company to have sugar mileage rates placed on parity with those from Montreal to Toronto and Hamilton), 30 April 1913; *Dominion Sugar Co.* v. *Grand Trunk, Canadian Pacific, Chatham Wallaceburg and Lake Erie and Pere Marquette Railway Cos* (1913), 17 *C.R.C.* 231–40.

26 BRC Transcripts, vol. 84, file vol. 185, 7255–65 (Application for readjustment of rates from Wallaceburg to Toronto and Hamilton by Dominion Sugar Company), 14 October 1913; *Dominion Sugar Co.* v. *Grand Trunk, Canadian Pacific, Chatham Wallaceburg and Lake Erie, & Pere Marquette Railway Cos*, 240–7 (Drayton's comment, 245).

27 See e.g., *Doolittle & Wilcox* v. *Grand Trunk and Canadian Pacific Railways* (1908), 8 *C.R.C.* 10; *Canadian Portland Cement Co.* v. *Grand Trunk and Bay of Quinte Railways* (1909), 9 *C.R.C.* 209; *Welland* v. *Canadian Freight Association* (1911), 13 *C.R.C.* 140.

28 NA, Records of the Department of Railways and Canals, RG 43, vol. 331, file 4965, pt 1, "Rate Making – Public Carriers," Address by S.J. McLean to Montreal Branch of the Engineering Institute of Canada, 15 November 1925; the phrase "not a mere arbiter of logic" is also that of Commissioner McLean, *Kemp Manufacturing & Metal, and Winnipeg Ceiling & Roofing Cos* v. *Canadian Pacific Railway* (1909), 10 *C.R.C.* 163.

29 BRC Transcripts, vol. 3, file vol. 6, 2491–503 (Toronto Board of Trade presentation), 24 June 1904.

30 NA, Records of the Canadian Transcript Commission, RG 46, Central Registry Files, vol. 1542, file 710: Toronto Board of Trade to Board, 24 June 1904; Advisory Committee Canadian Freight Association to Chief Commissioner A.G. Blair, 29 August 1904; F. Morley (Toronto Board of Trade to Cartwright), 22 November 1905; James Mills to fellow commissioners, 20 December 1905; Advisory Committee, Canadian Freight Association to Cartwright, 11 January 1906; Morley to

Board, 15 February 1906; BRC Transcripts, vol. 13, file vol. 31, 3049–
3360 (Case 368, Toronto Board of Trade application for reduced
rates), 29, 30 May 1906.

31 Ibid., 3067–9 (Killam), 29 May 1906; RG 46, Central Registry Files,
vol. 1542, file 710, Memorandum from James Hardwell re Toronto
Board of Trade Complaint, 30 July 1906.

32 BRC Transcripts, vol. 12, file vol. 30, 2605–72 (Cases 382, 383, 384,
Kerr Engine Company, Walkerville Brewing Company, Standard
Paint and Varnish re rates charged; Case 374, William Grey and
Sons), 4 May 1906.

33 Ibid., vol. 13, file vol. 32, 3623 (Bosworth), 6 June 1906.

34 Ibid., 3591–605 (F.H. Chrysler); 3615–39 (G.M. Bosworth); 3791–
803 (A.G. Blair), 6, 7 June 1906.

35 Ibid., 3811–12 (Killam), 7 June 1906; RG 46, Central Registry Files,
vol. 1542, file 710, Report of Chief Traffic Officer re International
and Toronto Board of Trade Rate Cases, 27 June 1907, 3–4 [this,
Hardwell's supplementary report and the various orders related to
the case were published in *Annual Report* (1908), 5–23].

36 In Canada, all other rates always were fixed in relation to the fifth-
class rate. For example, the railways charged twice as much for first-
class as for fifth-class freight. No such fixed relationship existed in the
United States, and first-class generally represented quite a bit more
than double fifth-class. American railway officials were willing to
adopt the Canadian general freight tariff, but not if it meant an adjustment of all rates on the basis of the current fifth-class rate that
would involve a large number of reductions and adjustments in
American rates. Instead, they agreed to maintain their current first-
class rates into Canada, while adjusting all others using the Canadian
proportions. For example, instead of doubling the existing fifth-class
rates to get new first-class rates, the new tariff on fifth-class freight
would represent one-half of the existing tariff on first-class freight. As
a result, with the exception of first-class freight, which remained the
same, all other rates from Detroit were increased.

37 Ibid., 4–5; BRC Transcripts, vol. 15, file vol. 38 (Meeting in Grand
Trunk Railway office re discrimination Michigan v. Western Ontario),
6480–531.

38 RG 46, Central Registry Files, vol. 1542, file 710, Report of Chief
Traffic Officer re International and Toronto Board of Trade Rate
Cases, 27 June 1907, 6–7.

39 Ibid., 7–16.

40 Hawley, *The New Deal and the Problem of Monopoly*, 187–90. See e.g.,
the different treatment of fruit growers by the railways after the establishment of the commission: CNR, Canadian Freight Association,

Minutes, vol. 10820: minute 1205, 28 April 1898; minute 1248, 30 June 1898; RG 46, Central Registry Files, vol. 1440, file 441; W.H. Bunting to Board, 24 March 1904; W.L. Dawson to Cartwright, 27 May 1904; John Loud to Commissioner Mills, 2 September 1904; BRC Transcripts, vol. 5, file vol. 11, 10 October 1904.

41 See, for example, the grumblings of Charles M. Hays of the Grand Trunk Railway: CNR, Grand Trunk Railway – General Manager's Letterbooks, vol. 1791, 337, 353, Hays to A.C. Killam, 23 October 1907, 24 October 1907.

42 BRC Transcripts: vol. 3, file vol. 6, 2491 (Bernier), 24 June 1904; vol. 62, file vol. 140, 9761 (Mabee), 19 December 1911.

43 Roger Noll, "Government Regulatory Behaviour: A Multidisciplinary Survey and Synthesis" in Noll, ed., *Regulatory Policy and the Social Sciences*, 45.

CHAPTER SEVEN

1 E.g. BRC Transcripts, vol. 70, file vol. 157, 7443–5 (Alexander McDonald), 19 July 1912.

2 Ibid., vol. 66, file vol. 148, 4128 (Bicknell), 16 April 1912.

3 Much of the discussion which follows is based on Paul Voisey, "The Urbanization of the Canadian Prairies, 1871–1916," Alan F.J. Artibise, "Boosterism and the Development of Prairie Cities, 1871–1913," in Francis and Palmer, *The Prairie West*, 383–434.

4 Robert A.J. McDonald, "Victoria, Vancouver and the Economic Development of British Columbia, 1886–1914," in Ward and McDonald, *British Columbia*, 369–95; L.D. McCann, "Urban Growth in a Staple Economy: The Emergence of Vancouver as a Regional Metropolis," 1886–1914," in Evenden, ed., *Vancouver*, 17–42; Patricia Roy, *Vancouver*.

5 Lamb, *Canadian Pacific Railway*, 233–5; Regehr, *Canadian Northern Railway*, 157–218, 285–302; Glazebrook, *History of Transportation*, 135–40.

6 Canada, Parliament, *Sessional Papers*, no. 20, 1908, 1911, 1915, Annual Report of the Department of Railways and Canals, 1907, 1910, 1914.

7 See Argo, "Historical Review of Canadian Railway Freight Rate Structure, 1876–1938" in Henry, *Railway Freight Rates in Canada*.

8 CNR, Canadian Northern Railway Legal Files, vol. 8566 A, file 3–8: George H. Shaw (Traffic Manager) to William Mackenzie, 23 May, 2 September 1902, 7 January, 28 July, 12 October 1903, 8 November, 27 December 1904; Shaw to Z.A. Lash (Chief Solicitor), 22 June 1905.

9 Ibid., Shaw to Lash, 22 June 1905; NA, Records of the Canadian Transport Commission, RG 46, Central Registry File, vol. 1515,

file 5664, pt 1: F.W. Peters (Assistant Freight Traffic Manager, Canadian Pacific) to Killam, 6 August 1907; Killam to Peters, 12 August 1907; Herbert Baker (Portage La Prairie Board of Trade) to Board of Railway Commissioners, 13 August 1907; BRC Transcripts, 4057–61, 21 August 1907.

10 RG 46, Central Registry Files, vol. 1515, file 5664, pt 1: C.N. Bell (Winnipeg Jobbers and Shippers Association and Council of Board of Trade), to Killam, 14 November 1907; Winnipeg Wholesale Implement Association to Killam, 19 November 1907; Winnipeg Branch of Canadian Manufacturers' Association to Killam, 16 November 1907; Portage La Prairie Board of Trade to Killam, 15 November 1907; Brandon Board of Trade to Killam, 20 November 1907; Killam to Charles Drinkwater (Canadian Pacific), 21 November 1907; Moose Jaw Board of Trade to Killam, 22 November 1907; Regina Board of Trade to Board, 23 November 1907; Victoria Board of Trade to Killam, 23 November 1907; Vancouver Board of Trade to Killam, 23 November 1907; Killam to Bell, 25 November 1907.

11 BRC Transcripts: vol. 23, file vol. 56, 1a–34, 7, 9 January 1908, file vol. 58, 930–1457, 29–31 January, 1, 3 February 1908; vol. 24, file vol. 59, 1461–816, 5, 6, 14 February 1908; vol. 28, file vol. 67, 7143–448, 16–18 September 1908.

12 RG 46, Central Registry Files, vol. 1515, file 5664, pt 1: Regina Board of Trade to Board, 18 December 1907, 24 January 1908; Brandon Board of Trade to Killam, 25 January 1908; vol. 1441, file 12682, pt 1, H.C. Lawson (Regina Board of Trade) to Board of Railway Commissioners, 9 October 1909.

13 BRC Transcripts, vol. 41, file vol. 96, 14000–171, 12623–33 (Regina Rates case), 8, 15 November 1909.

14 *Canadian Pacific and Canadian Northern Railway Cos* v. *Regina Board of Trade* (1909), 11 *C.R.C.* 380–94; affirmed (1911), 13 *C.R.C.* 203–15. BRC Transcripts, vol. 53, file vol. 122, 1181–1220 (Application to appeal), 21 February 1911.

15 During the original hearings, a Regina merchant claimed that the Fort William to Winnipeg rate was based on a "constructive mileage," so that a tariff was charged applicable to 290 miles instead of the actual 424 miles. Although freight traffic officers denied that they had used such a system, they used the concept of "constructive mileage" as the foundation of the new tariffs. Merchants in Regina would pay the rate for the "constructive mileage" of 290 miles from the Lakehead to Winnipeg plus the actual distance of 357 miles from Winnipeg to Regina, making for a charge on a total of 647 instead of 781 miles. The railways, however, continued to apply the higher Saskatchewan–Alberta tariff on this constructed distance.

16 BRC Transcripts: vol. 64, file vol. 145, 1824–52, 13 February 1912; vol. 67, file vol. 151, 4751–93 (Application for Order to Lower Tariff to Regina), 21 May 1912; RG 46, Central Registry Files, vol. 1441, file 12682, pt 1, M.K. Cowan (Regina Board of Trade) to D'Arcy Scott, 16 May 1912; file 12682, pt 3, Response of Canadian Northern and Canadian Pacific to Regina Board of Trade Complaints, 10 June 1912.

17 *British Columbia Pacific Coast Cities* v. *Canadian Pacific Railway Co.* (1906), 7 *C.R.C.* 139–41; BRC Transcripts, vol. 48, file vol. 11, 9933–6 (E.K. Beeston, Nelson Board of Trade), 6 September 1910.

18 Ibid., vol. 10, file vol. 26, 404–58, 6 March 1906.

19 Ibid.: vol. 4, file vol. 9, 4163–77 (Eastbound rates to Calgary), 31 August 1904; vol. 10, file vol. 26, 404–98 (B.C. Coast Cities v. Canadian Pacific), 6 March 1906; vol. 11, file vol. 27, 501–717 (Killam's remark as to investigation, 532), 6, 7, 8 March 1906; *British Columbia Pacific Coast Cities* v. *Canadian Pacific* (1906), 7 *C.R.C.* 125, at 143.

20 Ibid., 135–41.

21 Ibid., 141–7. Commissioner James Mills dissented from the majority ruling, arguing that the commission should accept the report and recommendations of Hardwell, "whose technical knowledge and experience specially fit him for dealing with such questions," 148–9.

22 BRC Transcripts, vol. 53, file vol. 121, 620 (MacInnes of CPR describes voluntary concessions), 26 January 1911.

23 BRC Transcripts: vol. 41, file vol. 96, 14530–588 (Presentation of Vancouver Board of Trade), 27 October 1909; vol. 48, file vol. 11, 9906–37 (Application of Vancouver Board of Trade re discrimination, Vancouver vs Montreal), 6 September 1910; vol. 49, file vol. 112, 1304–8 (Vancouver Board of Trade case), 9 September 1910; vol. 53, file vol. 121, 643–84 (Vancouver Board of Trade case), 26, 27 January 1911; 769–819, 908–13 (Testimony of Sullivan, Moule, and Lanigan), 27, 28 January 1911.

24 Ibid., vol. 53, file vol. 121; 819–33, 27 January 1911; 938–41, 28 January 1911.

25 Ibid., vol. 64, file vol. 145, 1870–1935, 13, 14 February 1912.

26 RG 46, Central Registry Files, vol. 1464, file 18755, pt 1, Petitions re western rates, beginning 14 November 1911, last dated 15 February 1912.

27 Ibid., vol. 1464, file 18755, pt 4: Mabee to Winnipeg Board of Trade, 24 November 1911; Mabee to Rogers, 25 November 1911; C.N. Bell (Winnipeg Board of Trade) to Minister of Railways and Canals, 4 December 1911; Mabee to Frank Cochrane (Minister of Railways and Canals), 21 December 1911; Board of Railway Commissioners Order 15754, 8 January 1912.

28 A third lawyer, F.A. Morrison from the Maritimes appears on some of the documentation but took no active part, and is never even mentioned during the investigation.

29 BRC Transcripts, vol. 64, file vol. 145, 1807–16, 13 February 1912; vol. 65, file vol. 146, 2825–55, 8 March 1912.

30 Ibid., vol. 69, file vol. 154, 6467 (Phippen), 19 June 1912.

31 Ibid., vol. 65, file vol. 146, 4104–32, 16 April 1912.

32 RG 46, Central Registry Files, vol. 1464, file 18755, pt 3: H.W. Whitla to Drayton, 5 September 1912; M.K. Cowan to Drayton, 6 September 1912; Cowan to Drayton, 22 October 1912; BRC Transcripts, vol. 72: file vol. 160, 9228–39, 28 September 1912; file vol. 161, 9562–747, 7, 8 October 1912; vol. 73, file vol. 162, 9752–977, 9, 10 October 1912. Drayton was formerly solicitor for the city of Toronto and a member of the Toronto Hydro-Electric Commission.

33 Ibid.: vol. 73, file vol. 163, 10236 (Cowan), 4 November 1912; vol. 76: file vol. 168, 53–382, 7, 8, 9 January 1913; file vol. 169, 404–662 (Drayton comment at 628, cf. 528, 641, 652, 654), 10, 11 January 1913; vol. 82, file vol. 180, 4735–5663 (Almost entire hearing focuses on U.S. comparisons) 18, 19, 20, 25 June 1913, (Further comments by Drayton), 5548, 5663–5, 25 June 1913.

34 Ibid., vol. 88, file vol. 192, 10254–5, 12 December 1913.

35 RG 46, Hearings Exhibits, vol. 585, file 18755, 0.106–7, Exhibit Series I–IV prepared by Jean Paul Muller (1913) [hereafter Muller Exhibits Series], I, 56–7.

36 Ibid., 1–55; BRC Transcripts, vol. 86, file vol. 188, 8696–749 (Muller testimony), 25 November 1913.

37 Ibid., 8750–71 (Muller testimony), 25 November 1913; Hearing Exhibits, vol. 585, file 18755, no. 106–7 (Muller Exhibits Series IV), 1913.

38 RG 46, Hearing Exhibits, vol. 585, file 18755, no. 108–10, Brief Filed on Behalf of Canadian Pacific Railway, 21 November 1913, 2–8; BRC Transcripts, vol. 86: file vol. 188, 8849–59, 8877, 25 November 1913; file vol. 189, 9258, 29 November 1913.

39 Ibid., vol. 86, file vol. 188, 8728, 8850–95, 25 November 1913; RG 46, Hearing Exhibits, vol. 585, file 18755, no. 108–10, Canadian Pacific Brief, 21 November 1913, 12–20.

40 BRC Transcripts, vol. 86, file vol. 188, 9079–83, 9208, 29 November 1913; RG 46, Hearing Exhibits, vol. 585, file 18755, no. 106–7, Muller Exhibits Series VI, 1913, 11–13.

41 Ibid., 7–8.

42 BRC Transcripts, vol. 86, file vol. 189, 9225–6, 29 November 1913, cf. 9110–22, 28 November 1913.

43 See Sharfman, *The Interstate Commerce Commission*, vol. III, pt B, 98–161. Kolko (*Railroads and Regulation*) thinks it of the utmost signifi-

cance that regulators and governments sought to ensure the railway companies a fair rate of return, which accounts for his concluding with the 1920 *Transportation Act*. Such an approach overlooks many more interesting questions – including why regulators found it impossible to follow this mandate.

44 *In re Western Tolls* (1914), 17 *C.R.C.* 123, at 156–71 (quote re Grand Trunk at 167).

45 Ibid., 162, 164–6.

46 Ibid., 196–214 (Interstate Commerce Commission decision cited at 209–10).

47 Ibid., 171–96.

48 Ibid., 217–29; BRC Transcripts, vol. 92, file vol. 200, 109–44, *In re Western Tolls*, 6 April 1914 [includes many of the specific recommendations not published in *C.R.C.*]; RG 46, Central Registry Files, vol. 1464, file 18755, pt 1, Western Rates Case – Report of Chief Traffic Officer, 16 March 1914.

49 In the course of the western rate inquiry, the commission had also been asked to consider a number of special commodity rates in the west. In the decision, the board agreed to adjust and reduce tolls on grain, dairy, and packing house products, cement, and coal shipped within the region, but refused to lower livestock, vegetable, and few other special rates: ibid.

50 *In re Western Tolls* (1914), 17 *C.R.C.* 123 at 230.

51 BRC Transcripts, vol. 88, file vol. 192, 10254–5, 12 December 1913.

52 NA, Department of Railways and Canals Records, RG 43, vol. 331, file 4965, pt 1, "Rate Making – Public Carriers," address by S.J. McLean to Montreal Branch – Engineering Institute of Canada, 15 November 1925.

53 "Sops Instead of Justice," *Manitoba Free Press*, 9 April 1914; "Extensive Reduction in Canadian Rates Ordered – Comments of President Shaughnessy," *Railway Age Gazette*, 17 April 1914. For a sample of more favourable editorial comments, see "A Great Victory for Saskatchewan," Regina *Morning Leader*, 8 April 1914, "Rate Decision," Edmonton *Journal*, 8 April 1914; "Freight Rates Decision," *Calgary Weekly Herald*, 9 April 1914.

54 E.g., RG 46, Central Registry Files, vol. 1464, file 18755, pt 2, Victoria Board of Trade to Cartwright (Board of Railway Commissioners), 9 July 1914; "Jeremiads versus Justice," *Manitoba Free Press*, 13 December 1913.

CHAPTER EIGHT

1 BRC Transcripts, vol. 110, file vol. 236, 6003–4 (Edwards), 29 June 1915.

2 See Simon, "New British Investment in Canada," 238–54.

3 Eagle, "Sir Robert Borden and the Railway Problem," 197–9.

4 Figures calculated in this and following paragraphs from Canadian Northern and Grand Trunk Pacific statistics published in *Poor's Manual of Railroads*, 1913–20.

5 Eagle, 167–86.

6 Ibid., 238–58, 297, 315–32.

7 Royal Commission on Railways and Transportation, *Report* (Ottawa, 1917), xlvii, xciii; Eagle, "Borden and the Railway Problem," 344–60.

8 Ibid., 343–4.

9 Ibid., 371–436 on the Canadian Northern takeover; and for the Grand Trunk, see Eagle, "Monopoly or Competition," 3–30.

10 Canada, Parliament, *Sessional Papers*: 1919, no. 20b, Railway Statistics, xxix–xxxvii; 1921, no. 20b, Railway Statistics, 21–3.

11 It has been argued that from 1907 onward, internally generated revenues became important to American railways: Neal, "Investment Behaviour by American Railroads," 126–35.

12 For the work of the Canadian Railway War Board, see NA, Records of Department of Railways and Canals, RG 43, vol. 606, file 19173, particularly W.M. Neal (Secretary to Hon. J.D. Reid, Minister of Railways and Canals), 11 March 1919; Hopkins, *Canadian Annual Review – 1918*, 515–20.

13 Application of Maritime Nail Company against rate from Saint John to points on the Quebec Central Railway, Canadian Freight Association, *Decisions of the Board of Railway Commissioners*, III, case no. 222, 23 December 1909; *Canadian Lumbermen's Association* v. *Grand Trunk, Canadian Pacific, and Canadian Northern Railways* (1910), 10 *C.R.C.* 306–19; *International Paper Co.* v. *Grand Trunk, Canadian Pacific, and Canadian Northern Railways Cos* (1913), 15 *C.R.C.* 111–18.

14 NA, Records of the Canadian Transport Commission, RG 46, Central Registry Files, vol. 1519, file 25547, pt 1, J.G. Ransom (Canadian Freight Association) to A.D. Cartwright, 17 February 1915; BRC Transcripts, vol. 102, file vol. 221, 488–517, 1 March 1915. On the 5 per cent case in the United States, see Sharfman, *Interstate Commerce Commission*, vol. III B, 63–71.

15 The official response of a number of business organizations can be found cited in *In re Eastern Tolls* (1916), 22 *C.R.C.* 4, at 8–18.

16 RG 46, Central Registry Files, vol. 110, file vol. 236, 6259–66 (J.F. Orde, Dominion government), 20 June 1915; *In re Eastern Tolls*, 17–18; RG 46, Central Registry Files, vol. 105, file vol. 225, 1200–4 (J.W. Wood, Toronto Board of Trade), 29 March 1915; file vol. 226, 2158–63 (Dunn, International Harvester), 14 April 1915.

17 Ibid., vol. 105, file vol. 225, 1249–54 (Anglo-Canadian Company –

leather); vol. 107, file vol. 229, 3477–500; vol. 110, file vol. 236, 6088–99, 1 June 1915; *In re Eastern Tolls*, 26–8.

18 Ibid., 20–5, 28–40, 42–9.

19 In the matter of the application, commonly referred to as the Eastern Rates case *In re Eastern Tolls* (1916), 6 *J.O.R.R.* 155–64. [The discussion of the various specific increases is excluded from the *C.R.C.* report, as cited above, note 15.] Rates on general merchandise shipped more than twenty-five miles in central Canada and in parts of New Brunswick were advanced one or two cents; rates on goods shipped between the Maritimes and most Quebec communities, including Montreal were advanced two to four cents; freight rates between the Maritimes and southwestern Ontario increased three to six cents.

20 Ibid., 164–250.

21 *In re Eastern Tolls* (1916), 22 *C.R.C.* 4, at 40–2.

22 BRC Transcripts, vol. 110, file vol. 236, 6160–1 (T. Marshall), 1 June 1915.

23 CNR, Canadian Northern Legal Files, vol. 8577, file 3–249: Phippen to Beatty, 6 March 1917; W.H. Biggar to Phippen, 8 March 1917; Beatty to Phippen, 12 March 1917; Phippen to Drayton, 15 March 1917; Drayton to Phippen, 16 March 1917.

24 *In re Increase in Passenger and Freight Tolls* (1917), 22 *C.R.C.* 49, at 53–5; BRC Transcripts, vol. 127, file vol. 269: 2886–932 (Toronto Board of Trade, Canadian Manufacturers' Association, St Catherines Fruit Growers, National Livestock Record Board, United Farmers of Ontario, Kitchener Board of Trade), 12 June 1917; 3199–202 (Montreal Board of Trade), 20 June 1917; 3679–80, (Vancouver Board of Trade), 6 June 1917; 4121–4 (Kootenay Fruit Growers), 16 June 1917; 4135 (Calgary Board of Trade), 17 June 1917; 4189–90 (Edmonton Board of Trade), 19 June 1917; 4284–90 (Winnipeg Board of Trade), 4337–45; (Government of Manitoba), 23 June 1917; 4401 (Fort William Board of Trade), 25 June 1917; 4379 (Phippen, Canadian Northern).

25 Ibid., 4348–9 (Pitblado), 23 June 1917.

26 *In re Increase in Passenger and Freight Tolls*, 63–6.

27 Ibid., 57–63, 77, 81–2.

28 Ibid., 74–5; NA, Robert Borden Papers, MG 26 H: 125500, Canadian Council of Agriculture to Borden, 26 December 1917; 125504, H.J. Symington to Borden, 26 December 1917; 125391–4, Winnipeg Board of Trade to Borden, 5 January 1918; 125395, 12398, Western Retail Lumbermen, 8, 16 January 1918; NA, Privy Council Records, RG 2, Series 3, Dormants, vol. 197, file 1918, no. 229, pt 3; Peter White (lawyer on behalf of Canadian Livestock Interests) re 15 per cent advance, 22 February 1918; Winnipeg Board of Trade memo

re 15 per cent advance, 5 January 1918; H.J. Symington, Appeal from 15 per cent case [n.d.]; Peter White (on behalf of Canadian Livestock interests) to Hon. J.A. Calder, 7–15, 18 February 1918; Reply of Winnipeg Board of Trade Shippers Section in Appeal on 15 per cent case, 3–4, 25 February 1918; Ibid., file 1918, 36–229, pt 1, Transcript of Hearings on Appeal re Increase of Railway Rates, 5–6, 52–4, 69–70 (Symington), 24 January 1918.

29 RG 46, vol. 618, file Appeal from Board of Railway Commissioners, Factum of the Respondents the Canadian Pacific Railway Company, 1–2; RG 2, Series 3, vol. 197, file 1918, 36–229, pt 1, Transcript of Hearings on Appeal re Increase of Railway Rates, 10 (Phippen), 22 (Beatty), 1 March 1918.

30 Borden Papers, 50998, Thomas White to J. Reid, 11 February 1918; NA, George E. Foster Papers, MG 27 II D7, Diaries, vol. 7, 11 March 1918. cf. Borden Papers: 50996, Thomas White (Minister of Finance) to J. Reid (Minister of Railways), 1 February 1918; 55031, Arthur Meighen to Borden, 15 February 1918.

31 RG 2, Series 1, PC 631, PC 632, 14 March 1918. PC 632 also stipulated that the total tax bill of the Canadian Pacific could not be less than the company's total net earnings in excess of a 10 per cent return on its common stock, nor could it be less than the amount by which the company's net earnings might exceed those in the year prior to the rate increase.

32 Unlike its Canadian counterpart, the Interstate Commerce Commission granted the 15 per cent advance on eastern lines only. In March 1918, as the American government prepared to take over that country's railways, the commission quietly ordered first a 15 per cent advance in rates into Canada and then reversed its earlier position and granted the general advance to railways in all parts of America: Sharfman, *Interstate Commerce Commission*, vol. III B, 83–97; cf. Martin, *Enterprise Denied*, 319–35 for the events surrounding the McAdoo award.

33 RG 2, Series 1, PC 1768, 16 July 1918; Drayton to C.J. Doherty, 15 July 1918; Peitchinis, *Labour-Management Relations in the Railway Industry*, 101–15.

34 RG 2, Series 1, PC 1863, 27 July 1918.

35 Canada, Parliament, *Sessional Papers*, 1921, no. 20b, Railway Statistics, 21–3; Peitchinis, *Labour-Management Relations*, 115–19; NA, Robert Borden Diaries, MG 26 H, 6 July 1920; NA, Arthur Meighen Papers, MG 26 I, 26178–80, Howard D. Kelley (President, Railway Association of Canada) to Meighen, 9 July 1920.

36 Ibid., 26180, Meighen to Kelley, 14 July 1920; BRC Transcripts, vol. 165, file vol. 337: 2–19, Exhibit 2 – Application for Advance; 52–9, Exhibit 11 – Statement of Grand Trunk Railway in Connection

with Proposed Canadian Rate Case 1920; vol. 162, file vol. 332, 4273–93 (Phippen for Railway Companies), 10 August 1920; for Meighen's political situation in 1920, see Graham, *Arthur Meighen*, vol. 3–11.

37 "Carvell, Frank Broadstreet," Wallace ed., *Macmillan Dictionary of Canadian Biography*, 137; Hopkins, *Canadian Annual Review – 1918*, 437–8 discusses his role as minister of public works; English, *The Decline of Politics*, 175–6, 212; Eagle, "Monopoly or Competition," 6–7, 10–11; Armstrong and Nelles, *Monopoly's Moment*, 278–9.

38 BRC Transcripts: vol. 162, file vol. 332, 4260–686, 10–12 August 1920; vol. 163, file vol. 333, 5000–336, 18–19 August 1920; file vol. 334, 5345–500, 20–1 August 1920.

39 Ibid., vol. 162, file vol. 332, 4334, 4601–2 (Carvell), 10, 11 August 1920; *Railway Association of Canada* v. *Canadian Manufacturers Association* (1920), 26 *C.R.C.* 135–6; *Debates*, 30 March 1920, 864–6.

40 Ibid., 132–40.

41 Ibid., 141–7.

42 Meighen Papers: 24116–9, Meighen to C.A.C. Jennings, 5 October 1920; 26239, Toronto City Clerk to Meighen, 9 September 1920; 26140–2, Hugh Blain (Canadian Wholesale Grocers Association) to Meighen, 9 September 1920; 26243–5, J.B. Coyne to Meighen, 9 September 1920; 26521–2, Edmonton Board of Trade to Meighen, 10 September 1920; Halifax Board of Trade to Meighen, 10 September 1920; 26523, T.C. Norris to Meighen, 10 September 1920; 26254–62, J.B. Coyne to Meighen, 10 September 1920; 26178–80, Saskatchewan Associated Boards of Trade to Meighen, 22 September 1920; 26286–93, Press Statement re Appeal (and Drafts of Statement) [n.d.].

43 RG 2, Series 8, Appeals from Board of Railway Commissioners, vol. 1, file Increase in freight rates, 1920: D'Arcy Scott, Appeal from Railway Commission on behalf of Province of Saskatchewan, 20 September 1920; H.J. Symington, Appeal of Manitoba from General Advance Case, 11 September 1920 [no transcript of the hearing]; Meighen Papers, 26397, Meighen to Hugh Armstrong, 5 October 1920.

44 *Governments of Manitoba and Saskatchewan* v. *Railway Association of Canada* (PC 2434) (1920), 26 *C.R.C.* 147, at 149–50, 152–3.

45 Ibid., 150–2.

46 Ibid., 152–3; cf. Meighen Papers, 28559–663, S.J. McLean to Meighen, 28 September 1920, which contains yet another estimate of the impact of the rate advance. The historical image of Meighen, largely shaped by Roger Graham's biography, can be found most recently in Thompson and Seager, *Canada, 1922–39*.

47 Meighen Papers, 26423, Meighen to Drayton, 26 October 1920; BRC Transcripts, vol. 171, file vol. 348, 11724 (Carvell), 14 December 1920; *Application of Governments of Manitoba and Saskatchewan et al. for*

an Order Suspending the Railway Rate Increases (1920), 22 *C.R.C.* 298–307.

48 Hopkins, Canadian Annual Review – 1921, 381–2; BRC Transcripts, vol. 178, file vol. 361: 7106–8 (Calgary), 18 April 1921; 7130–6 (Edmonton), 20 April 1921; 7145, 7158–60, 7167–72 (Regina), 22 April 1921; 7197 (Brandon), 23 April 1921; 7309 (Carvell), 27 April 1921.

49 *In re Proposed Reductions in Freight Rates* (1921), 11 *J.O.R.R.* 255–62, 329–31; on wage reductions on the railways after 1920, see Peitchinis, *Labour-Management Relations*, 119–30.

50 BRC Transcripts, vol. 194, file vol. 390, 3398–9, 23 March 1922.

51 NA, William Lyon Mackenzie King Papers, MG 26 J1, 64155–8, N. Lambert to King, 1 June 1922 enclosing resolution of Canadian Council of Agriculture, 22 December 1921. Russenholt's classic cartoon, "Separating the farmer from his profits" *Grain Growers' Guide*, 28 December 1921, has been reprinted in Chodos, *The C.P.R.*, illustrations between 54 and 55, and more recently in Friesen, *The Canadian Prairies*, 187.

52 The most thorough, credible, and elegant argument is presented by Albro Martin in *Entreprise Denied*. There are echoes of his views in Alan Green, "Growth and Productivity Change in the Canadian Railway Sector," 808–9 and Stevens, *Towards the Inevitable*, 469–70.

53 For an econometric analysis which also suggests that finance rather than freight rates are the key to understanding the Canadian railway problem, see Lewis and MacKinnon, "Government Loan Guarantees and the Failure of the Canadian Northern Railway," 175–96.

CHAPTER NINE

1 NA, William Lyon Mackenzie King Diaries, MG 26 J13, 17 October 1924, 4 December 1924; F.R. Scott, "W.L.M.K.," in Scott and Smith, *The Blasted Pine*, 36–7.

2 King Diaries, 4 December 1924.

3 Thompson, *Harvests of War*, 59–72; Fowke, *The National Policy and the Wheat Economy*, 199–202; Dominion Bureau of Statistics, *Grain Statistics 1922*, (Ottawa, 1922), 19–21, and Graph, "Monthly Average Price Per Bushel of Grain"; ibid., *Livestock and Animal Products Statistics 1923*, 2.

4 Forbes, *Maritime Rights Movement*, 54–66; Henry Veltmeyer, "The Capitalist Underdevelopment of Atlantic Canada," in Brym and Sacouman, *Underdevelopment and Social Movements*, 21–4.

5 *Canada Year Book*: 1919, 385–9; 1921, 474–5; 1925, 408–9, 455; 1927, 573–4; Bliss, *Northern Enterprise*, 390–1.

6 Morton, *Manitoba*, 373–86; Smith, *Prairie Liberalism*, 84–92, 163–83; Carl F. Betke, "The United Farmers of Alberta, 1921–35," in Caldarola, ed., *Society and Politics in Alberta*, 14–32; Ormsby, *British Columbia*, 416–8; Robin, *Rush For Spoils*, 184–5, 205–7; Forbes, *Maritime Rights*, 38–53, 73–157.

7 Thompson and Seager, *Canada, 1922–39*, 14–17, 28–37; Morton, *Progressive Party*; Dawson, *Mackenzie King*, 356–94.

8 Forbes, *Maritime Rights*, 124–30; Thompson and Seager, *Canada 1922–39*, Tables 1b, 1c.

9 BRC Transcripts: vol. 178, file vol. 361, 7135–6, 7299–300 (Symington), 20, 27 April 1921; vol. 192, file vol. 387, 2247–53 (Symington), 15 March 1922.

10 Ibid.: vol. 191, file vol. 386, 1483–97 (Symington), 21 February 1922; vol. 193, file vol. 388, 2533–69 (Symington), 16–17 March 1922.

11 Ibid.: vol. 178, file vol. 361, 7108–10, 7117 (William Innes, G.W. Green, Calgary and Lethbridge Boards of Trade), 18 April 1921; vol. 185, file vol. 375, 13175–8 (F.T. Fisher, Edmonton Board of Trade), 2 November 1921; *Re Freight Tolls* (1922), 27 *C.R.C.* 175–6.

12 BRC Transcripts: vol. 184, file vol. 374, 12617–49 (Premier Oliver), 17 October 1921; vol. 185, file vol. 375, 13086–108 (McGeer, D.O. Lewis), 20 October 1921; vol. 191, file vol. 386, 1583–1654 (Lewis), 22 February 1922; vol. 192, file vol. 387, 1944–2090 (Lewis), 13 March 1922; vol. 193, file vol. 388, 2854–84 (McGeer on Kicking Horse Pass), 20 March 1922.

13 Ibid., vol. 184, file vol. 374: 12652–69 (W.H. Malkin, Vancouver Board of Trade), 12680–962 (Testimony of various British Columbia merchants and manufacturers), 17–19 October 1921; vol. 185, file vol. 375, 12975–13034 (Further testimony of business leaders), 20 October 1921; vol. 193, file vol. 389, 2940–62 (McGeer), 21 March 1922. For opposition to British Columbia's application see e.g. ibid., 13142–5, 13175–8, 13241–2, 132452 (Innes, F.T. Fisher, H. Henry, C. Cook, Calgary, Edmonton, Saskatoon, Regina Boards of Trade), 31 October, 2–4 October 1921; 13304–353 (I. Pitblado, Winnipeg Board of Trade and a series of local merchants and manufacturers), 8 November 1921.

14 Ibid., vol. 189, file vol. 383: 391–419, 462–536 (Representative business leaders from Amherst Foundry Ltd., Cummings Manufacturing Co., Amherst Boot and Shoe, Moir's, Ganong Brothers, T.S. Sims and Co., Maritime Nail, T. McCavity and Sons, Charles Fawcett Ltd., Atlantic Underwear, Marven Biscuit, Altantic Sugar), 17, 19 January 1922; 402 (Finn); 460–1 (Rand), 17, 19 January 1922; vol. 194, file vol. 390, 3433–5 (Rand), 24 March 1922.

15 Ibid., vol. 194, file vol. 390, 3486 (Rutherford), 24 March 1922.

16 Ibid., vol. 193, file vol. 388, 2522–5 (McLean and Symington),
    16 March 1922.

17 NA, Privy Council Records, RG 2, Series 1, PC 1863, 27 July 1918;
    Railway Act, 1919, S.C. 1919, c. 68, s. 325(5). The House of Com-
    mons pressed the 1919 amendment over the objections of the Senate.
    A number of senators feared that the language of the statute would
    allow the railway commission to override contractual agreements be-
    tween municipalities and street railways with respect to fares. In the
    end, the Senate agreed to s. 325(5) but only after it had been
    amended so that it would lapse in three years. Ironically then, it was
    the Senate, usually portrayed as sympathetic to the railways and to
    large corporations, which made the subsequent debate over the Crow
    rates possible. This suggests that the senators were more concerned
    with constitutional propriety and the sanctity of contracts than with
    any particular business interest: Debates, 4136–9, 27 June 1919; Can-
    ada, Senate, Debates, 668–9, 674, 6 June 1919, and 808–11, 2 July
    1919.

18 NA, William Lyon Mackenzie King Papers, MG 26 J1, 63851, Special
    Committee Appointed to Consider Railway Transportation Costs, Re-
    port to the House, 24 June 1922 reproduced in "Memo as to Crow's
    Nest Pass Agreement," W.C. Kennedy (Minister of Railways and Ca-
    nals) to King, 1 August 1922. Kennedy briefly discusses the appoint-
    ment of the committee at 63842–7. My discussions of the Crow's Nest
    Pass rate issue in chapters 8 and 9 have been greatly assisted by the
    solid, detailed account in Lane, "Freight Rate Issues," 55–80.

19 Lane, "Freight Rate Issues," 81–98; Re Freight Tolls (1922), 27 C.R.C.
    153, at 162–3; King Papers, 63847–8, "Memo as to Crow's Nest Pass
    Agreement," 1 August 1922.

20 Lane, "Freight Rate Issues," 100–8; King Papers, 65522–3, A.E.
    MacLean to King, 23 June 1922. For the kind of support given the
    restoration of the Crow rates, see the petitions in the King Papers:
    61142–4, Saskatchewan Associated Boards of Trade to King,
    18 March 1922; 62900, Calgary Board of Trade to King, 3 May 1922;
    62720, Premier Herbert Greenfield (Alberta) to King, 17 May 1922;
    68010–11, Lethbridge Board of Trade to King, 19 May 1922; 69284–
    5, Red Deer Board of Trade to King, 16 May 1922.

21 Lane, "Freight Rate Issues," 108–12; Dawson, Mackenzie King, 395–7;
    King Papers, 63850–5, "Memo as to Crow's Nest pass Agreement,"
    1 August 1922; An Act to Amend the Railway Act, 1919, S.C. 1922,
    c. 41. The involvement of officials of Canadian National in the Special
    Committee Meeting seems to confirm contemporary rumours that of-
    ficials on the public railway were more willing to accept the eastbound
    grain rates than their conterparts on the Canadian Pacific.

22 King Papers, 63850–5, 1 August 1922.

23 *Re Freight Tolls*, 161–4.

24 Ibid., 171–8.

25 Ibid., 164–71.

26 King Papers, 67058–9, John Oliver to King, 28 June 22; RG 2, Series 8, Appeals from Board of Railway Commissioners: vol. 2, file "Appeal versus Order of 30 June 1920," Transcript of Hearing, 3 February 1923; vol. 1, file Typescript of Hearings, 9–14 August 1923; NA Records of the Canadian Transport Commission, RG 46, vol. 618, file 30682.2, Petition of Attorney General of the Provinces of British Columbia and Alberta, 1 December 1922; King Diaries, 3 February 1923.

27 RG 2, Series 8, vol. 2: file Appeal versus Order of 30 June 1920, Transcript of Hearing, 3 February 1923, b58–72 (McGeer); file Appeal versus Order of 30 June 1920: John Blue (Edmonton Board of Trade) to Clerk of Privy Council, 22 February 1923; H. Greenfield to A. Chard, 9 February 1923; Memo of Edmonton Board of Trade, 9 February 1923; Memo in relation of Alberta joining British Columbia in Appeal to Privy Council, 21 February 1923.

28 Ibid., vol. 1, file Typescript of Hearings, 9–14 August 1923, b26 (King); for the Speaker's ruling, see *Debates*, 1912–14, 17 April 1923.

29 RG 2, Series 8, vol. 1, file Typescript of Hearings, 9–14 August 1923, b26–30 (Chrysler), b58–61 (Flintoft), c27 (Pitblado).

30 *Debates*, 1911–71, 17 April 1923. For opposition to British Columbia's application, see RG 2, Series 8, vol. 1, file Typescript of Hearings, 9–14 August 1923, c23–d2–3 (Pitblado, Province of Manitoba and Winnipeg Board of Trade); King Papers: 72520–2, Premier Charles A. Dunning to King, 13 January 1923; 72219, J. Davidson, (Winnipeg Board of Trade), 23 January 1923.

31 RG 2, Series 8, vol. 1, file Typescript of Hearings, 9–14 August 1923, a44–8 (McGeer); RG 2, Series 1: PC 1848, 12 September 1923; PC 2007, 2 October 1923.

32 *In re Rates on Grain from Prairie Points to Pacific Coast Ports for export* (1924), 13 *J.O.R.R.* 173–86.

33 RG 2, Series 1, PC 2166, 24 October 1923.

34 King Papers, 90120–6: King to Oliver, 17 January 1924; Oliver to King, 25 January 1924; King to Oliver, 4 February 1924; Oliver to King, 20 February 1924; King to Oliver, 8 March 1924; 90141–43, Oliver to King, 25 April 1924; Darling, *Politics of Freight Rates*, 65–7.

35 Cruikshank, "The People's Railway."

36 Forbes, *Maritime Rights*, 22–95, 124–30; NA, Records of Department of Railways and Canals, RG 43, vol. 372, file 6949, no. 162, History of

Intercolonial Rates, Appendix 2; King Papers, 72888–95, R.E. Finn to King, 25 January 1923.

37 Forbes, *Maritime Rights*, 97–9; King Papers, 93688–90, Thornton to King, 17 March 1924; BRC Transcripts, vol. 253, file vol. 502, 4620–32 (Frank J. Watson, Canadian National Railways, describing 1924 changes), 10 March 1927; RG 43, vol. 372, file 6949, no. 162, History of Intercolonial Rates, Appendix 1.

38 Forbes, *Maritime Rights*, 116.

39 Neatby, *Mackenzie King*, 12–22; Morton, *Progressive Party*, 194–7; King Papers, 76947–50, W.R. Motherwell to King, 29 December 1923.

40 RG 2, Series 8, vol. 4, file Freight rates, "Memorandum in the Matter of Section 325(5) Of the Railway Act of 1919 and of the Statutes of 1922 Chapter 41," Thornton and Beatty to King, 15 May 1924.

41 RG 2, Series 8, vol. 4, file "Transcript of Hearings re Crow's Nest Pass Agreement Transportation Rates," a5–48 (Symington), 28 June 1924, 40–5 (H.H. Stevens, British Columbia's case), 27 June 1924, a59–60 (W.F. Carrol, Maritime case); cf. ibid., file Freight Rates – Crows Nest Pass 1924, Exhibits 1–52 for examples of letters and petitions supporting and opposing the restoration of the westbound rates.

42 King Papers, 91059–64, King to Oliver, 30 July 1924.

CHAPTER TEN

1 See NA, William Lyon Mackenzie King Papers, MG 26 J1, 94434–7, 94438–43, George W. Yates (Assistant Deputy Minister Department of Railways and Canals) to King, 29 September, 2 October 1924; NA, Arthur Meighen Papers, MG 26 I, 74466–71, Memo from Canadian Manufacturers' Association, 13 March 1925; Board of Railway Commissioners, *In re Freight Tariffs* (1924), 14 *J.O.R.R.* 147, at 153–5. Between June and October 1924, the wholesale price of high-priced binders or of relatively inexpensive common plows sold in Winnipeg, Regina, and Calgary remained unchanged. The prices of barbed wire, nails, spikes, bar-iron, and building paper did not respond to the restored Crow rates in Calgary, although they were reduced slightly in Winnipeg and Regina: King Papers, 88551–61, Chief Commissioner McKeown to Mackenzie King, 3 December 1924.

2 King Papers: 83729–30, A.B. Copp to King, 17 September 1924; 8549, King to McKeown, 20 September 1924; NA, William Lyon Mackenzie King Diaries, MG 26 J 13, 12 September 1924, 20 December 1924.

3 BRC Transcripts, vol. 216: file vol. 429, 5904–6031 (Complaints arising from restoration of Crow rates), 22 September 1924; 6226–31, 23 September 1924; file vol. 430, 6238–494, 24 September 1924.

4 Ibid.: vol. 216, file vol. 430, 6508–47, 24 September 1924; vol. 217, file vol. 431, 6551–692, 26 September 1924; *General Order No. 408* (1924), 14 *J.O.R.R.* 193.

5 *In re Freight Tariffs*, Commissioner Boyce at 160–71.

6 Ibid., Boyce at 159, 171.

7 King Papers, 85196–99, King to G. Graham (Minister of Railways and Canals), 25 October 1924; Lane, "Freight Rate Issues," 201–16.

8 NA RG 2, Privy Council Records, Series 8, vol. 4, file Freight Rate – Crow's Nest Pass, 1924, Transcript, b24–33, c6–d17 (Symington and McGeer arguments), 4–5 December 1924.

9 King Diaries, 6 December 1924; RG 2, Series 1, PC 2220, 25 December 1924; cf. Lane, "Freight Rate Issues," 231–42.

10 *Re Crow's Nest Pass Rates* (1925), 30 *C.R.C.* 32, at 42–9.

11 RG 2, Series 1, PC 886, 5 June 1925 [reproduced in *In re General Freight Rates Investigation* (1927), 33 *C.R.C.* 127, at 365–70].

12 *Manitoba Free Press* editorial comment cited in Lane, "Freight Rate Issues," 274; An Act to amend the Railway, Act, 1919, S.C. 1925, c. 52. For a good account of the fate of the Progressive party, see Thompson and Seager, *Canada, 1922–39*, 24–37.

13 King Papers, 90130–43, John Oliver to King, 25 April 1924; *In re Rates on Grain from Prairie Points to Pacific Coast Ports* (1924), 13 *J.O.R.R.* 183–6; *In re Freight Tariffs*, 183–92.

14 BRC Transcripts, vol. 218: file vol. 433 (Hearing re Grain Rates to Vancouver), 5, 6 November 1924, 7335–707; file vol. 434, 7874–8002 (Discussion of disposition of case and McKeown's decision), 11 November 1924; *Application of the Government of British Columbia for an Order Reducing Rates on Grain Moving Westward for Export* (1925), 15 *J.O.R.R.* 271, at 283–4.

15 King Papers: 103415–24, telegraphic exchange: Oliver to King, King to Oliver, 6 June 1925; Oliver to King, 8 June 1925; King to Oliver, 11 June 1925; Oliver to King, King to Oliver, 13 June 1925; 107373–5, Henry Thornton to King, 26 August 1925; King Diaries, 24 August 1925.

16 King Diaries, 27 July 1925; 118–9, 19 August 1925. Commissioner Boyce describes the Board meetings at which the issue was discussed in *Application ... to rescind Order No. 36769* (1925), 15 *J.O.R.R.* 364, at 370–1.

17 *Application of the Government of British Columbia for an Order reducing Rates on Grain Moving Westward for Export*, 271–86, quoted comments of Commissioner Boyce at 279, 285. King Diaries, 1 September 1925, reveals the displeasure of the Prime Minister upon learning that McKeown might delay the decision.

18 BRC Transcripts, vol. 223, file vol. 443, 1573–683 (Application to Re-

scind Order 36769), 29 September 1925; King Diaries, 7 November 1925, 8 November 1925; *Application ... to rescind Order No. 36769*, 333–81, McLean at 333–4, Boyce at 364–6 both discuss some of the events leading to the decision; Boyce's statement on leaving rates at 380–1.

19 Ibid., McLean at 334, Boyce at 367–71.

20 *Application of the Government of British Columbia for an Order Reducing Rates on Grain Moving Westward for Export*, McKeown at 277–8; *Application ... to rescind Order No. 36769*, McLean at 336, Boyce at 377–9.

21 BRC Transcripts, vol. 232, file vol. 461, 6595–901 (Ralston), 6–8 April 1926; vol. 256, file vol. 508, 6991 (McGeer), 12 April 1927; vol. 232, file vol. 461, 6008–517 (Quebec Harbour Commissioners presentation and subsequent discussion), 23–5 February 1926; vol. 255, file vol. 506, 6049–140 (Cannon and St Laurent), 1 April 1927.

22 Ibid.: vol. 254, file vol. 505, 5625–40, 5840–57, 5869–6020; vol. 255, file vol. 506, 6042–3, 6316–9 (Woods for Alberta) 29, 31 March, 1, 5 April 1927; 6155–81, 6211–13, 6247–71, 6274–315, 6323–54 (McEwen for Saskatchewan), 4–5 April 1927; file vol. 507, 6411–16, 6417–61, 6463–81, 6483–512, 6543–57 (Symington for Manitoba), 6–7 April 1927.

23 Ibid.: vol. 249, file vol. 494, 1245–52 (Woods), 1278–9 (McGeer), 26 January 1927; vol. 250, file vol. 496, 1835–62 (Discussion of development policies and Board, and "new national policy" comment by McGeer), 3 February 1927. Cf. vol. 255, file vol. 506, 6168–76 (McEwen, discussion of PC 886), 1 April 1927; vol. 232, file vol. 461, 6127 (McLean), 24 February 1926. Cf. ibid., 7759–61 (Further discussion of PC 886's impact), 27 April 1927.

24 Ibid., vol. 257, file vol. 510, 7750–4 (McLean), 26 April 1927.

25 Province of Nova Scotia, *Submission to Royal Commission on Maritime Claims* (21 July 1926).

26 Forbes, *Maritime Rights*, 147–60; Canada, Parliament, Royal Commission on Maritime Claims, *Report* (Ottawa, 1927), 3, 20–1.

27 Ibid., 22–3; The Maritime Freight Rates Act, S.C. 1927, c. 44, King Papers, vol. 140, 118865–75, Henry Thornton to King, 11 March 1926; Darling, *Politics of Freight Rates*, 107–9.

28 Royal Commission on Maritime Claims, *Report*, 23–6; cf. King Papers, 121202–3, C.A. Dunning to King, 24 August 1927.

29 King Papers: 119963–8, E.W. Beatty to King, 6 August 1927; 127661–2, Thomas Vien to King, 1 June 1927; King Diaries, 7 August 1927.

30 *In re General Freight Rates Investigation* (1927), 33 *C.R.C.* 127, at 135–7, 153–62 (McKeown), 203–4 (McLean), 234 (Vien), 247–9 (Boyce), 272–3, 274 (Lawrence), 274–99 (Oliver).

31 Ibid., 168–74 (McKeown), 331–57 (Oliver), 204–27 (Vien), 196–9 (McLean), 249–69 (Boyce), 273 (Lawrence).
32 King Papers: 120159–60, A.C. Boyce to Charles Dunning (Minister of Railways), 21 July 1927; 121193, Dunning to King, 22 July 1927; 126264, John Stevenson, Traffic Managers, and Customs Brokers to King, 13 August 1927.
33 *Re Freight Rates Investigation*, 162–3 (McKeown), 299–320 (Oliver), 232–4 (Vien), 202–3 (McLean), 245–7 (Boyce), 271 (Lawrence). Vien agreed that the grain rate from Calgary to Vancouver could be calculated on the basis of the longer Canadian National route from Edmonton, because the original decision had been based on the superior operating conditions on the Edmonton to Vancouver route.
34 Ibid., 137–53 (McKeown), 320–7 (Oliver), 179–85 (McLean), 229–32 (Vien), 243–5 (Boyce), 271–2 (Lawrence).
35 Ibid., 165–7 (McKeown), 235–42, 270, quote at 240 (Boyce), 180, 201–2 (McLean).
36 *Canadian National Railways* v. *Quebec Harbour Commissioners* (1929), 36 *C.R.C.* 81–91; RG 2, Series 8: vol. 6, file General Order no. 448 of 26 August 1927, Petitions in Appeal of: United Farmers of British Columbia, 16 January 1929; Attorney Generals of Provinces of British Columbia, Alberta and Saskatchewan, 20 May 1929, Attorney General of Saskatchewan, 15 November 1929; vol. 7, file General Order no. 448 of 26 August 1927, PC 349, 25 February 1933.
41 For the Duff Commission and the 1933 legislation see Fournier, *Railway Nationalization in Canada*, 253–347.

CHAPTER ELEVEN

1 T.C. Keefer, "Montreal," in *Philosophy of Railroads*, 88.
2 On the vote seeking behaviour of politicians see Trebilcock, *The Choice of Governing Instrument*. For a thorough discussion of the limits of interest group pressure analysis and of the importance of the "relative autonomy" of the state in the creation of the Interstate Commerce Commission, see Skowronek, *Building A New Administrative State*, 121–50, I would be the first to admit that my analysis is far less structural than Skowronek's. My approach to the creation of the Canadian railway commission more closely resembles that of Thomas McCraw, who emphasizes the importance of individuals and their ideas in the shaping of specific regulatory legislation throughout his fine *Prophets of Regulation*.
3 For a discussion of business organizations and government policy in an earlier era, see Forster, *A Conjunction of Interests*.

4 BRC Transcripts, vol. 194, file vol. 391, 4052 (Rutherford), 30 March 1922; on the private use of public power theme, see McCraw, *Prophets of Regulation*, 300–9.

5 Armstrong and Nelles refer to a "pluralist, or at least dualist approach" to regulation in Canada in *Monopoly's Moment*, 326–7. Their own analysis does tend to focus on and explain the selection of one particular instrument within particular regulatory jurisdictions. I hope that my analysis makes it even clearer that governing instruments can also coexist. I borrow the term "regulatory pluralism" more directly from Harry Arthurs, whose work on "legal pluralism" has greatly influenced my own thinking on the subject of regulation. Arthurs' analysis is directed primarily to a legal debate over proceduralism and administrative law, so that I prefer to use a broader term, "regulatory pluralism": Arthurs, *'Without the Law.'*

6 On transportation policy after 1930, see: Darling, *Politics of Freight Rates*; Purdy, *Transport Competition and Public Policy in Canada*; Studnicki-Gizbert, *Issues in Canadian Transport Policy*. For more recent developments, see Government of Canada, *Freedom to Move*; Howard I. Wetston, "Transportation Reform and the Proposed National Transportation Agency," in Finkelstein and Rogers, *Recent Developments in Administrative Law*, 321–40; National Transportation Act, 1987, R.S.C. 1985, c. 28 (3rd Supp.), ss. 1–273; National Transportation Agency, *Annual Review*, 1989.

Bibliography

UNPUBLISHED SOURCES

ARCHIVES OF ONTARIO
John Fiskin Papers (MU 1040)

NATIONAL ARCHIVES OF CANADA: MANUSCRIPTS
Robert Borden Papers, Correspondence and Diaries (MG 26 H)
Canadian Manufacturers' Association Papers (MG 28 I 230)
Canadian Pacific Railway Records (MG 28 II 20):
  Thomas Shaugnessy Letterbooks
  William Van Horne Letterbooks
George E. Foster Papers (MG 27 II D7)
Alexander Galt Papers (MG 27 I D8)
George P. Graham Papers (MG 27 II D8)
Great Britain, Colonial Office Records
  v. 540, 529–31, Earl of Gladstone's Circular, 15 January 1846
Joseph Hickson Papers (MG 29 A 29)
William Lyon Mackenzie King Diaries, Typewritten Transcripts (MG 26 J 13)
William Lyon Mackenzie King Papers (MG 26 J1)
Wilfred Laurier Papers (MG 26 G1)
John A. Macdonald Papers (MG 26 A1)
Arthur Meighen Papers (MG 26 I)
Department of Railways and Canals Records, Railways Branch, Correspondence (RG 43)
Clifford Sifton Papers (MG 27 II D 15)
John S. Willison Papers (MG 30 D 29)

UNIVERSITY OF TORONTO ARCHIVES
Department of Graduate Records, file Simon J. McLean (A73–0026/228)

UNIVERSITY OF TORONTO RARE BOOK ROOM
James Mavor Papers (MSS 119)

GOVERNMENT PUBLICATIONS

CANADA
Board of Railway Commissioners, *Annual Reports*, 1904–1930.
Department of Transport [R. Dorman]. *A Statutory History of the Steam and Electric Railways of Canada, 1836–1937*. Ottawa: King's Printer 1938.
Dominion Bureau of Statistics.
  Grain Statistics. Ottawa 1922–29.
  Livestock and Animal Products Statistics. Ottawa 1923–29.
  Railway Freight Index. Ottawa 1934.
Freedom to Move – A Framework for Transportation Reform. Ottawa: Transport Canada 1985.
House of Commons, *Debates*.
Journals of the House of Commons, 1883, Appendix no. 1, Third Report, Select Standing Committe on Railways and Canals, 43–6.
Royal Commission on Maritime Claims, *Report*. Ottawa, 1927.
Royal Commission on Railways and Transportation, *Report*. Ottawa, 1917.
Senate, *Debates*.

SESSIONAL PAPERS
Report of the Department of Railways and Canals, 1879–1917.
Report of the Railway Rates Commission, no. 30, 1895.
Report of the Royal Commission on Railways, no. 8a, 14 January 1888.
Reports Upon Railway Commissions, Railway Rate Grievances and Regulative Legislation, no. 20a, 1902.
Trade and Navigational Returns, 1876, 1886, 1901.

CANADA, PROVINCE OF
1849, Journals of the Legislative Assembly, Appendix N.

UNITED STATES
Senate. 51st Congress, 1st Session. Report no. 847, *Report on the Transportation Interests of the United States and Canada*. 1889.

PUBLIC RECORDS

CANADIAN NATIONAL RAILWAYS RECORDS (RG 30)
Canadian Freight Association/Association of General Freight Agents of Canada, Minutes, 1896–1925

Canadian Northern Railway, Legal Files
Grand Trunk Railway and Canadian Northern Railway, Freight Tariffs
Grand Trunk Railway, General Manager's Letterbooks
Grand Trunk Traffic Rates, 1858–65 (vol. 2001)
Historical Material on Freight Rates (vol. 8546)
History of the Grand Trunk Railway (vol. 10934)

PUBLIC SERVICE COMMISSION, HISTORICAL PERSONNEL FILES, VOL. 181,
SIMON JAMES MCLEAN (RG 32)

RECORDS OF CANADIAN TRANSPORT COMMISSION (RG 46)
Board of Railway Commissioners, Transcripts of Hearings
Board of Railway Commissioners, Hearing Exhibits
Board of Railway Commissioners, Central Registry Files
Railway Committee of the Privy Council, Minutes
Railway Committee of the Privy Council, Correspondence

RECORDS OF DEPARTMENT OF RAILWAYS AND CANALS
Railways Branch, Correspondence (RG 43)

CITY OF TORONTO
City Council, Minutes (1872–1882)

STATUTES

CANADA
An Act to Amend an Act to Incorporate the Ontario and Quebec Railway
    Company, S.C. 1883, c. 58.
An Act to Amend an Act Respecting the Credit Valley Railway Company,
    S.C. 1883, c. 57.
An Act to Amend the Railway Act, 1919, S.C. 1922, c. 41.
An Act to Amend the Railway Act, 1919, S.C. 1925, c. 52.
An Act to authorize a Subsidy for a Railway through the Crow's Nest Pass,
    S.C. 1897, c. 5.
An Act to incorporate the Canadian National Railway Company, S.C. 1919,
    c. 13.
An Act Respecting certain aid for the extension of the Canadian Northern
    Railway, S.C. 1903, c. 7.
An Act Respecting the Canadian Pacific Railway Company, S.C. 1883, c. 55.
An Act Respecting the Northern Railway of Canada, S.C. 1878, c. 26.
An Act Respecting Railways, S.C. 1888, c. 29.
Canadian Pacific – Canadian National Railways Act, S.C. 1933, c. 33.

Maritime Freight Rates Act, 1927, S.C. 1927, c. 44.

National Transportation Act, 1987, R.S.C. 1985, c. 28 (3rd Supp.), ss. 1–273.

Railway Act, The, 1903, S.C. 1903, c. 58.

Railway Act, 1919, S.C. 1919, c. 68.

CANADA, PROVINCE OF

Railway Clauses Consolidation Act, 1851 (14 & 15 Vict.), c. 51.

BRITISH COLUMBIA

An Act to Ratify an Agreement ... between His Majesty the King and the Canadian Northern Railway Company, S.B.C. 1910, c. 3.

MANITOBA

An Act Confirming a Certain Agreement Respecting Certain Railways and Passenger Rates, S.M. 1901, c. 39.

ONTARIO

An Act to Amend Several Acts Relating to the Credit Valley Railway Company, S.O. 1873, c. 80, s. 4.

An Act to Incorporate the Credit Valley Railway Company, S.O. 1871, c. 38, s. 41.

An Act Respecting the Credit Valley Railway Company, S.O. 1883, c. 50.

UNITED KINGDOM

Constitution Act, 1867 (30 & 31 Vict.), c. 3.

CASES

Application of Government of British Columbia for an Order Reducing Rates on Grain Moving Westward for Export (1925), 15 *J.O.R.R.* 271

Application of Governments of Manitoba and Saskatchewan et al for an Order Suspending the Railway Rate Increases (1920), 22 *C.R.C.* 298

Application to Rescind or Suspend the Operation of Order of Board No. 36769 pending Decision of General Freight Rate Investigation (1925), 15 *J.O.R.R.* 364

Attorney General v. *Ontario, Simcoe & Huron Railways* (1858), 6 *Grant's Chancery Reports* 446

British American Oil Co. v. *Grand Trunk Railway Co.* (1909), 9 *C.R.C.* 178

British Columbia Pacific Coast Cities v. *Canadian Pacific Railway Co.* (1906), 7 *C.R.C.* 125

Campbell v. *Northern Railway* (1879), 26 *Grant's Chancery Reports* 522

Canadian Lumbermen's Association v. *Grand Trunk, Canadian Pacific and Canadian Northern Railways* (1910), 10 *C.R.C.* 306

Canadian National Railways v. *Quebec Harbour Commissioners* (1929), 36 *C.R.C.* 81

Canadian Pacific and Canadian Northern Railway Cos v. *Regina Board of Trade* (1909), 11 *C.R.C.* 380; affirmed (1911), 13 *C.R.C.* 203

Canadian Portland Cement Co. v. *Grand Trunk and Bay of Quinte Railway Cos* (1909), 9 *C.R.C.* 209

City of St Thomas v. *Credit Railway* (1884), 7 *Ontario Reports* 332; decision affirmed (1885), 12 *Ontario Appeal Reports* 273

Crow's Nest Pass Rates, Re (1925), 30 *C.R.C.* 32

Dominion Sugar Co. v. *Grand Trunk, Canadian Pacific, Chatham Wallaceburg, and Lake Erie & Pere Marquette Railway Cos* (1913), 17 *C.R.C.* 231

Doolittle & Wilcox v. *Grand Trunk Railway and Canadian Pacific Railways* (1908), 8 *C.R.C.* 10

Eastern Tolls, In re (Eastern Rates Case) (1916), 22 *C.R.C.* 4, 6 *J.O.R.R.* 155

Freight Tariffs, In re (1924), 14 *J.O.R.R.* 147

Freight Tolls, Re (Reduction in Freight Rates Case) (1922), 27 *C.R.C.* 153

General Freight Rates Investigation, In re (1927), 33 *C.R.C.* 127

General Order No. 408 (1924), 14 *J.O.R.R.* 193

Governments of Manitoba and Saskatchewan v. *Railway Association of Canada* (1920), 26 *C.R.C.* 147; application refused (1920), 26 *C.R.C.* 298

Grand Trunk Railway v. *British American Oil* (1910), 43 *Supreme Court Reports* 311

Grand Trunk Railway v. *Credit Valley Railway* (1879), 26 *Grant's Chancery Reports* 572

Increase in Passenger and Freight Tolls, In re (1917), 22 *C.R.C.* 49

International Paper Co. v. *Grand Trunk, Canadian Pacific and Canadian Northern Railway Cos* (1913), 15 *C.R.C.* 111

Joint Freight and Passenger Tariffs, In re (1909), 10 *C.R.C.* 343

Kemp Manufacturing & Metal and Winnipeg Ceiling & Roofing Cos v. *Canadian Pacific Railway* (1909), 10 *C.R.C.* 163

Proposed Reductions in Freight Rates, In re (1921), 11 *J.O.R.R.* 255

Railway Association of Canada v. *Canadian Manufacturers' Association (Forty Per Cent Increase Case)* (1920), 26 *C.R.C.* 135

Rates on Grain from Prairie Points to Pacific Coast Ports for Export, In re (1924), 13 *J.O.R.R.* 173

Regina Board of Trade v. *Canadian Pacific and Canadian Northern Railway Cos* (1909), 11 *C.R.C.* 380

Scott v. *Midland Railway* (1873), 33 *Upper Canada Queen's Bench Reports* 580–92

Stamford Junction Case (1904), 3 *C.R.C.* 256

Sydenham Glass Co. Case (1904), 3 *C.R.C.* 409

Town of Welland v. *Canadian Freight Association* (1911), 13 *C.R.C.* 140

United Factories v. *Grand Trunk Railway* (1904) 3 *C.R.C.* 424

Western Tolls, In re (Western Rates Case) (1914), 17 *C.R.C.* 123

NEWSPAPERS AND PERIODICALS

Brandon Daily Mail, 1894
Calgary Daily Herald, 1895
Calgary Weekly Herald, 1914
Canada Farmers' Sun, 1893–99
Canadian Manufacturer, 1882–90
Chatham *Daily Planet,* 1901
Edmonton Bulletin, 1895, 1912–15
Edmonton *Journal,* 1912–15
Hamilton *Daily Spectator,* 1873
Industrial Canada, 1900–30
Manitoba Free Press, 1894–1930
Monetary Times (Toronto), 1867–1930
Montreal Gazette, 1856
Montreal *Gazette,* 1870–1930
Montreal *Star,* 1900–30
Railway Age Gazette, 1910–20
Railway and Marine World (also entitled *Railway and Shipping World*), 1896–
    1930
Regina *Morning Leader,* 1900–14
Toronto *Globe,* 1856, 1870–1905
Toronto *World,* 1900–15
Windsor *Evening Record,* 1901
Winnipeg *Daily Tribune,* 1894–95, 1901

BOOKS AND ARTICLES

Abbott, Harry. *A Treatise on the Railway Law of Canada.* Montreal: C. Theoret
    1896.
Aitken, Hugh G.J. *The Welland Canal Company.* Cambridge, Mass.: Harvard
    University Press 1954.
Alderman, Geoffrey. *The Railway Interest.* Leicester: Leicester University
    Press 1973.
Argo, J.A. "Historical Review of Canadian Railway Freight Rate Structure,
    1876–1938." In R.A.C. Henry and Associates. *Railway Freight Rates in
    Canada.* Ottawa: Queen's Printer 1939.
Armstrong, Christopher, and H.V. Nelles *Monopoly's Moment: The Organi-
    zation and Regulation of Canadian Utilities, 1830–1930.* Philadelphia: Tem-
    ple University Press 1986.
Arthurs, Harry. *'Without the Law': Administrative Justice and Legal Pluralism*

in Nineteenth-Century England. Toronto: University of Toronto Press 1985.

Baggeley, Carmen. *The Emergence of the Regulatory State in Canada, 1867–1939*. Ottawa: Economic Council of Canada 1981.

Baker, William. "Isaac Burpee", *Dictionary of Canadian Biography*, vol. II. Toronto: University of Toronto Press 1982.

Baskerville, Peter. "Railways in Upper Canada/Ontario: The State, Entrepreneurship and the Transition from a Commercial to an Industrial Economy." Unpublished paper. 1987.

Bellan, Ruben. *Winnipeg First Century*. Winnipeg: Queenston House Publishing 1978.

Bercuson, David, ed. *Canada and the Burden of Unity*. Toronto: MacMillan 1977.

Bernier, Ivan, and Andrée Lajoie. *Regulations, Crown Corporations and Administrative Tribunals*. Toronto: University of Toronto Press 1985.

Bernstein, Marver H. *Regulating Business by Independent Commissions*. Princeton: Princeton University Press, 1955.

Berton, Pierre. *The Last Spike*. Toronto: McClelland and Stewart 1971.

– *The National Dream*. Toronto: McClelland and Stewart 1970.

Bliss, Michael. *A Canadian Millionaire: The Life and Business Times of Sir Joseph Flavelle, Bart., 1858–1939*. Toronto: MacMillan 1978.

– *A Living Profit: Studies in the Social History of Canadian Business*. Toronto: McClelland and Stewart 1974.

– *Northern Enterprise: Five Centuries of Canadian Business*. Toronto: McClelland and Stewart 1987.

Brown, Robert Craig. *Robert Laird Burden: A biography*, vol. I. Toronto: MacMillan 1975.

– and Ramsay Cook. *Canada, 1896–1921: A Nation Transformed*. Toronto: McClelland and Stewart 1974.

Brym, Robert J., and R. James Sacouman. *Underdevelopment and Social Movements in Atlantic Canada*. Toronto: New Hogtown Press 1979.

Cain, P.J. "British Railway Rates Problem, 1894–1913." *Business History* 20 (1978): 87–99.

– "Traders versus Railways." *Journal of Transport History* 2 (1973): 65–84.

Caldarola, Carlo, ed. *Society and Politics in Alberta*. Toronto: Methuen 1979.

Canadian Freight Association. "History of Canadian Freight Association." Pamphlet courtesy Canadian Freight Association.

Chandler, Alfred. *The Visible Hand: The Managerial Revolution in American Business*. Cambridge, Mass.: Harvard University Press 1977.

Chodos, Robert. *The C.P.R.: A Century of Corporate Welfare*. Toronto: James Lewis and Samuel 1973.

Clark, John Maurice. *Standards of Reasonableness in Local Freight Discriminations*. New York: AMS Press 1968.

Clark, S.D. "The Canadian Manufacturers' Association: A Political Pressure Group." *Canadian Journal of Economics and Political Science* 4 (1938): 505–23.

Clegg, Stewart, and David Dunkerly. *Organization, Class and Control.* London: Routledge and Kegan Paul 1980.

Clippingdale, Richard. "J.S. Willison, Political Journalist: From Liberalism to Independence, 1881–1905." PHD. diss., University of Toronto 1970.

Cooper, Charles. *Rails to the Lakes: The Story of the Hamilton and Northwestern Railway.* Cheltenham, Ontario: Boston Mills Press 1980.

Cox, Mark. "The Limits of Reform: Industrial Regulation and Management Rights in Ontario, 1930–7." *Canadian Historical Review* 68 (1987): 552–75.

Craven, Paul, *'An Impartial Umpire': Industrial Relations and the Canadian State, 1900–11.* Toronto: University of Toronto Press 1980.

Crick, Bernard. *In Defence of Politics.* Chicago: Wiedenfeld-Nicholson 1972.

Cruikshank, Ken. "Law versus Common Sense: Judicial Regulation of Railways, 1850–1903." Unpublished Conference Paper. Law in History Conference. Ottawa 1986.

– "The People's Railway: The Intercolonial and the Canadian Public Enterprise Experience." *Acadiensis* 16 (1986): 78–100.

– "The Transportation Revolution and its Consequences: The Railway Freight Rate Controversy of the Late Nineteenth Century." *Historical Papers/Communications historique* (1987): 112–37.

Cruise, David, and Alison Griffiths. *Lords of the Line.* Toronto: Viking Penguin Canada 1988.

Currie, A.W. "Freight Rates and Regionalism." *Canadian Journal of Economics and Political Science* 14 (1948): 421–40.

– "Freight Rates on Grain." *Canadian Historical Review* 21 (1940): 40–55.

– "The Board of Transport Commissioners as an Administrative Body." *Canadian Journal of Economics and Political Science* 11 (1945): 342–58.

– *Economics of Canadian Transportation.* Toronto: University of Toronto Press 1954.

– *The Grand Trunk Railway.* Toronto: University of Toronto Press 1957.

Darling, Howard. *The Politics of Freight Rates.* Toronto: McClelland and Stewart 1980.

Dawson, R. MacGregor. *William Lyon Mackenzie King*, vol. 1. Toronto: University of Toronto Press 1958.

de T. Glazebrook, G.P. *A History of Transportation in Canada*, vols. 1 and 2. Toronto: McClelland and Stewart 1964.

Doern, G. Bruce, ed. *The Regulatory Process in Canada.* Toronto: MacMillan 1978.

Drummond, Ian M. *Political Economy at the University of Toronto.* Toronto: University of Toronto Press 1983.

Dwivedi, O.P. *The Administrative State in Canada.* Toronto: University of Toronto Press 1982.

Eagle, John A. *The Canadian Pacific Railway and the Development of Western Canada, 1896–1914.* Montreal: McGill-Queen's University Press 1989.

– "Monopoly or Competition: the Nationalization of the Grand Trunk Railway." *Canadian Historical Review* 62 (1981): 3–30.

– "Sir Robert Borden and the Railway Problem in Canadian Politics, 1911–20." PHD. diss., University of Toronto 1972.

Easterbrook, W.T., and Hugh G.J. Aitken, *Canadian Economic History.* Toronto: Macmillan 1956.

Economic Council of Canada. *Reforming Regulation.* Ottawa: Economic Council of Canada 1981.

Evans, J.M. et al., eds. *Administrative Law: Cases, Texts and Materials.* Toronto: Emond-Montgomery 1980.

Evenden, L.J., ed. *Vancouver: Western Metropolis.* Victoria: University of Victoria 1978.

Fellmeth, Robert C. *The Interstate Commerce Commission.* New York: Grossman 1970.

Filby, James. *Credit Valley Railway: The Third Giant.* Cheltenham, Ontario: Boston Mills Press 1974.

Finkelstein, Neil R., and Brian MacLeod Rogers, eds. *Recent Developments in Administrative Law.* Toronto: Carswell 1987.

Fleming, Howard. *Canada's Arctic Outlet.* Los Angeles: University of California Press 1957.

Forbes, Ernest R. *The Maritime Rights Movement, 1919–1927.* Montreal: McGill-Queen's University Press 1979.

Forster, Ben. *A Conjunction of Interests: Business, Politics and Tariffs, 1825–79.* Toronto: University of Toronto Press 1986.

– "Finding the Right Size: Markets and Competition in Mid- and Late-Nineteenth Century Ontario." In Hall, Roger et al., *Patterns of the Past: Interpreting Ontario's History.* Toronto: Dundern Press 1988: 150–73.

Fournier, Leslie T. *Railway Nationalization in Canada.* Toronto: MacMillan 1935.

Fowke, Vernon. *The National Policy and the Wheat Economy.* Toronto: University of Toronto Press 1957.

Francis, R. Douglas, and Howard Palmer. *The Prairie West: Historical Readings.* Edmonton: Pica Pica Press 1985.

Friesen, Gerald. *The Canadian Prairies.* Toronto: University of Toronto Press 1984.

Furner, Mary O. *Advocacy and Objectivity: A Crisis in the Professionalization of American Social Science, 1865–1905.* Lexington: University Press of Kentucky 1975.

"George Moberly," *Canadian Biographical Dictionary*, Ontario vol. Toronto 1888.

Gilbert, Heather. *Awakening Continent: The Life of Lord Mount Stephen*, vol. 1. Aberdeen: Aberdeen University Press 1965.

Goodnow, Frank J. *Politics and Administration*. New York: Russel & Russel 1967 [orig. 1900].

Goodrich, Carter. *Government Promotion of American Canals and Railroads, 1800–1890*. New York: Columbia University Press 1960.

– "State In, State Out: A Pattern of Development Policy." *Journal of Economic Issues* 2 (1968): 365–72.

Graham, Roger. *Arthur Meighen*. Vol. 1: *The Door of Opportunity*. Toronto: University of Toronto Press 1960.

– *Arthur Meighen*. vol. 2: *And Fortune Fled*. Toronto: University of Toronto Press 1963.

Grant, Hugh M. Foreign Ownership and the history of the Canadian Oil Industry. Early draft of his PHD diss., University of Toronto 1986.

Green, Alan G. "Growth and Productivity Change in the Canadian Railway Sector, 1871–1926." In S. Engerman, and R. Galloner, eds. *Long Term Factors in American Economic Growth*, Studies in Income and Wealth, vol. 51. Chicago: University of Chicago Press 1986.

Grodinsky, Julius. *Transcontinental Railway Strategy, 1869–93*. Philadelphia: University of Pennsylvania 1962.

Hall, D.J. *Clifford Sifton*. vol. 1: *The Young Napoleon*. Vancouver: University of British Columbia Press 1981.

– *Clifford Sifton*. vol. 2: *The Lonely Eminence*. Vancouver: University of British Columbia Press 1985.

Hammack, David C. *Power and Society: Greater New York at the Turn of the Century*. New York: Russell Sage Foundation 1982.

Hammond, M.B. "Railway Rate Theories of the Interstate Commerce Commission." *Quarterly Journal of Economics* 25 (1910–11): 1–66, 279–336, 471–538.

Hardin, Herschel. *A Nation Unaware*. Vancouver: J.J. Douglas 1974.

Haskell, Thomas. *The Emergence of Professional Social Science: The American Social Science Association and the Nineteenth-Century Crisis of Authority*. Urbana: University of Illinois Press 1977.

Hawley, Ellis. *The New Deal and the Problem of Monopoly*. Princeton: Princeton University Press 1966.

Hays, Samuel P. *American Political History as Social Analysis: Essays by Samuel P. Hays*. Knoxville: University of Tennessee Press 1980.

– *Conservation and the Gospel of Efficiency*. Cambridge, Mass.: Harvard University Press 1959.

Heaver, T.D. and James C. Nelson, *Railway Pricing Under Commercial Freedom*. Vancouver: University of British Columbia Press 1977.

Hopkins, Castell., ed. *Canadian Annual Review of Public Affairs* 1901–1930.

Horwitz, Robert Britt. *The Irony of Regulatory Reform* New York: Columbia University Press 1989.

Humphries, Charles W. *'Honest Enough to Be Bold': Sir James Pliny Whitney.* Toronto: University of Toronto Press 1985.

Hunter, Andrew F. *A History of Simcoe County*, vol. 1. Barrie, Ontario: Simcoe County Council 1909.

Hurst, Willard. *The Legitimacy of the Business Corporation.* Charlottesville: University of Virginia Press 1970.

Innis, Harold A. *A History of the Canadian Pacific Railway.* Toronto: University of Toronto Press 1971.

– *Essays in Canadian Economic History.* Toronto: University of Toronto Press 1956.

Inwood, Kris. "Effective Transportation and Tariff Protection." Working Paper no. 85–24, Department of Economics, Saint Mary's University, Halifax.

Jackman, W.T. *Economic Principles of Transportation.* Toronto: University of Toronto Press 1935.

Jackson, James A. "The Disallowance of Manitoba Railway Legislation in the 1880s." MA thesis, University of Manitoba 1945.

Janisch, H.N. *The Canadian Transport Commission.* Ottawa: Law Reform Commission 1977.

Johnson, Leo. *History of the County of Ontario, 1615–1875.* County of Ontario: Corporation of the County of Ontario 1973.

Kasson, John F. *Civilizing the Machine: Technology and Republican Values in America, 1776–1900.* New York: Grossman Publishers 1976.

Kealey, Greg. "Introduction." In Kealey, ed. *Canada investigates industrialism.* Toronto: University of Toronto Press 1973.

Keefer, T.C. *Philosophy of Railroads.* Ed. H.V. Nelles. Toronto: University of Toronto Press 1972.

Kerr, Donald. "Wholesale Trade on the Canadian Plains in the Late Nineteenth Century: Winnipeg and its Competitors." In Howard Palmer, ed. *Settlement of the West.* Calgary: University of Calgary Press 1977.

Kirkland, Edward Chase. *Men, Cities and Transportation: A Study in New England History, 1820–1900*, vols. 1–2. Cambridge, Mass.: Harvard University Press 1948.

Kolko, Gabriel. *Railroads and Regulation, 1877–1916.* New York: Norton and Co. 1965.

Laidlaw, George. *The Credit Valley Railway.* Toronto: Copp Clark 1876.

Lamb, W.K. *A History of the Canadian Pacific Railway.* New York: MacMillan 1977.

Lane, W.A. "Freight Rate Issues in Canada, 1922–25: Their Economic and Political Implications." PHD diss., McGill University 1983.

Law Reform Commission of Canada. *Independent Administrative Agencies*. Ottawa: Law Reform Commission 1980.

Lewis, Frank, and Mary MacKinnon. "Government Loan Guarantees and the Failure of the Canadian Northern Railway." *Journal of Economic History* 47 (1987): 175–96.

Locklin, D. Philip. "The Literature on Railway Rate Theory." *Quarterly Journal of Economics* (February, 1933): 167–230.

MacGibbon, D.A. *Railway Rates and the Canadian Railway Commission*. New York: Houghton-Mifflin 1917.

MacMurphy, A., and Shirley Denison, eds. *Canadian Railway Act 1903*. Toronto 1905.

Manchester, A.H. *A Modern Legal History of England and Wales, 1750–1950*. London: Butterworths 1980.

Martin, Albro. *Entreprise Denied: The Origins of the Decline of American Railroads*. New York: Columbia University Press 1971.

McCalla, Douglas. "The Decline of Hamilton as a Wholesale Centre." *Ontario History* 65 (1973): 247–54.

– *The Upper Canadian Trade, 1934–72: A Study of the Buchanans' Business*. Toronto: University of Toronto Press 1979.

McCraw, Thomas K. "Regulation in America: A Review Article." *Business History Review* 49 (1975): 159–83.

– *Prophets of Regulation*. Cambridge, Mass.: Belknap Press 1984.

McLean, S.J. "An Early Chapter in Canadian Railway Policy." *Journal Of Political Economy* 8 (1898): 323–52.

– "Canadian Railways and the Bonding Question." *Journal Of Political Economy* 9 (1899): 500–42.

– "Federal Regulation of Railways in the United States." *Economic Journal* 10 (1900): 151–71.

– "The Railway Policy of Canada, 1849–67, Parts I and II." *Journal of Political Economy* 9 (1899): 191–217, 351–83.

– "Railway Policy of Canada." PHD diss., University of Chicago 1897.

– "Railway Rate Regulation in Canada." *Forum* 33 (1902): 419–29.

– "State Regulation of Railways in the United States." *Economic Journal* 10 (1900): 349–69.

– *The Railway Commission and Its Work*. Ottawa: King's Printer 1930.

– *The Tariff History of Canada*. Toronto: University of Toronto Studies in Political Science 1895.

Miller, J.R. "As A Politician He Is A Great Enigma": The Social and Political Ideas of D'Alton McCarthy." *Canadian Historical Review* 58 (1977): 399–422.

Mills, David. "Railway Reform – The CPR." *Canadian Monthly and National Review* 2 (1872): 437–9.

Mitnick, Barry M. *The Political Economy of Regulation*. New York: Columbia University Press 1980.

Morton, W.L. *Manitoba: A History*. Toronto: University of Toronto Press 1957.
– *The Progressive Party of Canada*. Toronto: University of Toronto Press 1950.
Neal, Larry. "Investment Behaviour by American Railroads, 1897–1914." *Review of Economics and Statistics*, 51 (1969): 126–35.
Neatby, H. Blair. *William Lyon Mackenzie King*. Toronto: University of Toronto Press 1963.
Nelles, H.V. *The Politics of Development*. Toronto: MacMillan 1974.
Noll, Roger, ed. *Regulatory Policy and the Social Sciences*. Los Angeles: University of California Press 1985.
North, D.C. "Ocean Freight Rates and Economic Development." *Journal of Economic History* 18 (1958): 537–55.
Ormsby, Margaret. *British Columbia: A History*. Vancouver: University of British Columbia Press 1958.
Owram, Doug. *The Government Generation*. Toronto: University of Toronto Press 1986.
Peitchinis, Stephen G. *Labour-Management Relations in the Railway Industry*. Task Force on Labour Relations Study no. 20. Ottawa: Information Canada 1971.
Poor's Railroad Manual of the United States [later *Poor's Manual of Railroads*] 1860–1925.
Purdy, H.L. *Transport Competition and Public Policy in Canada*. Vancouver: University of British Columbia Press 1972.
Rabin, Jack, and James S. Bowman, eds. *Politics and Administration*. New York: Marle-Dekker 1984.
Regehr, T.D. *The Canadian Northern Railway*. Toronto: MacMillan 1976.
Ripley, William Z. *Railroads: Rates and Regulations*. New York: Arno Press 1973.
Risk, R.C.B. "Lawyers, Courts and the Regulatory State." Unpublished Paper, 1983.
– "The Nineteenth Century Foundations of the Business Corporation in Ontario." *Unitersity of Toronto Law Journal* 23 (1973): 270–306.
Robin, Martin. *The Rush For Spoils*. Toronto: McClelland and Stewart 1972.
Roy, Patricia. "Progress, Prosperity and Politics: The Railway Policies of Richard McBride." *BC Studies* (1980): 3–28.
– *Vancoucer* Toronto: James Lorimer and Company 1980.
Saywell, John T. "The Early History of Canadian Oil Companies: A Chapter in Canadian Business History," *Ontario History* 53 (1961): 67–72.
Scott, F.R. and A.J.M. Smith, *The Blasted Pine*. Toronto: MacMillan 1967.
Sharfman, I.L. *The Interstate Commerce Commission: A Study in Administrative Law and Procedure*, vols. 1–4. New York: Commonwealth Fund 1931–37.
Simon, Matthew. "New British Investment in Canada, 1865–1914." *Canadian Journal of Economics* 3 (1970): 238–54.
Skowronek, Stephen. *Building a New Administrative State: The Expansion of*

National Administrative Capacities, 1887–1920. Cambridge: Cambridge University Press 1982.

Smith, David E. *Prairie Liberalism: The Liberal Party in Saskatchewan, 1905–71*. Toronto: University of Toronto Press 1975.

Sproat, John G. *The Best Men: Liberal Reformers in the Gilded Age*. New York: Oxford University Press 1968.

Stevens, G.R. *Canadian National Railways: Towards the Inevitable*. Toronto: Clarke Irwin 1962.

– *History of the Canadian National Railways*. New York: MacMillan 1973.

Stevens, Paul D. "Laurier and the Liberal Party in Ontario, 1887–1911." PHD. diss., University of Toronto 1966.

Stigler, George J. "The theory of economic regulation." *Bell Journal of Economics and Management Science* 2 (1971): 3–21.

Studnicki-Gizbert, K.W. *Issues in Canadian Transport Policy*. Toronto: MacMillan 1974.

Sugarman, David, ed. *Legality, Ideology and the State*. London: Academic Press 1983.

"T.E. Kenny," *Morgan's Canadian Men and Women of the Time*. Toronto: William Briggs, 1898.

Thompson, J.H. *The Harvests of War*. Toronto: McClelland and Stewart, 1978.

Thompson, J.H., Seager, Allen. *Canada, 1922–1939: Decades of Discord*. Toronto: McClelland and Stewart 1985.

Traves, Tom. *The State and Enterprise*. Toronto: University of Toronto Press 1979.

Trebilcock, Michael J. et al. *The Choice of Governing Instrument*. Ottawa: Economic Council of Canada 1982.

Ulen, Thomas. "Railroad Cartels Before 1887." *Research in Economic History* 8: 125–44.

Urquhart, M.C., and K.A.H. Buckley, eds. *Historical Statistics of Canada*. Toronto: University of Toronto Press 1965.

Veblen, Thorstein. *The Theory of Business Enterprise*. New York: New American Library 1958.

Vietor, R.H.K. "Businessmen and the Political Economy." *Journal of American History* 14 (1977): 47–66.

Waite, P.B. *Canada, 1874–1896: Arduous Destiny*. Toronto: McClelland and Stewart 1971.

– *The Man From Halifax*. Toronto: University of Toronto Press 1985.

Wallace, W. Stewart, ed. *Macmillan Dictionary of Canadian Biography*, Fourth Edition. Toronto: MacMillan 1978.

Ward, W. Peter, and Robert A.J. McDonald. *British Columbia: Historical Readings*. Vancouver: Douglas and McIntyre 1981.

Weaver, John. "Order and Efficiency: Samuel Morley Wickett and the Urban

Progressive Movement in Toronto, 1900–15." *Ontario History* 61 (1977): 220–34.

Who's Who in America, vol. 2 (1901–03).

Williams, David R. *Mayor Gerry: The Remarkable Gerald Grattan McGeer*. Vancouver: Douglas and McIntyre 1986.

Willison, John Stephen. *The Railway Question in Canada*. Toronto: Warwick Brothers and Rutter 1897.

Wilson, James Q., ed. *The Politics of Regulation*. New York: Basic Books 1980.

Wood, L.A. *A History of Farmers' Movements in Canada*. Toronto: University of Toronto Press 1975.

Wright, Arthur R. "An Examination of the Role of the Board of Transport Commissioners for Canada as a Regulatory Tribunal." *Canadian Public Administration* 6 (1963): 349–86.

Young, Brian. *Promoters and Politicians: The North Shore Railways in the History of Quebec*. Toronto: University of Toronto Press 1978.

Index